MAKING SENSE OF
ALGEBRA

MAKING SENSE OF
ALGEBRA

Developing Students' Mathematical Habits of Mind

E. Paul Goldenberg

June Mark

Jane M. Kang

Mary K. Fries

Cynthia J. Carter

Tracy Cordner

HEINEMANN
Portsmouth, NH

FOREWORD BY **Steven Leinwand**

Heinemann
361 Hanover Street
Portsmouth, NH 03801–3912
www.heinemann.com

Offices and agents throughout the world

© 2015 by Education Development Center, Inc.

The authors and publisher wish to thank those who have generously given permission to reprint borrowed material:

Excerpts from Common Core State Standards © Copyright 2010. National Governors Association Center for Best Practices and Council of Chief State School Officers. All rights reserved.

Excerpts adapted from "An algebraic-habits-of-mind perspective on elementary school" by E. Paul Goldenberg, June Mark, and Al Cuoco in *Teaching Children Mathematics* (Volume 16, Issue 9, May 2010). Published by National Council of Teachers of Mathematics. Reprinted by permission of the publisher conveyed via Copyright Clearance Center.

Sample dialogue adapted from *Implementing the Mathematical Practice Standards: Anita's Way to Add Fractions with Unlike Denominators*, www.mathpractices.edc.org. Copyright © 2012–2013 by Education Development Center, Inc. Reprinted by permission. All rights reserved.

Library of Congress Cataloging-in-Publication Data
Making sense of algebra : developing students' mathematical habits of mind / E. Paul Goldenberg [and five others].
    pages cm
  ISBN 978-0-325-05301-1
1. Algebra—Study and teaching.   I. Goldenberg, E. Paul (Ernest Paul)
  QA141.M27 2015
  512.9071—dc23

                                 2015004344

Editor: Katherine Bryant
Production: David Stirling
Cover and interior designs: Suzanne Heiser
Typesetter: Shawn Girsberger
Manufacturing: Steve Bernier

Printed in the United States of America on acid-free paper
19 18 17 16 15   PAH   1 2 3 4 5

CONTENTS

Foreword   VI
Acknowledgments   IX
Introduction   X

Chapter 1: **Algebraic Habits of Mind**   1
What Are Mathematical Habits of Mind?   3
Algebraic Habits of Mind   5
Conclusion   36

Chapter 2: **Mental Mathematics Is More Than Mental Arithmetic**   37
Slow Learners and Struggling Students   39
Arithmetic, Mathematics, and Executive Functions   43
Why Use These Exercises in High School?   50
Designing and Using Mental Mathematics Exercises   53
Conclusion   58

Chapter 3: **Solving and Building Puzzles**   59
What Makes a Puzzle a Puzzle?   60
Why Do People Invent Puzzles, Do Them, and Like Them?   63
Who Am I? Puzzles   67
Mobiles and Mystery Number Puzzles   70
Latin Square-Based Puzzles   76
Teaching with Puzzles   80
Conclusion   86

Chapter 4: **Extended Investigations for Students**   88
Experience Before Formality: Try It Yourself   90
Principles: What Makes a Good Investigation?   92
Aspects of Investigation: Entering, Shaping, and Extending Investigations   107
Teaching Through Investigation   117
Conclusion   125

Chapter 5: **A Geometric Look at Algebra**   127
The Number Line: Numbers as Locations and Distances   127
Area as a Model for Multiplication, Division, and Factoring   147
Conclusion   156

Chapter 6: **Thinking Out Loud**   157
Benefits of Discussion in the Classroom   157
Teaching Students How to Discuss   159
When Discussions Falter   164
Models of Mathematical Discussions   171
Conclusion   181

References   182

FOREWORD

Steven Leinwand

Think about how often we hear something close to "I was fine until Algebra!" or "Algebra was my mathematical Waterloo!" or more bluntly, "I just hated algebra!" The world is littered with those for whom algebra made no sense. These negative, and often even debilitating, perceptions both poison one's view of algebra and color one's overall sense of mathematical ability. How sad that algebra, this incredibly powerful set of skills and concepts that enable generalization, predicting, and making sense of the patterns all around us, should be remembered with such negative passion because it never made sense.

Rather than just lamenting this pervasive situation, in *Making Sense of Algebra,* Paul Goldenberg and his EDC colleagues take an upbeat, practical, and proactive approach to building a set of algebraic habits of mind that support far more effective teaching and learning of algebra. Building on years of research, curriculum development, and evaluation, this important book doesn't just identify this set of habits of mind, but presents each habit with examples, classroom illustrations, and the underlying research within the context of specific high-leverage "instructional ingredients."

But, as always, the question that teachers face is "How much can I possibly do?" Teaching is already incredibly challenging. How much help can it be to go through the effort of adopting new lenses to my planning, implementation, and reflection? Why shift mindsets to accommodate these habits of mind? Change always makes life more difficult; why should we believe *this* change will help enough to be worth it? The answer, in the form of a deductive argument, is simple:

Fact 1: Algebra is clearly not working for enough students.

Fact 2: Societal and workplace needs require that algebra work for a far greater proportion of our students.

Fact 3: Students themselves benefit from higher paid work opportunities and, as a result, better quality of life, when they've succeeded at algebra.

Hypothesis 1: Algebra can work for a much larger proportion of students if and when we change some of how we teach algebra.

Conclusion (assuming one accepts the three facts and the hypothesis): Algebra can and will work for a much larger proportion of students if and when we adopt and implement a set of research-affirmed practices that guide our curriculum and teaching and our students' learning. As for why *this* change, the authors help complete that argument logically, too.

That's why the ideas in this book are so important, why they are worthy of study and implementation, and why they are such powerful antidotes to approaches that have not proved successful.

But none of this is easy. Nearly everywhere I go I hear questions like: "How can I get my algebra students to care?" and "How can I get my students to engage in discussion?" and "How can I get them to think?" These are the practical questions the authors have long wrestled with, and these are the questions for which we are provided helpful, nuanced, research- and classroom-based answers.

Consider, for example, Chapter 3, "Solving and Building Puzzles." The ideas in this chapter help shift our mindsets from seeing algebra as the drudgery of learning procedures for solving equations to seeing it as the engaging inquisitiveness of solving puzzles using powerful mathematical ideas. The notion of puzzles reminds me of the extensive de-bugging that occurs in the workplace—a puzzling out of where the problem is located and how it can be resolved. Think of how National Transportation Safety Board inspectors puzzle out the causes of air crashes from the clues they gather or of how medical professionals at the National Institutes of Health puzzle out the origins of and cures to dangerous pathogens. I am also reminded of a remedial algebra class I observed that was rousingly launched with a 5×5 KenKen puzzle (discussed in detail in Chapter 3) and how students eagerly justified their conjectures about numbers and operations. Algebra is the perfect place to interweave the habits of puzzling with the processes of reasoning and communication and exploration, and Chapter 3 is chock-full of ideas—like Who Am I, mobile, and Mystery Number puzzles—for how best to do this.

We are reminded in Chapter 4 that "the world's real problems require not just the stamina to apply methods and knowledge one already has, but also the disposition (and skill) to investigate and gather new knowledge and develop new methods. For students to learn to think like problem solvers, they need regular experience doing such investigative work in which one must think, experiment, organize information, follow hunches, interact, take wrong turns, discover, think more, and synthesize one's findings as a conclusion." Too often such reminders are simply presented and, as teachers, we are left asking, "That's fine, but how?" One of the joys of *Making Sense of Algebra* is how clearly and practically the "how" question is answered. Not only are we provided with wonderful "low threshold, high ceiling" examples, but we are also shown how to transfer these examples directly to algebra lessons along with insightful and honest guidance on advantages and disadvantages, pitfalls and opportunities, important ideas, and connections to algebraic thinking.

Of course, it's not as simple as merely incorporating the cross-product of the five Common Core-aligned habits of 1) describing repeated reasoning, 2) puzzling and persevering, 3) seeking and using structure, 4) using tools strategically, and 5) communicating with precision with the five creative ingredients of 1) mental mathematics activities, 2) mathematical puzzles, 3) exploration-based learning, 4) broadly useful mathematical tools, and 5) classroom discussions. But shifting practice in every algebra classroom in some of these twenty-five directions can make a tremendous difference in the learning of algebra and thus long-term perceptions of algebra.

In fact, one can almost dream of a world where, because teachers adopt, adapt, and incorporate these ideas into their teaching, "algebra" is no longer the subject of so many laugh lines in the popular culture because it finally actually makes sense and isn't so alienating to the next generation of students.

ACKNOWLEDGMENTS

This book was long on our minds, but never quite in our plans until Katherine Bryant at Heinemann planted it there, and Anita Gildea and others helped it take root. It was daunting, and very hard work, but also a great deal of fun. We gratefully acknowledge that initial (strong!) nudge, and all the suggestions, editing, design, and other help we've received since that time from Katherine Bryant, David Stirling, and Josh Evans at Heinemann.

The book makes explicit some of the thinking behind curriculum development and teacher professional development that we have been doing for a long time. That thinking was strongly influenced by teachers and students, refining and extending it over the course of, now, nearly three decades. Stories from some of those teachers and classes appear in this book. Thank you so much, high school students and teachers of Malden and Lowell, MA; middle school students and teachers at The Rashi School in Dedham, MA; and yet other teachers, students, and schools in Attleboro, Chelsea, and Newton, MA, and many other schools across the country, whose hard work and thoughtful feedback helped us develop the *Transition to Algebra* curriculum, which led to this book. Even more, thank you for the memories of *you* in your classrooms. They are, all of them, very good memories!

And thank you to colleagues and friends, Al Cuoco, Marion Walter, and Deborah Spencer for important contributions to the editing. Deb diagnosed and suggested major surgery for one of the chapters that found itself in the ICU. Marion Walter referred to her editing of multiple chapters as nit-picking, but what valuable nit-picking it was, including finding mathematical slips and unhygienic wordings. And Al worked through the book to protect mathematical fidelity and to help us all keep our sanity. We'd also like to thank Brian Harvey for a generous and careful reading that helped correct and clarify the text.

EDC's LTD NBDI initiative provided the initial support that enabled us to develop the book proposal for Heinemann, including an outline and a sample chapter, now very much revised. Major funding for this work came from a grant from the National Science Foundation. We are very grateful to both benefactors, who can claim the credit for making the work possible but are not responsible for opinions of the authors, who try to do well but can, of course, slip up.

Thank you all—funders, publisher, and EDC colleagues, friends, editors, teachers, students. We hope the work ultimately returns the favor you have done us.

INTRODUCTION

Helping all students succeed in algebra is an urgent and persistent national challenge.
Success in algebra is not merely a gateway to more advanced mathematics and science but
is linked to high school graduation, college enrollment and completion, and workforce
preparation. Unfortunately, many students enter high school algebra underprepared, and
those numbers are greater for students from groups underrepresented in mathematics and
other STEM disciplines. As a result, school districts across the country are seeking new,
research-based approaches that go beyond simply providing additional instructional time or
basic skills practice, neither of which, alone or in combination, has proven sufficient to solve
the problem.

Improving this situation requires understanding that algebra is both a language for expressing
things we already know and a systematic way of thinking that lets us use that language to
figure out things we don't already know. Developing the mathematical habits of mind that
support that thinking—a set of *algebraic* habits of mind—helps students make the transition
from arithmetic to algebra. In this book, we explain and illustrate these habits of mind
and offer ideas, tools, and specific instructional strategies to assist you as educators to help
your students develop these mathematical habits of minds by building on students' prior
knowledge, using intuitive models that illustrate the logic of algebra, and posing problems that
encourage perseverance and strategy.

Our team has spent close to two decades working out how to organize curricula around
mathematical habits of mind, sparking students' and teachers' curiosity and engagement with
mathematics, and studying teachers' implementation of these ideas. Building mathematical
habits of mind and leading students to expect mathematics to make sense have become central
to EDC's mathematics curricula, which span the grades K to 12, including, most recently,
Transition to Algebra, as well as our earlier curricula, *Think Math!* and *CME Project*. We
have tested these ideas in our work in mathematics classrooms from early childhood through
college and through our work with teachers across grades. This book, like those curricula,
builds on our lineage of work around mathematical habits of mind (e.g., Cuoco, Goldenberg,
and Mark 1996; Goldenberg 1996; Cuoco, Goldenberg, and Mark 2012; Mark et al. 2012).

We develop habits through practice; to make mathematical ways of thinking into habits, students need to be engaged in activities that exercise those ways of thinking. Using a combination of mathematical and pedagogical discussion, stories from classrooms, and suggestions for teaching, this book aims to give more teachers the tools to integrate a habits-of-mind approach into their practice.

Five specific teaching ingredients are described in this book, all used in ways that develop the algebraic habits of mind we want. All of the following can be adapted to a variety of educational contexts, teaching styles, and core curricula:

- *mental mathematics activities* that build computational fluency and strengthen executive function
- *mathematical puzzles* to support algebraic reasoning, arithmetic facility, and perseverance in problem solving
- *exploration-based learning* to support pattern identification and description with algebraic notation
- *broadly useful mathematical tools* such as number lines and area models that offer students spatial ideas to support their understanding of numbers and algebra
- *classroom discussions* that support meaningful mathematical communication and precision and that broaden problem-solving techniques.

A habits-of-mind approach to making sense of algebra provides a basis for effective instructional practices that challenge past paradigms of algebra support (e.g., extra time with the same approaches and materials) that so often fail. In our own classrooms, and in the many classrooms that we have observed, teachers have used this structure and logic to help students make sense of ideas traditionally deemed hard to learn. Perhaps even more importantly, students have learned to use these tools independently to think about, learn, explain, and enjoy new algebraic ideas.

ABOUT THIS BOOK

Each chapter in this book addresses an instructional strategy, tool, or idea for developing students' mathematical habits of mind and for developing the logic that students need to succeed in algebra.

Chapter 1, "Algebraic Habits of Mind," introduces a set of mathematical habits of mind that are central to proficiency in algebra and therefore essential in helping students transition from arithmetic to algebra. We have named these "describing repeated reasoning," "puzzling and persevering," "seeking and using structure," "using tools strategically," and "communicating with precision," with an obvious nod to the most closely related Common Core State Standards for Mathematical Practice, which mandate these habits of mind as part of mathematical instruction and learning. This chapter gives examples of each, helping to clarify the related mathematical practices that are central to the CCSSM.

Developing these mathematical habits of mind is important for many reasons: they are essential to mathematical proficiency, critical thought, college and career readiness, access to future opportunities, and productive participation in society. The specially honed ways of thinking that mathematicians and others have evolved to create mathematics—the ability to puzzle through unknown problems with solid analytic ways of thinking—serve people in all domains and prepare *all* students well for the future.

Chapter 2, "Mental Mathematics Is More Than Mental Arithmetic," describes the use of mental mathematics exercises to build a logical system for arithmetic that reflects algebraic ideas, providing a solid foundation for learning algebra. Like standard math fact drills, these exercises build fluency with number, but their purpose goes well beyond fast recall. These daily exercises are designed to develop a "commonsense feel" for algebraic properties of operations, capacity to juggle multiple pieces of information simultaneously, and mastery and confidence in mental computation. These brief, lively, highly focused exercises provide students with experiences that help to build the logic of algebra by connecting arithmetic pattern and algebraic structure.

Success in algebra requires not only a good foundation in arithmetic but a "mathematical infrastructure" of cognitive tools that include working memory adequate to hold several numbers, ideas, and processes in mind while attacking a problem; the metacognitive ability to monitor one's thinking and keep one's place in a process; the metacognitive skill to talk oneself through what's familiar in a problem situation and what isn't; and more. The mental mathematics exercises we describe can help to hone this mathematical infrastructure.

This chapter provides a variety of examples of such mental mathematics exercises and describes the algebraic ideas they help to build. When students have a solid experiential foundation for learning algebra, they need less explanation of the new ideas of algebra and they have a better idea how to incorporate and use that new learning; and when explanation *is* still needed, teachers have that experiential background to refer to and build upon. The chapter also offers a few principles to guide the design and implementation of mental mathematics exercises.

Chapter 3, "Solving and Building Puzzles," focuses on the use of mathematical puzzles, explaining why and how puzzles can help to develop the logic needed for strong algebraic reasoning and foster mathematical habits of mind, in particular the puzzling and persevering habit of mind. The chapter describes a number of puzzle types and the mathematics underlying them. The puzzle types featured include Who Am I? puzzles, mobile puzzles, Mystery Number puzzles, and Latin square-based puzzles. In this chapter, we show how solving and inventing certain kinds of puzzles can help students develop mathematical habits that are useful (even necessary) in making sense of familiar topics in high school algebra: modeling with equations, solving equations and systems of equations, seeking and using algebraic structure, and more. The chapter closes with ideas for teaching with puzzles: a way to introduce puzzles, a way to help focus students' thinking, and the value of encouraging students to *build* their own puzzles.

As a complement to many of the typical shorter problems that students often encounter in mathematics class, Chapter 4, "Extended Investigations for Students," focuses on extended investigations, opportunities for students to explore problems that require stamina, experimentation, and analysis. This chapter identifies some features of investigatory problems, examines mathematical themes well suited to research by students making the transition to algebra, and shares ways in which such investigations can help students develop valuable mathematical habits over time. These kinds of investigations engage them in *doing* mathematics similar to the ways in which mathematicians investigate problems—seeking patterns, developing and testing hypotheses, reasoning about the mathematics. These investigations also demonstrate that the language of algebra is accessible and is used to express patterns that can be found almost anywhere.

Geometric notions—in particular, location, distance, and area—can help us to understand and reason about arithmetic operations and to organize algebraic calculations as well. In Chapter 5, "A Geometric Look at Algebra," we discuss two models that are useful in both pre-algebra and algebra classrooms: number lines, primarily for order, addition, and subtraction, and the area model, primarily for multiplication, division, and (in algebra) factoring. Both models give students a visual lens through which to look at mathematical ideas—subtracting negative numbers or factoring algebraic expressions—clarifying what they already know and helping them extend and deepen their understanding. The chapter offers some classroom activities for developing and using these geometric models with students.

Chapter 6, "Thinking Out Loud," focuses on discussion: teaching *how* to discuss; troubleshooting, moderating, and maintaining discussions; and choosing, using, and possibly creating models of mathematical discussions. We explore the ways in which discussions can

Background of This Book

This book grows out of years of work, but most directly out of a research and development project, *Transition to Algebra: A Habits-of-Mind Approach*, that we conducted over the past several years, with support from the National Science Foundation (grant no. DRL-0917958). That project developed and tested a set of instructional materials, now published by Heinemann, for a full-year intervention course to support students enrolled in high school algebra but underprepared and at risk of failure. That course aims to ensure students' success in algebra by building their algebraic habits of mind: engaging them in developing the logic of algebra, in making sense of problems and persisting in solving them, and in expecting algebra—and all of mathematics—to make sense. In that course, students learn to treat the language and logic of algebra as precise forms of their natural language and as "common sense"; they extend the logic of whole numbers to negatives, fractions, and even negative and fractional exponents; and they derive algebraic ideas and principles from arithmetic experience and knowledge. Though originally designed to be used concurrently with an algebra course, that course has also found a broader audience as a middle school introduction to algebra.

be a useful resource in the mathematics classroom and offer some suggestions for helping students learn how to hold a logical mathematical discussion. Challenges to productive mathematical discussion in classrooms and some ideas for countering those challenges are also discussed. Last, the chapter introduces student dialogues as a way to model good mathematical discussion and provides some examples of scripted student dialogues that aim to illustrate mathematical discourse and argument.

This book is designed to be useful to anyone interested in learning more about the mathematical habits-of-mind approach and improving classroom practice—especially with a focus on algebra—with fun, logic-building activities that are in alignment with the CCSSM: mathematics teachers in grades 6–10 working with introductory algebra students as well as mathematics coaches, administrators, professional development providers, preservice educators, and curriculum coordinators.

In the same spirit that gets you as reader and us as authors to want students to enjoy the logic and beauty of mathematics, we hope you will enjoy this book.

Algebraic Habits of Mind

Although it is necessary to infuse courses and curricula with modern content, what is even more important is to give students the tools they will need in order to use, understand, and even make mathematics that does not yet exist. A curriculum organized around habits of mind tries to close the gap between what the users and makers of mathematics do."

—(Cuoco, Goldenberg, and Mark 1996, 376)

The Common Core State Standards for Mathematics (CCSSO, NGA 2010) set proficiency standards in two areas: mathematical *content* and mathematical *practice*.

The content standards—though adjusted to achieve focus and coherence, and updated to reflect known new needs—are essentially familiar in form. They are organized by grade (except in high school) and then by topic, to comprise a list of facts, procedures, conventions, forms, symbols, skills, and so on that students must know, understand, and be able to use and apply correctly.

The Standards for Mathematical Practice have a different purpose and are not so familiar. They aim at preparing students for an economy that is increasingly knowledge-based and a world that is increasingly complicated and unpredictable, in which change is more likely to speed up than slow down. Competing in such a world requires great adaptability to unexpected challenges. For that, workers need not only the skills for solving problems that we already know about but also the stamina and disposition to puzzle through totally unfamiliar problems for which we cannot now provide methods and procedures. The ability to solve new and unforeseen problems requires mastery not just of the *results* of mathematical thinking (the familiar facts and procedures) but of the ways that mathematically proficient individuals do that thinking. This is especially true as our economy increasingly depends on fields that require mathematics.

In fact, changes in technology, economics, suppliers, regulations, and so on mean that even traditional businesses—not just high-tech start-ups—frequently encounter brand-new problems to solve, ones for which no method, formula, or procedure has already be invented. When the real world throws us a problem, it never asks what chapter we've just studied!

The I-can-puzzle-it-out disposition—the intrepid readiness to tackle problems with only the knowledge one has or can find and without a prelearned solution method—is an important starting place. Mathematical proficiency depends also on other mental habits that dispose one to characterize problems (and solutions) in precise ways, to subdivide and explore problems by posing new and related problems, and to "play" (either concretely or with thought experiments) to gain experience and insights from which some regularity or structure might be derived. And there are still other habits of mind: a readiness to seek and articulate underlying structure that might relate new problems to ones that have already been solved, to choose approaches both strategically and flexibly, and so on.

These habits of mind (and others) characterize the practice of mathematicians, but their utility extends well beyond mathematics. The I-can-puzzle-it-out perspective and all of its supporting habits of mind are necessary foundations for science, medical diagnosis (or diagnosis of a computer or car), law, economics, inventing a business plan, the building trades, and essentially all inventive or investigative work and critical thought.

The idea of using mathematical habits of mind as an organizer for the curriculum has been around since at least the early 1990s, but even then the idea wasn't new. Mathematicians and good educators have always known that mathematics is more than the results of mathematics: more than the ideas, facts, methods, and formulas that are the content of math books and classes.

Mathematics is also about the ways of thinking that generate these ideas, facts, and methods. For people who are proficient at mathematics, these ways of thinking are "second nature," *habits*, which is why we refer to them as *habits of mind*.

Though the *idea* is old, new attention has been focused on it, under the new name of the Standards for Mathematical Practice, which aggregate into eight clusters many of the mathematical habits of mind we have described in our work.

What Are Mathematical Habits of Mind?

If the name is to make sense, a mathematical habit of mind must reflect how mathematicians think, and must also be a habit. A *habit of mind*, then, is a way of thinking—almost a way of *seeing* a particular situation—that comes so readily to mind that one does not have to rummage in the mental toolbox to find it. Acquiring a habit may require a fair amount of experience doing things self-consciously, just as learning to drive is self-conscious before it becomes habit and fluid and natural.

Habits of Mind
Some important mathematical habits of mind include:
- the I-can-puzzle-it-out disposition
- using precision in thought and communication; characterizing problems and solutions in precise ways
- subdividing and exploring problems by posing new and related problems
- tinkering with problems (concretely or with thought experiments)
- seeking, articulating, and using underlying structure
- choosing approaches both strategically and flexibly.

There are three things to know about mathematical habits of mind in general.

1. They are *not* "classroom processes." Mathematicians often collaborate, of course, but no more or less than people in other fields: collaboration is not a mathematical habit of mind. They communicate, too—it's often how a problem arrives on our desk, it can sometimes be helpful as we're thinking things through, and it's the only way to report results—but communication, too, is not unique to mathematics: it's not a mathematical habit of mind, though, as we'll see, certain aspects of communication can be. And some mathematicians write neatly and organize their notes. Or they don't. These are not mathematical habits of mind.

2. Even though some habits of mind are nearly universal in this discipline, not all mathematical thinkers think the same way, so one cannot make a list and declare that "this is how mathematicians think." In our 1996 book (Cuoco, Goldenberg, and Mark 1996), we distinguished some general mathematical habits of mind from others that are peculiarly algebraic or peculiarly geometric. Statisticians, too, have ways of thinking that are peculiar to their discipline. Many of the commonalities in mathematical thinking find their way into sharp problem solving beyond mathematics.

3. The eight Common Core Standards for Mathematical Practice, and even the shorter list of habits of mind we describe below, are not totally disjoint categories. Mathematical habits of mind are interconnected. In part, that's because mathematical *content* is, itself, highly interconnected.

Why Habits of Mind?

When we first set out to describe these mathematical habits of mind, our goal was to emphasize the particular ways of thinking that mathematicians use in their work. There were two reasons for this.

The first reason was pure fidelity to the subject that was being taught: for students to learn to think mathematically, they cannot just be spectators, simply using and perhaps appreciating the results of mathematicians' work; they must be mathematicians (at their own level, of course), *doing* and *making* mathematics themselves. The experience of making mathematics is not the only way to develop these mathematical ways of thinking and make them automatic—that is, habits—but it is the most available way in school, probably the easiest, and possibly the best.

The second reason was related to equity and opportunity. Many of the results and methods in mathematics—like the quadratic formula, the Pythagorean theorem, methods of proof, or a general method for adding fractions—are things we must teach, not just because tradition or some set of standards says so, but because without such background, students are barred from choosing and succeeding in mathematics-intensive fields such as engineering, technology, science, and, of course, mathematics. These fields offer good jobs, needed by society and paid better than many others. They also appeal to many students who have been given the foundations that allow them further access. An education that skips the facts and skills or that prejudges who gets them deprives students of choice and a better livelihood, and it deprives society of a strong workforce. But even as we try to permit more students, and a more diverse group of students, to pursue mathematics-intensive careers, there are naturally many others whose interests lie elsewhere. Ultimately, knowing how to calculate $\frac{2}{7} + \frac{3}{5}$ or how to prove the Pythagorean theorem serves only some people, but the specially honed ways of thinking that mathematicians and others have evolved to create mathematics—the ability to puzzle through unknown problems with solid analytic ways of thinking—serves people in all domains and prepares *all* students well for the future.

Students with a history of unsuccessful experiences in mathematics should not be excluded from mathematics. Those "slow learners" or "struggling students" are often given *more* formulaic/algorithmic instruction, on the assumption that knowing one way of doing each kind of problem—a fixed, simplified set of rules—is easier to learn than some more lofty and amorphous "way of thinking" or a set of alternative strategies. Research, not philosophy, should ultimately dictate whether or not this is the best approach, but it certainly is not an obvious open-and-shut case. We expect that it is, in fact, wrong. Hand a couple of fourteen-year-olds a smart phone or tablet that they have never seen before, or a new puzzle or game on one of those devices, and they'll most likely have it figured out in minutes. And the kid who is "good with his hands"—a "natural" mechanic on cars, for example—is figuring things out, not following memorized rules. In fact, memorizing sets of rules is hard for many people; the experience of learning a foreign language and trying to deal with gender or case or some other structure that feels (for the nonnative speaker) like arbitrary rules is really hard. Stuff that you can figure out or think your way through—stuff that "makes sense"—is generally much easier.

Moreover, rules are easy to mix up. Students often apply the "two negatives make a positive" mantra in inappropriate ways, such as in addition or subtraction rather than the multiplication and division it should be restricted to. We've even heard students say "two positives make a negative" in algebraic contexts, even though that defies their own direct experience in arithmetic contexts. By contrast, a mental image of the "geography of the number line"—an image showing negatives as naming their distance to the left of 0, positives to the right—helps students make sense of the arithmetic of negative numbers and be able to follow its logic. (See "Using Tools Strategically" later in this chapter.) Students' lack of success may be precisely *because* they are taught to use rules, rather than logic. Treating previously unsuccessful students to the same approach yet again is not a solution; building mathematical habits of mind may be their best, or only, route back in.

ALGEBRAIC HABITS OF MIND

There are many habits that the mathematical mind develops. This chapter focuses on five clusters of habits that are particularly important for proficiency in algebra and therefore for the successful transition from arithmetic to algebra. We have named them "describing repeated reasoning," "puzzling and persevering," "seeking and using structure," "using tools strategically," and "communicating with precision," with an obvious nod to the most closely related Common Core State Standards for Mathematical Practice, which mandate these important habits of mind as part of mathematical instruction and learning from kindergarten on.

Each of these five clusters is described here. As we said earlier, they are not entirely disjoint—one's way of thinking about a problem will often feel like a blend of two or more of the habits of mind, and it can sometimes be hard to decide which of two habits of mind is more prominent in a given example of thinking. Nor is this a comprehensive list of mathematical habits of mind; it does not include even all of the ways of thinking that become second nature to a proficient algebraic thinker, let alone the habits of mind of geometers, analysts, or statisticians. And each of the five habits of mind is, in reality, not a single thing but a cluster of several related subhabits. The rationale for clustering in this way is that it is easier to remember and understand five things than twenty-five.

Describing Repeated Reasoning

Beginning with concrete examples and abstracting regularity from them is one nearly automatic approach mathematicians take to attack unfamiliar problems; it is a *habit* of the mathematical mind. The name that the Common Core invented for this element of mathematical practice is "Look for and express regularity in repeated reasoning." Although students are still building this habit, they are—like novice drivers—*not* so natural and smooth, and they may need to be told to perform repeated experiments and describe their method. Accordingly, in this chapter, we named only a part of the process for this particular habit of mind: describing repeated reasoning. Here's an example of it.

Generalizing Equations

Ignore, for the moment, any anachronisms in the following odd scenario and just imagine that you are the first person ever to need to devise an equation that, if graphed, would describe all of the points on a circle whose center is point (-1, 3) and whose radius is 7. Let's also suppose that you *do* know how to use Pythagoras' rule for finding the distance between two points on a coordinate plane. You can't Google the equation for a circle, because nobody has yet invented the equation (or Google). You are solving a brand-new, previously unsolved problem! How can you start?

Of course, there are many ways, but here's one that mathematicians do almost automatically in situations where a problem is brand-new. You experiment. You might sketch the situation roughly on graph paper, just to get a look. You see, instantly, four points that must be on the circle: (6, 3) and (-8, 3) are each 7 units away from the center horizontally, and (-1, 10) and (-1, -4) are each 7 units away vertically. But no insight about the other points pops to mind.

So you just guess a point and *test* it to see if it's exactly 7 units from the center. Even a silly guess like (100, 100) would do—the purpose is not to happen accidentally on the "right answer" but to use the way you *test* your guess to gain insight into the problem. But because you have a sketch, you can, if you like, pick a plausible point, like (4, 8), or (−7, 6).

You decide to start with (4, 8), so you sketch in the right triangle, see that both of its legs are 5 units long, and calculate that the hypotenuse—the distance from the center of the circle to the point (4, 8)—is $\sqrt{50}$ units long.

Really close to 7. But to be *on* the circle, the distance must be *exactly* 7. Because your goal is to find an equation, you record the *calculation*, not just the result, for the point you picked, (4, 8).

$$(4 - {}^-1)^2 + (8 - 3)^2 \stackrel{?}{=} 7^2$$

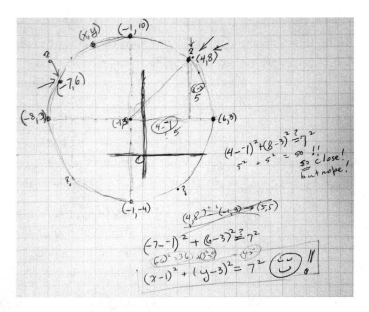

And you try another point. Again, it hardly matters what point you pick—the goal is to get *insight*. You choose (−7, 6) and check to see if it is on the circle. From the drawing, you see that the triangle's sides are 3 and 6, and you know that $3^2 + 6^2 \neq 7^2$, but you write out the calculation anyway.

$$({}^-7 - {}^-1)^2 + (6 - 3)^2 \stackrel{?}{=} 7^2$$

You might take a few more points before the "rhythm of the calculation" becomes clear. You are not looking for a pattern in numbers; you are looking for a pattern in your own actions, the way you check to see if a point is exactly 7 units from (3, −1). So you compare your calculations:

$$(4 - {}^-1)^2 + (8 - 3)^2 \stackrel{?}{=} 7^2$$

$$({}^-7 - {}^-1)^2 + (6 - 3)^2 \stackrel{?}{=} 7^2$$

$\vdots$

Although you can gain insight whether or not the point you pick is actually on the circle, thinking about what might be a likely candidate—when you have enough clues to do so—is another way to develop insight.

They are really the same, except for the numbers that correspond to the coordinates of the point you are checking! So you sketch some (arbitrary) point (x, y), and "test" *it* as if to see if it is exactly 7 units from $(3, {}^-1)$. Doing with (x, y) what you've already done with $(4, 8)$ and $({}^-7, 6)$, you write:

$$(4 - {}^-1)^2 + (8 - 3)^2 \overset{?}{=} 7^2$$

$$({}^-7 - {}^-1)^2 + (6 - 3)^2 \overset{?}{=} 7^2$$

$$(x - {}^-1)^2 + (y - 3)^2 \overset{?}{=} 7^2$$

Really, there's no need for the "?" anymore, because we can *choose* any value for y between 10 and $^-4$ (which we already know are the most extreme values it can take) and *calculate* a value of x that is certain to make $(x - {}^-1)^2 + (y - 3)^2$ equal 7^2. Done! You have an equation!

$$(x - {}^-1)^2 + (y - 3)^2 = 7^2$$

First attempts at using this Guess-Check-Generalize method are usually messier, with calculations all over the page, not so recognizably parallel to each other. One of the key skills to learn is how to *organize* the guesses and the calculations that check those guesses.

> You might try this yourself using points (1, 2) and (16, 7) as an example. What's the line's slope? Is (5, 4) on that line? That is, does it make the same slope with (1, 2)? What about (100, 35)?

This way of approaching a problem is not specific to this one purpose of finding the equation for a circle. You can use this way of thinking to generate the equation for a line through two points.

Without knowing the equation for that line, you can still calculate the slope between those two points. Then guess some arbitrary point that might be on the line and test it to see if it is. We do that by checking to see if the slope between *it* and one of the original points is the same as the slope between those two original points. Do that for a few more guessed numerical examples, keeping track of the structure of the calculation—what you are actually *doing* and not just the results of that arithmetic. Finally, "guess" and "check" the arbitrary point (x, y). Your final formula will probably look something like

$$\frac{y - \boxed{\text{some number}}}{x - \boxed{\text{another number}}} \overset{?}{=} \text{a slope}$$

That, without the question mark, is the equation you sought! If you want, you can manipulate it algebraically into other forms, but such changes are cosmetic.

Likewise, if you want to develop a rule that tells you the coordinates of the reflection of an arbitrary point (a, b) over an arbitrary line $y = cx + d$, you would, again, start with specific cases—a *specific* line like $y = 2x - 3$ and a set of *specific* points. Then you would track the calculations you use (not just the results), figure out what you are repeatedly doing, and capture the (abstract, algebraic) description of that repeated reasoning.

Generalizing in Arithmetic

Generalizing from repeated reasoning does not always involve algebra. Here are two examples.

We sometimes refer to automatic behaviors as "second nature" rather than habit, something we do naturally without having to think about it. Quite early, children "naturally" feel that doubling ⚅⚄ should give ⚅⚅⚄⚄. Whatever makes that feel natural generalizes, with experience, to doubling 43 or 24, and to halving 68 or 112. But these are *second* natures. The built-in part is the cognitive feature that, if exercised, makes doubling ⚅⚄ or 43 *become* "natural" quickly and fairly easily; the facts, themselves—twice 40 and twice 3—are not built in, nor is the ability to double and halve. The cognitive built-in feature lets the ability grow quickly from experience, but experience is what generates the knowledge and skill. Repeated experience with the intuitive reasoning learners use as they double and halve numbers builds a foundation for the generalization and abstraction that they will later encode formally as the distributive property. This is a definitive example of abstracting regularity from repeated specific calculations and expressing that regularity, first just by *enacting* it (applying it to new cases like tripling or multiplying by 21), and later by *encoding* it as a general rule. (See Chapter 2.)

The following exercise, at its simplest, is just a multiplication fact practice that might suit fourth or fifth grade, but it develops much more than fact memory and extends quickly to support algebraic goals. It is also a clear example of abstracting pattern from repeated reasoning. Students who know most but not all of the products of numbers less than or equal to 10, and who know how to use those to find simple products of multiples of 10, like 30×30, can enjoy this activity in which the teacher does not talk at all but produces a patterned calculation and invites students to join in.

> The circled x is just one extra visual clue to keep multiplication in mind.

Sketch a segment of a number line, draw a pair of arrows upward from some number and, where the arrows meet, write that number times itself, like this.

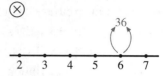

Still with no words of explanation, draw another pair of arrows from the nearest neighbors of that number and write their product.

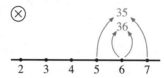

Start the same process at a new location.

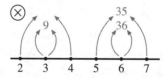

By now, most students see the pattern, so when you draw arrows up from that new number's neighbors, you can turn to them and wait for them to say what to write.

Continue in the same way, now writing *no* numbers until they say what to write. After a while, the display might look like this.

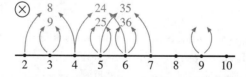

A few steps later, your display might look like this.

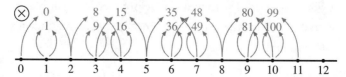

Still without you or your students saying anything about the pattern they've seen, draw a new segment of the number line and again invite students to call out the number.

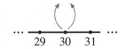

When they do, continue as before, drawing arrows from the nearest neighbors.

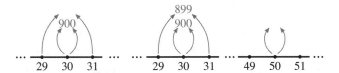

Everything up to this point has required only memory of known facts, but now, when they call out 899, they are using a pattern they abstracted from repeated reasoning. They have not, at this point, written the pattern in the language of algebra, or even expressed the pattern orally in their own native language, but they have enacted the pattern, shown that they see it and can use it.[1]

Generalizing a Process

There are two main ideas here. To summarize, they are:

1. Perform experiments to determine a process.
   When mathematicians face problems for which they know no way of deriving a solution, one of their most common approaches is to experiment to gain insight. Try some approaches and see where they lead. Even before they find a solution, mathematicians can develop a sense of how they'd know if a solution—perhaps a claim made by someone else—was correct. Then they'd make a complete guess—choosing a plausible solution without worrying whether it is a correct one—and test that "guessed" solution, because a process for testing a solution can give insights into how to derive a solution. Students can use this approach as well. At the beginning of this section, we described this process for finding the equation for a circle given a center and radius. Here is an example of the same process applied to solving a word problem.

   > Asher has a part-time job working 20 hours a week. He does so well that he is hired full-time (40 hours a week) and he is also given a $1 per hour raise. He

---

[1] See http://thinkmath.edc.org/resource/difference-squares for more detail.

is really happy, because now he will make $270 more each week than he made before. How much was he making per hour before the raise? How much is he making now?

Many students who can *solve* the algebraic equation that represents this problem can't *generate* that equation. But if students guess a starting wage, even randomly, calculate and compare the weekly earnings before and after the promotion, and then repeat that process for a different, still completely arbitrary, guess they begin to get a sense for what it takes to check the guess.

So let's try it. Could he have been making $9 per hour before the raise? We can check. At $9/hour for a 20-hour week, his old earnings per week are 20 × $9 = $180. With a raise and a 40-hour week, he his new earnings are 40 × ($9 + $1) = $400. Does it conform to what we were told?

$$40 \times (9 + 1) - 20 \times 9 \overset{?}{=} 270$$

> This guess seems totally unreasonable, but the reasonableness of the guess is not at all important. What we are looking for here is only a pattern in how we go about checking the guess, because that is how we will generate an equation.

Nope! So we guess again. Let's try $100 per hour before the raise. His old earnings per week are 20 × $100 = $2000. His new earnings are 40 × ($100 + $1) = $4040. Is that $270 more?

$$40 \times (100 + 1) - 20 \times 100 \overset{?}{=} 270$$

That may be enough to see the structure, or we may need more experiments, but, as we illustrated earlier, the goal is not to find the answer by guesswork, trial and error, or approximation and adjustment. The goal is . . .

2. Describe a pattern that results from repeated reasoning.

The goal is to notice the regularity in the process we use to check our guesses and then *express that process* when we've "guessed a generic case." In the word problem example, and in the examples given earlier, that means expressing the process involved using letters instead of specific numbers. So, in this case, if Asher used to make x dollars per hour, his old earnings are $20x$ and his new earnings are $40(x + 1)$. To compare these, we subtract and see if that equals 270.

$$40(x + 1) - 20x = 270$$

This process precisely expresses what we did in the concrete cases. As was true in the equation for a circle example, this test of a generic case is the equation we need. Solving the equation answers the word problem.

But algebra is not the only way to express regularity that one sees. Let's return to the multiplication pattern:

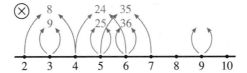

Recognizing regularity in both the process and the patterned results is typically easy even at grade 4. Expressing it precisely is much harder. At some point in algebra, students might recognize this as the familiar $(x - 1)(x + 1) = x^2 - 1$, or even the more general $(a - b)(a + b) = a^2 - b^2$, but even in early high school, first attempts at describing this pattern are generally inarticulate until students are given the idea of *naming* the numbers. They do not need algebraic symbols: they can just name the middle number "middle" and the outer numbers "outer." A more sophisticated scheme would describe the "outer" numbers as something like "middle plus 1" and "middle minus 1." With that idea, even early middle school children can state

$$(\text{middle} - 1) \times (\text{middle} + 1) = \text{middle}^2 - 1.$$

The step from this statement to conventional algebraic notation does not happen instantly, but notice how small that step is. It is just a matter of naming numbers with a single letter like *m* instead of a whole word like *middle* and omitting the × sign.

Similarly, knowing how to add 9 (or 99) by thinking "add 10 (or 100) and subtract 1" can be a discovery rather than a "rule" a child is taught. There are obviously many ways of setting up experiences from which young children might make this discovery, but one way is to have children start with some number like 28 and respond as the teacher repeats, "10 more" (38), "10 more" (48), "10 more" (58), and so on. The learners may first need to count to find the next number—or even to verify that these rhyming answers really *are* the results of adding 10—but they soon hear the pattern in their responses because no other explanatory or instruction words are interfering. (This is a reason why it is *important* that the teacher say only the words *ten more* and not longer and more distracting talk like "Now add 10 to 38.") Children begin to express that discovery from repeated reasoning by saying the 68, 78, 88, almost without even the request for "10 more." When the teacher later changes and asks for "*nine* more," even young learners often see, on their own, that this is almost 10 more, and they make the correction spontaneously. Describing the discovery then becomes a case of expressing the regularity that was found through repeated reasoning. Young learners find it very exciting to add 99 the same way, first by repeating the experience of getting used to a simple computation, adding 100, and then by coming up with their own adjustment to add 99. (See Chapter 2 for more about this process.)

Puzzling and Persevering

Seeing mathematics as a collection of magic spells that "just work" divorces it from common sense. One of our main goals—in the problems and projects we assign and in the way we conduct ourselves as teachers—is to lead students to *expect* mathematics to make sense, to feel coherent and not arbitrary, and to have understandable reasons behind its facts and methods. Building the puzzling and persevering habit of mind means engineering our instruction so that students look for that logic and coherence in each new situation they encounter, treating new problems as puzzles, looking for strategic starting places, and fitting the clues together.

The problems we encounter in the real world—our work life, family life, and personal health—don't tell us which parts of our prior knowledge to recall and use. They rarely even tell us exactly what question we must ask or answer, and they almost never tell us where to begin. To survive and succeed, we must figure out the right question to be asking and what additional information we might need, what relevant experience we have, and where to start. And we must have enough stamina to continue even when progress is hard (or imperceptible) and enough flexibility to try alternative approaches when progress seems *too* hard.

The same applies to the real-life problems of children, problems like learning to talk, ride a bicycle, play a sport, handle difficulties with friends, and so on. What makes a problem "real" is not the context. A good puzzle is more real to a child's "real world" than figuring out how much paint is needed for a wall; it is also a better model of the nature of the thinking that goes with *real* problems, because the first task in a puzzle of any kind is to figure out where to start. A satisfying puzzle is one that you don't know how to solve at first but can figure out. Newer assessments, and even the familiar older ones like college entrance exams, often design deliberately offbeat problems, for which students must (in the words of the Common Core State Standards) "[explain] to themselves the meaning," combine and sensibly string together knowledge they've gathered in various places (e.g., in different chapters!), and "[look] for entry points to its solution."

This collection of dispositions we're calling "puzzling and persevering" encompasses habits such as figuring out good questions to ask and what additional information we might need, looking for ways to apply what relevant experience we have, looking for a strategically easy place to start, and posing new problems.

Identifying Good Questions and Needed Information

We'll start with a problem type that we playfully call "tailless" word problems, and say more about the rationale later. You can create tailless problems yourself from any word problem you find worth thinking about, by omitting the question at the tail end. For example, you might start with a problem like the following, typical of many algebra texts:

> Right now, fewer than a dozen bicycles and tricycles are in the local playground. Altogether, there are at least 17 wheels. If *v* represents the number of vehicles and *w* represents the number of wheels, which system of equations describes this situation?

As one version of this problem appeared, it was then followed by four choices for students to choose among.

A "tailless" version of this problem would contain only the first two sentences, omitting the question that begins with "If *v* represents . . ." Instead, it would pose students one of two more generic questions: What can you say *for sure* about the situation? or What *questions* can you pose that might be answerable from this information?

Many responses are possible. Of course, a student *could* offer a question aimed at the same (presumed) goal of the original problem: How can you describe the situation using algebraic equations or inequalities? But there are other possibilities, like these:

- What is the largest (or smallest) number of wheels there can be?
- What is the largest (or smallest) number of vehicles?
- If we knew that there were *exactly* 17 wheels, could we figure out, for sure, how many bicycles there were?
- If we were told exactly how many wheels there were, what more could we figure out?
- Is it possible to have exactly $\frac{1}{2}$ (or $\frac{1}{3}$ or $\frac{2}{5}$) as many vehicles as wheels?

The answers to some of those questions are "trivial," explicitly given in the problem statement; others need some figuring out; and at least one leads to a general challenge.

Instead of questions, a student could make statements. Things that you could say *for sure* include:

- If we have *exactly* 17 wheels, then there must be at least 1 bicycle and at least 1 tricycle.
- If there were exactly 18 wheels, there could be *all* bicycles or *all* tricycles!

- There can't be more than 33 wheels.
- There can't be less than 17 wheels.
- There must be at least 6 vehicles.

The statement "There can't be less than 17 wheels" may feel trivial—it is more of a restatement of the given than a deduction—but even statements like that, especially early in learning how to do this kind of thinking, should not be discounted. Think of the work involved in understanding that "it is at least 17" means that it can *be* 17 and that it can be greater—expressed as $w \geq 17$ symbolically—but it cannot be less, $w \not< 17$.

Problem situations can be quite simple and still worthy of analysis in this way. For example, "Kayla has exactly 28¢ in her pocket. What can you say *for sure* about the coins in her pocket?"

At first, tailless problems are likely to be unfamiliar, and students won't be quick to respond. They may withhold good ideas, thinking that there is a "right answer" you are waiting for that they don't know. They may feel that their ideas are not worth saying or sound trivial. You want to encourage a variety of responses:

- Kayla could have 2 dimes and 8 pennies.
- Kayla could have 28 pennies.
- Kayla could have 5 nickels and 3 pennies.
- Kayla must have some pennies.
- Kayla must have at least 4 coins.

As in the previous example, even a response like "Kayla has more than a quarter," which seems trivial, is important to accept, partly because it helps free students to make observations—the goal is mathematical correctness, not profundity—but also because, in the right context, this is not trivial at all. If some life event requires one to have 25¢, then observing that 28¢ is more than enough is a completely legitimate conclusion. There are many good responses to this problem. The goal is not for students to get any *particular* one but to derive what they can from the given information, to reason with what they know, and, especially importantly—a skill grown over time, not all at once—to notice how many *different* sensible deductions can be made and to be creative at finding them. These challenges—developing good questions and starting with what one knows and figuring out what else can be known—ask learners for deeper analysis than typical problems do. They are also more like real-life situations, in which we have incomplete information, are left to find our own questions, and must find or invent our own methods. Here are two examples of more complex tailless problems, both adapted from grade 5 of the *Think Math!* curriculum (EDC 2008).

In 2014, there were estimated to be about 295 million egg-laying hens in the United States. A laying hen produces roughly 250 to 300 eggs per year. The population of the United States was estimated to be about 319 million people. List some mathematical questions that you can answer using this information.

Sam Houston Elementary School has nearly 1,000 children from kindergarten through fifth grade. Most classes have roughly 25 students, and no class has more than 27. What can you figure out from this information?

To be able to use mathematics well, one must build the ability to figure out what questions fit a mathematical situation. School problems are typically too tidy for that. Generally designed to let students cut their teeth on simplified situations, they give all required information and specify the question. That's fine for certain kinds of learning, but students also need regular exposure to problems in which the goal is to figure out the information needed, the methods to use, or what questions can sensibly be asked. In contrast to typical word problems, real-life problems almost never present the relevant information all at once; parts of the problem appear and other information dribbles in over time or requires us to take action to get it. Because the information *can* be incomplete, real-life problems always require us to analyze the situation to see *if* the information is complete. To do so, we must generally also make sure we've fully clarified what the problem is, because in real life, problems rarely come with neatly specified written questions. We must figure out what, exactly, we are trying to accomplish—what the question is—whether additional information is needed beyond what we already have, and if so, what information is needed. Cultivating this approach as a real *habit* of mind is useful!

Cutting the tail off standard problems is one way you can modify existing problems to create alternative problems that support this goal. Here are three other techniques you can use:

- Answer is a method: Keep the original question, but leave off some numbers and ask learners how they'd solve the problem if the numbers were known. The required answer is a *method* rather than a *number*. Here is an example from the 1909 book *Problems Without Figures* (Gillan 1909, 6): "I know how many gallons of water a horse will drink; how can I find how many quarts seven horses will drink?"
- Missing middle: Keep the original question, but leave off some numbers and ask what additional information would be required to answer the question. The required answer is a number, but it's the part of the required information that is not given, not the answer to the question that the problem poses. These variants of the fifth-grade problems posed above show how this is done.

What, if any, additional information is needed to solve this problem? "In 2014, there were about 295 million egg-laying hens in the United States and about 319 million people. Assuming all of these eggs are used in the United States, what is the average number of eggs used by each person?"

What, if any, additional information is needed to solve this problem? "Our elementary school contains kindergarten through fifth grade and has nearly 1,000 children. Roughly how many classes are there at each grade level?"

- "Frontless" problems: Only the question is retained. For example, "What is the area of the room?" or "How long will it take for the sink to drain?" Clearly the question *can't* be answered without information. But questions like these are, in many senses, as close to real life as we can get. In real life, the question poses itself first, and we must then figure out what information we need and what method we must use to answer it.

Identifying Relevant Experience
Sometimes, we search our memory for similar problems. Sometimes we choose tools (see "Using Tools Strategically," page 27) that structure the problem, represent it, or provide a useful (abstract) analogy to it. One way to help students make sense of the mathematics they learn is to put experience before formality, letting learners explore problems and derive methods from the exploration (see "Describing Repeated Reasoning," page 6, and see also Chapter 4 on extended investigations). That is one reason why the Common Core content standards put the logic of multidigit multiplication—properties, including especially the distributive property, that make possible the algorithms we use—*before* the algorithms for multidigit multiplication. The algorithms become capstones rather than foundations.

The principle applies to secondary school as well. Before we teach and practice a formula for computing arrangements of objects, giving students the concrete experience of trying to find all the possible ways to arrange a row of 7 coins—5 pennies and 2 nickels—is useful background. There are many possibilities, and it is hard to know when one has found them all without organizing the search and/or the listing in some systematic way. Once one has a system, the chances are good that the "answer," 21, will be discernible, in at least some students' work, as $6 + 5 + 4 + 3 + 2 + 1$. Starting from that, and the experience of doing the same with, say, 4 pennies and (again) 2 nickels, one can begin to see a reason *why* we are always summing consecutive integers starting with 1. One way to compute this sum is . . .

$$6 + 5 + 4 + 3 + 2 + 1 +$$

$$1 + 2 + 3 + 4 + 5 + 6 =$$

$$7 + 7 + 7 + 7 + 7 + 7 =$$

$$7 \cdot 6.$$

But that's twice what we really wanted, so $6 + 5 + 4 + 3 + 2 + 1 = \frac{7 \cdot 6}{2}$. At this point, both $\frac{n(n-1)}{2}$ and $\frac{n!}{2!(n-2)!}$ (where n is the number of coins and 2 is always the number of nickels) can be connected with the experience students have had. In $\frac{n(n-1)}{2}$, we directly see the $\frac{7 \cdot 6}{2}$. In $\frac{n!}{2!(n-2)!}$ we have to work a bit harder to notice that $\frac{n!}{(n-2)!}$ generates the $7 \cdot 6$. And then the full generalization can make sense. Again, we've presented this more neatly than naturally occurs in class—more investigation with arrangements, more *experience*, is useful before the formality—but the principle is correct. The algorithm is the capstone, not the foundation.

Finding a Strategically "Easy" Place to Start

When problems are genuine, not mere exercises, seeking a useful entry point is nearly *always* essential, and may need to be done more than once in attacking the problem. We must be in the habit of asking ourselves not "What am I supposed to do?" but "What *can* I do? What is a good way to look at this? What part might be easiest to attack first? What simplification can I make? Is there a clue in the structure, or the numbers, or the context that I can use? What *can* I do *now*, that might give me just enough traction to see a next step?"

This disposition to look for a "strategically lazy" place to start is also an essential real-life skill. Puzzles and problems provide useful practice contexts for this difficult-to-acquire skill. But typical classroom problems often leave us feeling that we are being tested. The problem may take work, but we feel (and are often enough told) that we should already *know* how to solve it. If we do *not* immediately see how to start it and know what steps to take after that, we are likely to feel anxious or embarrassed. Or we may feel that the problem is somehow unfair, that the teacher did not prepare us properly. By contrast, we *expect* puzzles to be puzzling. Puzzles are not tests: they give us permission to think a bit longer about where and how to begin.[2]

> There are often many good places to start. The point is to choose one that is convenient, because there are also many inconvenient places to start.

Puzzles place that particular skill—figuring out where to start—front and center. In a crossword puzzle, for example, *most* of the clues are likely to be obscure at first. Figuring out the best place to start may require examining many clues. Each time we use a clue correctly, we get new

---

[2]See discussion on Raven's Matrices in Chapter 3.

information, new clues that help us figure out other parts of the puzzle. The same is true of the Sudoku and KenKen puzzles that appear in many newspapers and even in-flight magazines. And the same is true of a genre of puzzle we call Who Am I? puzzles (see Chapter 3).

Who Am I?

· The sum of my digits is 20.
· My units digit is my largest digit.
· The product of my digits is not 0.
· $u = h + 1$.
· $u = 3t$.
· I am odd.
· My hundreds digit is even.

Taking the clues in order is not strategic: the first clue gives us an annoyingly large job to do, listing all the ways of making 20 with three single-digit numbers (9, 9, 2; 9, 8, 3; 9, 7, 4; . . .) and then all the ways of arranging each one of the sets we've created. That clue may be useful later—or it may turn out that we never need it—but it's a terrible place to start. By contrast, the last two clues are a good place to start because they quickly narrow things down.

And *now* the other clues suddenly become useful. The clue $u = 3t$ tells us that u can be only 3 or 9 and the puzzle falls quickly! (How can you decide if the answer is unique?)

h	t	u
		1
2		3
4		5
6		7
8		9

Teaching can, of course, include focused instruction—telling learners facts and showing them how to do things is not a sin and, in fact, at least some focused instruction is almost certainly necessary, not just for efficiency but to help students notice certain regularities or acquire certain habits like looking at extreme cases—but learners must also get lots of opportunities to tackle problems that they have not been taught explicitly how to solve and don't even know how to start. That is how real-life problems come to us: they never ask us if we're prepared. In class, where the object is to get students ready for these challenges, it's pointless to give problems that they *cannot* solve, but ones that they have not been *taught* to solve (and may not even know how to start) are excellent practice and fair game as long as the students have adequate background to figure out something that then lets them make progress.

Posing New Problems

The skill of posing new problems[3] is closely related to figuring out good questions to ask, finding good tails for a tailless word problem. Remember Kayla, who had exactly 28¢ in her pocket? Instead of asking, "What can you say for sure?" we could ask, "What problems can

---

[3] See Brown and Walter (2005); Moses, Bjork, and Goldenberg (1990 [1993]); and Goldenberg and Walter (2003).

you pose?" Over time, responses to tasks like this can evolve. Initially, one might expect few responses, and ones that closely resemble familiar word problem questions. At that stage, it is especially important to accept and encourage all responses, even ones that students might think are trivial. In time, the questions can become more sophisticated.

- What is the smallest number of coins Kayla could have?
- If Kayla has exactly 12 coins, what are they?
- How much more does Kayla need to make ___?
- With how many *other* people can Kayla share her money (assuming she has the right coins) so they all have equal shares?
- If Kayla has the right coins to share her money equally with one other student, but not to share it equally with three other students, what coins does she have?
- In what ways could Kayla's 28¢ be made with an odd number of coins?

By loosening the constraints, problem posing can go further. The last question above suggests a new one: Are there amounts of money and restrictions on coins that mean that *all* solutions require an odd number of coins? Can you come up with an amount of money and a restriction on coins so that all solutions require a number of coins that is some multiple of 4? And so on. The real mathematics is not so much in solving these problems but in the process of figuring out more and more interesting problems to pose.

Problem posing is, of course, a key ingredient in creative innovation—extending, deepening, enriching a problem with new, related problems—but it is also an essential tool in problem *solving*. This will be taken up in more detail at the end of Chapter 3, but for now it should be noted that looking for a place to start is often a case of posing a new and simpler problem than the (entire, original) problem that was presented. Even just simplifying the numbers to get traction on a problem is a case (perhaps only a trivial one) of posing a new problem. Students must feel permitted, even encouraged, to change problems at any time to explore them.

An example is useful. The following problem about sums of consecutive counting numbers has appeared in various forms and places (see, e.g., Goldenberg and Walter 2003). Here is one version of the problem:

> The precise term *positive integers* is less ambiguous than the informal term *counting numbers*, which is *generally* interpreted to include only positive integers but is used by some writers as if it also includes 0.

> The number 9 can be expressed as the sum of two consecutive counting numbers: 4 + 5. It can also be expressed as the sum of *three* consecutive counting

numbers: 2 + 3 + 4. *Perhaps there are other ways as well. The number 14 can be expressed as 2 + 3 + 4 + 5 (and maybe other ways).*

What claims can you make and defend about numbers that can be expressed as the sum of consecutive counting numbers?

First of all, this is an *enormous* problem as it was posed. The question is not at all vague—it asks for conjectures that are justified as claims supported by some form of proof—but it is very broad. For many students, their first thought is likely to be "Where do I even start?!"

With experiments. Try something. Gather some data. Some students might start with sums like these:

$$1 + 2$$

$$1 + 2 + 3$$

$$1 + 2 + 3 + 4$$

and so on.

Others might first investigate sums of only two consecutive numbers, or three, or four, like these:

6 + 7	4 + 5 + 6	2 + 3 + 4 + 5
3 + 4	2 + 3 + 4	3 + 4 + 5 + 6
8 + 9	3 + 4 + 5	5 + 6 + 7 + 8
⋮	⋮	⋮

Still others might start by seeing what numbers do make as they experiment with sums of consecutive numbers.

Each of these is a narrowing of the original problem, a new problem that the *student* poses. Though the student may not be aware of having invented a new problem, the student's claim naturally includes a "premise" that does state the new problem implicitly. For example, if a student claims, "Any time I add two consecutive counting numbers, the sum is always odd," the student is, in effect, solving the problem "What can you say about the sum of *two* consecutive counting numbers?" or, perhaps, "What claims can you make about sums that are *odd*?"

"What claims can you make *and defend*?" asks for a kind of proof, but the proof can be an informal sketch like "If two numbers are consecutive, one must be even and the other must be odd, so their sum is odd" or, depending on the student and class, it could be "Two consecutive counting numbers can always be expressed as n and $n + 1$, so their sum is $2n + 1$, which must be odd." A stronger claim is "Every odd number except 1 can be expressed as the sum of two consecutive counting numbers." Neither statement is about the generic case posed in the original problem: "[*All*] numbers that can be expressed as the sum of consecutive counting numbers." They are answers to a new problem, about a *specific* case that they specify (implicitly) when they say, "*Two* consecutive counting numbers."

In the course of the investigation, students may well do other kinds of problem posing that are more conscious than the subproblems that arise implicitly from experimentation.

- Are there any numbers that *can't* be expressed as sums of consecutive counting numbers?
- What numbers can be expressed as a sum of exactly three consecutive counting numbers?
- How *many* ways can a number be expressed as a sum of consecutive counting numbers? Is there some way to know this answer just by examining the number, or must I always experiment to find out?

Getting started on a tough investigation, or even a word problem, requires a sense of freedom to *ignore* the full task that is posed and just dive in somewhere. Even a vastly narrowed version of this investigation—short of spoon-feeding short-answer questions and completely circumventing investigation—requires that students' initial approach be some kind of further simplification.

Problem posing is discussed more in Chapter 3.

Seeking and Using Structure

Building the habit of seeking and using structure begins in the early grades. In elementary school, students meet structure in the notations and naming systems we use, in classification of mathematical objects, and in calculation. They also learn to seek structure by deferring evaluation. (See page 26.) Secondary school students see extensions and more complex expressions in algebraic notation, and they encounter and use more complex classifications in both algebra and geometry. They must often decide on an optimal level of evaluation—for example, whether to multiply/factor an expression or leave it as is. And they must often be able to see several alternative structures within an expression and decide which structure best suits the current purpose. For example, $x^6 - y^6$ might, depending on the context, be treated as a difference of cubes $\left(x^2\right)^3 - \left(y^2\right)^3$ or as a difference of squares $\left(x^3\right)^2 - \left(y^3\right)^2$.

Structure in Notation and Naming

Notation and naming are just conventions but, beyond some basic elements, they are not arbitrary. The words *seven*, *seventy*, and *seven hundred* express a conceptual connection among those three numbers; the written notation *7, 70, 700* shows their connection as well. The exact same structure of our number system is apparent in the notation *11, 110, 1100*, even though the words *eleven*, *one hundred ten*, and *one thousand one hundred* don't even hint at a connection. Though fraction notation is a convention—rational numbers like $\frac{3}{4}$ or $\frac{2}{7}$ could be expressed only through their decimal form or, as was the case historically in some places, only as sums of unit fractions—the convention that we have is not at all arbitrary: it represents the underlying structure of rational numbers, numbers that are expressible as the *ratio* (whence the word *rational*) of two whole numbers. Preserving the structure also preserves information that leads to insight. For example, the following expression looks, on the surface, as if it's saying, "Alternately subtracting and adding a bunch of fairly random-looking numbers (and infinitely more that we haven't been given) has a final sum that is pretty random looking."

$$2 - 0.666667 + 0.4 - 0.285714 + 0.222 - 0.2 + .181818 - 0.153846 + \ldots = 1.5707963\ldots$$

Well, *any* finite collection of numbers, added and subtracted, must equal *something*, so the fact that this obscure collection has that obscure sum is neither enlightening nor interesting. Here's what's missing: This expression shows the approximate *magnitudes* of all the terms in the sum but hides the *structure*—the source of those values. By contrast, here are two other views of that same sum showing how its terms are generated and organized—the structure of the series.

$$\frac{2}{1} - \frac{2}{3} + \frac{2}{5} - \frac{2}{7} + \frac{2}{9} - \frac{2}{11} + \frac{2}{13} - \cdots = \frac{\pi}{2} \text{ or } 2\left(1 - \frac{1}{3} + \frac{1}{5} - \frac{1}{7} + \frac{1}{9} - \frac{1}{11} + \frac{1}{13} - \cdots\right) = \frac{\pi}{2}$$

Now the numbers aren't arbitrary at all; we know where they come from, how they're related to each other, what the rest of them are, and why the result is interesting.

Structure in the Classification of Mathematical Objects

We classify and reclassify numbers flexibly as integer, rational, real, or complex, or as odd or even, or as prime or composite, or as multiples of 7, or in other ways to reflect properties that we need for particular purposes. Seeing a structure behind the definition of even and odd lets us generalize. We get these two categories, odd and even, from attempts to divide whole numbers by 2. What if we divide by 3? At first, we might again see just two categories: numbers that divide "evenly" and ones that don't. But we might try to preserve a different aspect of the structure that gave us "odd" and "even." If we think about those categories as reflecting the remainder when we divide by 2, we see *three* categories when we divide by 3: the multiples of 3 (they "divide evenly," or give a remainder of 0) and two sets of numbers that give two other remainders.

We classify geometric shapes flexibly as well, sometimes focusing only on how many dimensions a figure has, sometimes (with two-dimensional shapes) on whether its boundary consists only of straight sides or not, sometimes on the number of sides, sometimes even on relationships among those sides (e.g., angles between them, congruence, parallel sides), sometimes only on how vertices are connected.

It is possible, of course, to learn all of these classifying terms—*odd*, *prime*, *polygon*, *isosceles*—as arbitrary, unrelated vocabulary, but then one misses their purpose. Using structure lets us apply what we know about parallelograms to all of the figures that are part of the set we call *parallelograms*, even if we happen also to know those figures by other names.

Structure in Calculation

Elementary school arithmetic can be, and often is, taught without any attention to structure. Students can, for example, learn facts through random-order drills that rely on memory alone. But patterned practice—perhaps still pure drill, but organized around a particular property— builds structure that aids memory and skill. For example, consider what a student gains by learning to add 8 to any number—not just to single-digit numbers—by thinking of adding 10 and then adjusting. This approach can develop just as fluent fact-recall as random-order practice, but it also helps learners generalize to be able to add 18 or 28 to anything mentally. The structure is general, not just a set of memorized facts, so it is easy to adapt for adding 19 or 39 mentally, or for subtracting. Similarly, students can learn the 2 times table, learning facts for single-digit numbers only, or they can be taught in a way that allows them to multiply 43 by 2 because they can hold both 40×2 and 3×2 in their heads and then add them. Though the distributive property is a formal mathematical structure, the idea that underlies that property is built into children's thinking even before they know what multiplication is. They feel intuitively that doubling ⚬ ••••• gives ⚬⚬ ⫶⫶⫶⫶⫶, whatever number (or object) is in that bag.

But wait! Didn't we just encounter this very same example as a case of generalizing through repeated reasoning? How is this structure habit of mind different?

The repeated reasoning habit of mind—the way of thinking that becomes automatic for mathematicians—is to start with experiments and concrete cases. Mathematics is open to drawing general results (or at least good conjectures) from examples, looking for regularity, investigating, and describing the pattern both in what you have done and in the results. The structure habit is to look at the form of things, the structures in language, symbolic systems, calculations, systems, and classifications. To find that structure, one may well depend on significant experimentation and expressing the regularity in the repeated reasoning—that is, both may be interdependent—but the looking for and applying structure habit is not *about* the experimentation: it is about attention to and use of form.

Seeking Structure by Deferring Evaluation

In primary school, we can develop students' attention to structure, helping them learn to defer evaluation for certain kinds of tasks. For example, when presented with $7 + 5 \bigcirc 7 + 4$ and asked to fill in <, =, or > to compare the two expressions, young children are often drawn—and may even be explicitly told—to perform the calculations first. But competent adults, faced with a similar problem "Which is greater, $739 + 43$ or $739 + 44$?" would never perform the computation first. The competent adult is "strategically lazy" and uses the structure of the calculation, not the results of it, to answer the question.

This is where we want students' attention: we want them to see the structure, $\clubsuit + 5 \bigcirc \clubsuit + 4$ or [hand] $+ 5 \bigcirc$ [hand] $+ 4$, rather than focusing on the arithmetic. Without any reference to symbols "standing for" numbers—which is at least distracting and might even be confusing to young learners—they can readily see that it makes no difference what number is behind my hand: [hand] $+ 5$ must be greater than [hand] $+ 4$.

This same habit (and skill) of deferring evaluation—putting off calculation until one sees the overall structure—helps learners notice that they don't have to find common denominators or do any other "hard" work to compute $1\frac{3}{4} - \frac{1}{3} + 3 + \frac{1}{4} - \frac{2}{3}$. Instead, they see the computation as starting with 3, adding $1\frac{3}{4}$ and $\frac{1}{4}$ to that, and then subtracting both $\frac{1}{3}$ and $\frac{2}{3}$. For any student that could do this "the hard way" on paper, this new approach is a trivial computation that they can do in their heads.

Students need to develop this inclination to look for structure before jumping into calculation so that when they later begin to solve algebraic equations, they are able to use the same idea to treat $3(5x - 4) + 2 = 20$ as "something $+ 2 = 20$."

$$3(5x - 4) + 2 = 20$$

[hand] $+ 2 = 20$

Then, using common sense and not memorized (or mismemorized) rules, the "something" $3(5x - 4)$ must equal 18. From such reasoning, they can learn to derive rules that make sense. Students in beginning algebra are often taught to solve equations like $2(x + 3) + 4 = 24$ by going through a particular set of steps written in a particular way. On successive lines, they might write the original equation, then expand and write a new equation, then combine like terms and write a new equation, then write, on a new line, +10 under both sides, then . . . , each time writing a new equation. That method works for first-year algebra and helps students "see the steps." But it doesn't encourage students to "see beyond the trees" and perceive the overall structure. And it is really cumbersome for an equation like $\frac{80}{(x-7)} - 3 = 7$. Instead of the many steps needed for the conventional approach—add 3 to both sides, multiply both sides by $(x - 7)$, simplify, and so on—we could process this as $\frac{80}{(x-7)}$ minus 3 is 7, so $\frac{80}{(x-7)}$ must be 10, so $(x - 7)$ must be 8, making $x = 15$. It's not that one method is better than the other. *Both* methods are necessary, because each gives a different insight into the meaning of algebraic expressions and equations. Seeing the structure helps students see the logic of algebra; it often also makes calculation much easier.

Using Tools Strategically

Manipulatives, measurement instruments, calculators, and computers are all valuable tools. Paper and pencil is also a tool, valuable for much more than just calculation: competent use of that tool includes comfort with diagrams, tables, and graphs. Without diluting the meaning of "tool," some broad mental models should also be thought of as tools—and, as the Common Core requires, students should acquire the disposition "to make sound decisions about when each of these tools might be helpful, recognizing both the insight to be gained and [the tools'] limitations." Choosing when to pursue a calculation, look for an algorithm, or seek a contradiction is a clear example of choosing a tool strategically, a kind of thinking that, over time, becomes "second nature" for mathematicians: a *habit* of the mathematical mind.

All tools both aid and limit. Counters in grade 1 help develop skills and ideas connected with counting, but as a tool they strongly privilege positive integers. Though the Common Core sensibly puts the study of generalized fractions off until grade 3, even first graders come in knowing that they were 5, then $5\frac{1}{2}$, then 6, then $6\frac{1}{2}$, then 7, and counters don't let them represent what they already know about those numbers—especially their order—in a helpful way. Rulers and tape measures are concrete versions of number lines. Sensibly selected, they provide a way to show where numbers like $5\frac{1}{2}$ live. They extend thinking to positive rational numbers. The number line diagram extends thinking to negative numbers. The number line, an array/area model for multiplication/division, and tables all complement the use of counters, and remain important and faithful images of mathematics through secondary and university education. Tools help us organize and perform experiments and extend our reach, our memory, or our precision, but they don't *do* the problem. That remains our job.

Kinds of Tools

There are not just many tools but tools of different kinds. One kind of tool is the *labor-saver*. Tools like calculators—and their powerful siblings graphing calculators, and their superhero cousins computer algebra systems (CAS)—perform calculations that are enormously laborious without them. There were (*are*) ways of doing pretty much everything that they do without them, and pretty much everything that they do *was* done before they existed. In fact, if you're older than about 60, you were probably taught how to extract square roots using a paper and pencil method in high school, because square roots are often needed and there was no practical alternative before the 1970s to looking them up on a table or finding them yourself. The tables of logs and trig functions were all calculated by hand at one point and committed to books rather than teaching the methods to high schoolers because the computations were even slower, more tedious, and inaccessible than computing a square root. College and graduate school mathematics *still* teaches the methods, but no longer with the slightest interest in people using them for hand computation; the methods, and especially the way those methods were derived and interrelate, remain foundations for potential invention of new mathematical ideas and methods, even though the numbers that those methods compute are now available in an instant on your cell phone.

These labor-savers make mathematics and all the endeavors that depend on it not just easier but different, by changing the speed with which new ideas can be developed, which has contributed to the enormous growth in mathematics and physics and medicine (and other areas), and the speed with which old ideas can be applied (e.g., to guide vehicles or other equipment, or to analyze data). Because labor-saver tools have become indispensible in practice, learning how to use at least some of them—to get general principles and ideas—is now indispensible in school.

Data manipulation tools such as computer spreadsheets fall into this category, too. In principle, anything they do you could do without them, but as a matter of practicality, they change the world by handling more data with greater speed and accuracy than is possible without them.

A second kind of tool is an *aid to precision*. Drawing tools like rulers and compasses, measuring tools like rulers and protractors, and various electronic sensors are all tools of this type.

A third kind of tool is what we might reasonably call an *idea processor*. When we use a calculator to perform a calculation that arises en route to a solution, we are treating it as a labor-saver. But the very same set of tools can also be used to perform a set of interrelated experiments—for example, superimposing the graphs of $y = x^2 + bx + 7$ for various values of b to make or investigate a conjecture about the effect of the linear term. Here, the goal is not to perform a calculation and move on, but to experiment with variations on a theme until a clear idea emerges. By analogy to the term *word processor*, we might call this kind of tool an "idea processor." The word processor waits for you to enter your own ideas and contributes nothing at all except (perhaps) to catch certain recognizable errors in spelling or grammar, but you can rearrange the parts and tweak the wordings and adjust things until you feel your idea is clear. Word processors are specific to their domain, words; drawing and computer-aided design (CAD) tools do similar things for two- or three-dimensional graphic construction; and mathematical idea processors do the same thing in their various domains. We've already discussed CAS. Geometer's Sketchpad, Cabri Geometry, and Geometry Expressions are remarkably powerful mathematical environments for geometric exploration, construction, and proof, with such different features and capabilities that some people (such as the authors of this book) use all three. Fathom provides a similar kind of environment for exploration in statistics. Note that all of these—the computer algebra systems, calculators, spreadsheets, and interactive geometry and statistics tools—can be just labor-savers or idea processors, depending on what the student/mathematician is doing with them.

A fourth kind of tool is an *experimentation aid*. There is no generic description: depending on the problem, handwritten calculations on paper might be all the "aid" we require; or we might experiment by rearranging the order of objects in a sequence, using labeled bits of paper; or we might build structures from vertices and edges—polyhedra, tree structures, networks— using marshmallows for the nodes and toothpicks for the edges. The purpose, in any case, is to support experimentation, to allow an investigator to play around with ideas until some insight emerges. (By now, you may be noticing that these descriptions of kinds, or uses, of tools are not really disjoint: labor-savers can be experimentation aids; precision is often needed in experiments; idea processing and experimenting have enormous overlap, and both help build mental models.)

A fifth kind of tool is a *mental model builder*. It serves the purpose not of *getting* an answer, as the labor-saver does, but of building mental models (often mental visualizations) that allow one to get *mental* answers, or to organize or understand mathematical principles or properties and paper-pencil methods that use those principles or properties. This kind of tool is powerful if it is not just a special-purpose school aid but has mathematical fidelity and is versatile, extending and applying to many domains. Such tools help us make sense of mathematics; that's *why* they last. And that is also why good mathematical practice requires them.

The number line is one such tool, mandated in the Common Core State Standards not only because it is a good model for elementary arithmetic but because it stands as a mathematical model familiar and useful even to professional mathematicians. This and the application of the area model in algebra will be described in more detail in Chapter 5.

A word of clarification is needed because of the word *model*. The Common Core State Standards list "model with mathematics" and "use appropriate tools strategically" as distinct mathematical practices. The meanings *are* distinct, but connected.

When we use mathematics to model the growth of a bank account or the height of a plant or the expansion of the economy, or the spread of a disease or a fire, or the orbit of a planet, or relationship between the shadow of a stick and the shadow of a tree—that is, when we are modeling with mathematics—mathematics *itself* is a tool and we are using it to understand these physical or mathematical phenomena. This is what the Common Core's "model with mathematics" standard means. At other times, when we are trying to understand mathematical phenomena, we may use nonmathematical tools to model the mathematics: counters to model addition, for example. We are not modeling *with* mathematics but "using appropriate tools strategically" to understand the mathematics in the context of mathematical problem solving. The Common Core's "model with mathematics" standard is generally not construed to include this.

Chapter 5 focuses in detail on how geometric ideas can be used to model algebraic properties. Here we provide just a tiny preview of that, as an illustration of how mathematics can model mathematics.

Appropriate use of tools requires some reasoning about and picturing of results before they are fully derived. In arithmetic and algebra, that means reasoning about calculations and operations and predicting how part or all of a calculation would go without carrying it out fully. For example, if students understand $^-18 - 53$ as asking about the distance between $^-18$ and 53—specifically, moving *from* 53 *to* $^-18$—and if they understand the "geography" of the number line well enough to picture even roughly the relationship of these two numbers and 0 on the number line, they can set up that calculation mentally without needing special rules. Here is an image, drawn with no attention at all to precision. Imagine it sketched freehand without a ruler, by a kid.

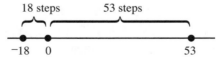

Such an image, mentally or on paper, shows that the distance between these two numbers is the total (the *addition*) of two distances (these numbers' distances from 0). The *distance*

between ⁻18 and 53 is therefore 71, but we haven't yet thought about the sign. There are two ways to think about that. One of the ways uses past experience. The sign of the result is negative, as students would expect when subtracting a larger number (53) from a smaller one (⁻18). Alternatively, they could think about the direction of change. Moving *from* 53 *to* ⁻18 involves change in the negative direction. Either way, we now see ⁻18 − 53 as ⁻71, without invoking special-case rules for the arithmetic of signed numbers.

The calculation ⁻18 − ⁻53 evokes a different mental image—one that students must first make with their hands and view with their physical eyes before they can hold it all in their heads and see it with their mind's eye.

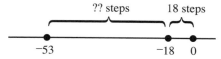

The distance from ⁻53 to ⁻18 is now the *difference* of the numbers' magnitudes (distances to 0). It makes sense that subtracting smaller numbers from larger ones gives positive results. (The change is in the positive direction.) In either case, the arithmetic—adding 18 to 53 or subtracting 18 from 53—is not performed on the number line (that takes mental manipulation or paper and pencil or a calculator), but knowing which operation to perform *is* made clear from the image. Other such mental-modeling tools organize multiplication (e.g., of polynomials) in the same way this tool organizes addition of signed numbers.

Tools may have different longevity, or may change purpose for a user over time. The labor-saver gets answers, allowing free and rapid experimentation while figuring out a situation, or it provides fast calculation to solve the problem, and remains a lifelong physical tool. The mental model starts out as a physical tool, but its purpose is to build lifelong mental tools—very possibly to be occasionally sketched on paper for communication or when new challenges arrive—and not to be a device for getting answers.

Choosing Tools Strategically

The Common Core State Standards for Mathematical Practice call not just for *using* tools but for students to "make sound decisions about when each of these tools might be helpful." Naturally, this requires that learners gain sufficient competence with the tools to recognize the differential power they offer. That may mean that from time to time, a particular tool is prescribed—or proscribed—until learners develop sufficient competency that they can make "sound decisions" about which tool to use.

But it also requires curriculum materials and teaching to include the kinds of problems that genuinely favor different tools and to give learners plenty of opportunities to decide for themselves which tool serves them best. For example, some computations are most sensibly done on a calculator, and some are most sensibly done in one's head; if a curriculum does not regularly switch among these, students make a habit of pulling out the calculator automatically without thinking.

When one is using tools to model the mathematics, the choice of model matters. When children first learn multiplication in elementary school, it is often modeled with images like multiple equal-sized collections of pencils, or multiple plates with a fixed number of cookies each. For example, 3 plates of cookies 4 four cookies in each is 12 cookies: $3 \times 4 = 12$.

Three plates, four cookies each   Four plates, three cookies each

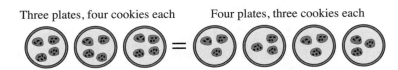

But with the "equal groups" model, it is nothing short of a miracle that 3 groups of 4 is the same as 4 groups of 3. This equal groups model illustrates one use of multiplication but hides a key property of the operation. A different image—the baking pan with the cookies laid out in an array—makes that entirely and intuitively apparent.

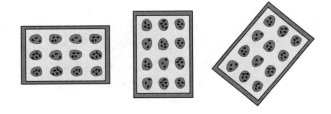

One can still use $3 + 3 + 3 + 3$, if one wants, as a description of the picture, and $4 + 4 + 4$ as a description of the same picture. Whether the multiplication expressions 3×4 and 4×3 are understood as "shorthand" for those addition expressions or as descriptions of rows and columns in the baking pan, it is clear that $3 \times 4 = 4 \times 3$.

That array model extends to allow 48×26 to be computed as $(40 + 8) \times (20 + 6)$.

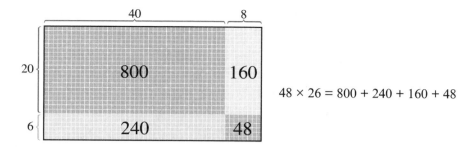

$$48 \times 26 = 800 + 240 + 160 + 48$$

There is no need for the tiny details—we're not counting anyway—so this becomes abstract.

	40	8
20	800	160
6	240	48

$$48 \times 26 = 800 + 240 + 160 + 48$$

And then, in secondary school, it generalizes to organize the multiplication of polynomials.

	a	b	8
b	ab	b^2	$8b$
6	$6a$	$6b$	48

$$(a + b + 8)(b + 6) = ab + b^2 + 8b + 6a + 6b + 48$$
$$= ab + b^2 + 14b + 6a + 48$$

The cookies on a plate model serves only for small repeated addition. The array/area image models the standard multiplication algorithm and generalizes for algebra: *that* is a practical tool.

Communicating with Precision

Mathematically proficient students . . . justify their conclusions, communicate them to others, and respond to the arguments of others. They . . . distinguish correct logic or reasoning from that which is flawed, and—if there is a flaw in an argument—explain what it is. (CCSS, MP #3)

Mathematically proficient students try to communicate precisely to others. They try to use clear definitions in discussion with others and in their own reasoning. They state the meaning of the symbols they choose, including using the equal sign consistently and appropriately. They are careful about specifying units of measure, and labeling axes to clarify the correspondence with quantities in a problem. (CCSS, MP #6)

The habit of striving for clarity, simplicity, and precision in both speech and writing is of great value in any field. In casual language, we are used to using context and people's reasonable expectations to disambiguate communication so that we don't burden our communication with specifics and details that the reader/listener probably can be expected to surmise anyway. But in mathematics, we need to base each new idea logically on earlier ones; to do so "safely," we must not leave room for ambiguity. Mathematics, in which such precision in communication is essential, is a good training ground for clarity. Communication is hard; it takes years to learn how to be precise and clear, and the skill often eludes even highly educated adults. If the teacher and curriculum serve as the "native speakers" of clear mathematics, students can learn the language from them.

See, for example, the really lovely *Plain English for Lawyers*, by Richard Wydick (2005). Though its intended audience is quite specific, its advice can be applied well by writers of any prose.

But what *is* "clear"? The term *mathematical hygiene* is slowly making the rounds now. We think it was first coined by Roger Howe, Yale mathematician, as a somewhat playful metaphor for getting language and terminology and symbol use "clean" (clear and unambiguous) as well as correct. For example, it's not incorrect to refer to the "sides" of a cube, but it isn't "clean": that is, without clarification, we don't know whether one means all the six faces, or only the "sides" as in the four sides of a room, or even, as we might well mean in a classroom, only the two sides (distinguished from front and back). Interestingly, precise language does not always mean fancier terms. Teachers (and curricula) push words like *numerator* and *denominator* on children because they are the "correct mathematical terminology," but because those words are often confused (especially at the start), it can be more mathematically "hygienic" to use *upstairs* and *downstairs*—as some mathematicians do themselves. The technical language may become important for other reasons—like tests—but in this case is not required for precision or clarity. Worse yet is the overzealous use of terms like *divisor* and *dividend* to describe the two numbers in a division problem, or *subtrahend* and *minuend* in subtraction: mathematicians themselves are often not sure which is which.

Correct use of mathematical terms, symbols, and conventions can always achieve mathematical precision but can also produce speech and writing that is opaque, especially to learners, often enough to teachers, and sometimes even to mathematicians. "Good mathematical hygiene" therefore requires being absolutely correct, but with the right simplicity of language and lack of ambiguity to maintain both correctness and complete clarity to the intended audience.

Defining terms is important, but children (and, to a lesser extent, even adults) almost never learn new words effectively from definitions. Virtually all vocabulary is acquired from use in context. Children build their own working definitions based on their initial experiences. Over time, as they hear and use these words in other contexts, they refine working definitions, making them more precise. For example, baby might first use *dada* for all men, and only later for one specific man. In mathematics, too, students can work with ideas without having started with a precise definition. With experience, the concepts become more precise, and the vocabulary with which we name the concepts can, accordingly, carry more precise meanings.

For learners, precision is also a way to come to understanding. By forcing their insight into precise language (natural language or the symbols of mathematics), they come to understand it better themselves.

For teachers in a class, this kind of clarity is important so that students understand exactly what a question means. Incorrect answers in class, or dead zones when students seem baffled and can't answer at all, are often the result of not being sure what question was asked, rather than not understanding how to answer it.

Clarity comes from developing a variety of subskills.

1. Use familiar vocabulary to help specify *which* object(s) are being discussed—which number or symbol or feature of a geometric object—using specific attributes, if necessary, to clarify meaning. For example, compare pointing at a rectangle from far away and saying, "No, no, *that* line, the long one, *there*," with saying, "The *vertical* line on the *right* side of the *rectangle*." Or compare "If you add three numbers and you get even, then all of the numbers are even or one of them is even" with "If you add *exactly* three *whole* numbers and the *sum* is even, then *either* all three of the numbers *must be* even or *exactly* one of them *must be* even." Note that the first statement is actually not correct: $7 + 1\frac{1}{2} + 5\frac{1}{2}$ is even but has no even numbers.

2. Use written symbols correctly. In particular, the equal sign (=) is used only between complete expressions, and it signals the equality of those two expressions. Also, the equal sign must not be misused to mean "corresponds to": writing "4 boys = 8 legs" is incorrect. Likewise, greater than (>) and less than (<) symbols are used only between complete expressions.

3. In writing numerical answers or speaking about quantities within problems, specify the nature and units of quantities whenever that is relevant. The purpose of precision is never to create work, only to create clarity. Sometimes a number is clear by itself, other times a unit is needed, sometimes a whole sentence is required: the situation determines the need.

4. Label graphs and diagrams sufficiently to make their meaning and, if necessary, the meanings of their parts completely clear to the reader. As students develop mathematical language, they learn to use algebraic notation to express what they already know and to translate among words, symbols, and diagrams. Possibly the most profound idea is *giving names* to objects. When we give numbers names, not just values, then we can talk about general cases and not just specific ones. That is exactly what (middle − 1) × (middle + 1) = middle^2 − 1 provided. And consider how much easier, and less ambiguous, it is to name the points in a geometric diagram like the one shown below and refer to objects by a name like $\overline{DE}$ than to say, "The shorter of the segments that go roughly northwest to southeast."

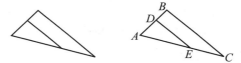

Clear communication requires the refinement of academic language as students explain their reasoning and solutions. Along with some new, specifically mathematical vocabulary, this includes the use of quantifiers (*all, some, always, sometimes, never, any, for each, only*, etc.), combination and negation (*not, or, and*), and conditionals (*if . . . then . . ., whenever, if not*, etc.).

CONCLUSION

Building strong mathematical habits of mind in students is a way of bringing coherence and meaning to mathematics. It also brings texture to the subject, highlighting significant insights over convention and vocabulary. Students learn that they can use their experiences to build habits—ways of thinking about and approaching problems. They move away from the belief that mathematics is a set of arbitrary rules and procedures to apply and begin to see mathematics as being about making sense of and solving complex problems. In the transition from arithmetic to algebra, students learn a powerful new language for expressing numerical ideas and for describing pattern and structure.

Mental Mathematics Is More Than Mental Arithmetic

Meghan (not her real name) was in ninth grade and enrolled in algebra. She was also enrolled in a supplementary support class. Like the others in that extra class, she was deemed at risk of failing algebra without the extra support. She was typical of that class in her past performance in mathematics: she could add, subtract, and multiply whole numbers mechanically on paper (but not well), and she used the paper even when it didn't really help, like for adding 7 + 5, which she'd count, and for multiplying by 10. She could divide haltingly (and not reliably) by a single digit and was generally stuck with other division. Some decimals seemed to make sense to her, but others did not; and she was utterly terrified by fractions. In fact, she was quite open about her terror, the most fearful—or most obviously so—in the class.

Meghan was also bright—as were most of her at-risk classmates. All of these students were called "slow learners," but it was not their learning, as I would see, that was slow. They were also called "struggling learners," and

> The authors have been working in several Massachusetts schools for the last few years, field-testing an approach to algebraic thinking aimed at helping students, especially "struggling" students, become fluent in the kind of arithmetic reasoning that's foundational for success in elementary algebra. Throughout this chapter, in the discussions of classroom events, "I" refers to one of them, E.P.G.

that, I was relieved to see, really *was* apt. As a whole class, they all tended to be passive, some of the students even a bit resistant, but when I worked with them as individuals, they were still actively, even eagerly, struggling to learn and succeed. And they wanted to learn algebra—*new* stuff, not just the second-grade stuff (even though they were not very good at that old stuff).

I first encountered Meghan when she was counting on her fingers to add 9 to 23 as part of a "number trick" intended to introduce algebraic notation. Without commenting on her fingers, I asked, "What's twenty-three plus *ten*?" She pulled back slightly and gave what would become a familiar look of terror and made it clear that she was having quite enough trouble with 9. Playfully, I said, "Oh! So would you mind if I annoy you with a couple of problems?" She shook her head with a forbidding no.

> "Please?"
> "OK."
> So I repeated, "What *is* twenty-three plus ten?" She counted on her fingers, speaking silently, and announced, "Thirty-three."
> "Fine. Add ten more." She counted again and said, "Forty-three."
> "Ten more." She counted, but this time, her tone changed.
> "Fifty-three?" Her questioning tone wasn't uncertainty about the answer, but surprise about the pattern. I smiled.
> "Ten more." She instantly said, "Sixty-three," but I asked her to count just this one more time to verify (and, by the way, to legitimize counting as *not* a sin).
> "Ten more."
> "Seventy-three," she said with conviction. I didn't ask for any more counting.
> "Ten more."
> "Eighty-three."
> "Ten more."
> "Ninety-three."
> "OK," I said, "*Nine* more than that!"
> She paused, but very briefly, and then, *without counting*, said, "A hundred and two?"
> I smiled broadly and genuinely, really pleased.
> "Am I right?" she asked, anyway. I said, "Of course!" and she smiled, too.

This new problem—adding only 9—required Meghan to use what she had just learned and required her to adapt it, relying only on her own common sense, and doing so at a spot, crossing 100, which I chose deliberately for its extra challenge. Her questioning tone this time did indicate some uncertainty about her answer, but the quickness of her response clearly meant that the mental act she had performed made complete sense to her. What she seemed to be asking was whether it was OK in math class to use her own common sense and not some rule she had learned.

This whole process took less than a minute.

Meghan and I played another minute or so, first adding 10 to any two-digit number and several three-digit numbers—I would say a random number, and just that number with no other words, and Meghan would respond with just a number 10 greater than mine—and then, after that became totally and obviously comfortable for her, doing the same with 9, and then 8. I was relentless, she was flawless, and she was awed with herself. She needed no praise or compliments.

SLOW LEARNERS AND STRUGGLING STUDENTS

At the end of that year, Meghan's algebra teacher, who had seen Meghan's work only in algebra class and not in this separate support class, recommended her for honors sophomore mathematics.

Proof! Meghan was *not* a slow learner. In less than a minute, she recognized the pattern and learned to apply and even adapt it. In a couple of minutes more, she became skilled at it. There would be many more indications that her learning wasn't slow.

And she didn't forget. Over the course of the year, Meghan continued to gain new mental mathematics skills and new confidence, and none of what she learned ever deteriorated.

So what happens to create kids like Meghan and so many of her age-mates? Adding 10 and 9 is, after all, second-grade stuff! Could it be that Meghan and her classmates really *couldn't* have learned it way back then, and had to mature seven years before they could make such gains in a minute's time? Yes, it's imaginable, but it's not believable. Close to half of Meghan's community (though not Meghan herself) and nearly all the students in two other communities we worked in were English language learners, but even with the added burden of nonfluency in English, we could routinely demonstrate in those

The lesson here is not, of course, that she succeeded because of five minutes a day of mental mathematics. Nor did most of her classmates get similar placements in honors (though there were three others). But it is a reminder that being on the bottom, even starting with a serious lack of confidence and skill, doesn't have to be permanent. Meghan's computational skill was abysmal, quite disabling her in mathematics, but the worst effect was her resulting disbelief that she *could* do mathematics, think logically, or learn this subject. She was quickly much better at algebra than arithmetic ($2x + 3x$ was mentally easier for her than 7×8) and wound up catching up in arithmetic via the algebra. There are many others like her. What made the difference for Meghan in her algebra class was her realization—a change that was visible in *both* classes—that she was *quite* capable. One of the best motivators is actual success at tasks one credits as hard (see, e.g., Bandura 1997).

communities' second grades that virtually all the children in all those classes performed as Meghan did in just a few minutes, given the same mental mathematics activity. It's not reasonable to think that Meghan's age group, seven years earlier, would have been, in such large numbers, so different from today's second graders.

The difference is not the students, but the activity. Knowing facts is important, but achieving that knowledge solely through memory drill is not efficient and works for relatively few children. By contrast, the drill that Megan did—let's be honest, it was drill—seems to work for almost all children. The way we create kids like Meghan from the curious, quick, and intrepid first graders they used to be is by focusing on memory *alone*, ignoring the parts of their minds that seek, and thrive on, pattern and structure. "Nine plus eight is seventeen" may well have been just a string of nonsense syllables for these children in first grade, rather than, as Meghan discovered in a mere minute, a perfectly logical deduction from knowing "ten plus eight."

Why Not Random Drill?

An alternative theory is very common, but it is based on logic that is flawed in two places. The argument goes like this: If Meghan had been fluent with all her basic facts, she would not have relied on her fingers; *therefore*, she and others like her should have had more random drills of "basic facts" (all one-digit addition and multiplication facts and the corresponding facts for subtraction and division) in early grades. The premise—if people have fluent access to single-digit facts (and a mental procedure for using them), they rarely use their fingers—is surely true. But it does not follow that only one particular (and complete) set of facts is the remedy, nor does it follow that the optimal way to achieve fluency with that (or any) set of facts is through random-order drill. For Meghan, seeing *structure*—in this example, the place-value structure of adding tens—easily substituted for an entire set of "nines facts" and, as she showed shortly after, all her "eights facts," too. Random-fact drill—randomness in general—hides structure.

> This activity with Meghan is an example of two of the habits of mind we named in Chapter 1. Through *repeated reasoning*, Meghan *abstracted a structure*—a pattern and an extension of that pattern— that she was then able to use to simplify her reasoning and improve her calculations.

Information processing theory suggests that the mental activity of memorizing facts does not leave enough processing space to see the structure and patterns underlying the mathematics. If you are *successful* at that memorization, and have the facts readily available, that frees up processing space and cognitive load, giving you a chance to discover the structure yourself. That works for some children. But if you get stuck at the memorizing stage, you both don't get the facts and don't see the structure. Then you may count yourself completely out—as Meghan clearly had done—until you have an experience (like the one described previously) that gives you a second chance, sufficiently different from the first that you dare to take it. By learning the structure, Meghan does not separately need to memorize the usual set of facts, because the structure gives her a different efficient route to process arithmetic mentally and, more incidentally, acquire mathematical facts as she goes.

Another reason to suppose that *more* random-fact drill is not the solution is that random-fact drill is common—sometimes in curricula but, even when not, often in classroom supplements with flash cards, computers, Round the World games, and so on—and still we get lots and lots and lots of Meghans. So, although we clearly do want students to get some set of numerical facts in their heads for fluency, and we even know that the more they can just retrieve, the less they'll have to work out, it should be clear that the random drill, however plausible it may seem, often does not work. Perhaps there is a better way to do random-order speed drill, one that does not generate tension in a way that decreases performance; or perhaps random-order speed drill is simply not the right approach.

The Value of Mental Mathematics Exercises

This event with Meghan was a spur-of-the-moment interruption of her work—an intervention based on a personal observation of her, and tailored to her, not a preplanned part of the lesson aimed at the whole class. But its design is nearly identical to mental mathematics exercises we do with whole classes. With a whole class, the management of the exercise is only slightly different, and the effectiveness, speed, and energy are exactly the same. Of course, in a large class, there are often a few students who try to disappear in the crowd, and the teacher must be watchful enough to notice and find a way to involve them. In fact, Meghan herself, even after such a positive personal experience with the adding-10/adding-9 drill, hid the first two times this kind of drill was done with the entire class. (More will be said about class management and involving all students later.)

Rational thought (at a personal or corporate level) tells us not to invest effort into ventures we think are likely to fail. Only when we believe there's a good chance of reward do we invest (even if we are wrong in our beliefs, as state lotteries prove all the time). So we shouldn't be surprised when the kids who most need to put in extra effort don't do it: if they see themselves as likely to fail, it is frankly quite rational of them not to try; they're better off investing that effort someplace where they think the chances of success are greater. So, if we want to change that pattern in students who see themselves as "bad" at mathematics, we have to craft activities that *surprise them with their competence*. Things that look easy to them are no reward at all, even if they succeed; after all, how proud can one be of doing something that looked easy in the first place? And things that look *too* hard will put them off. Things that look genuinely hard but at which they have success, though, draw them in.

Video game and weight-loss program designers use exactly this principle. They know that people stick with the program when they get the sense of racking up points, so they set goals that are real progress but achievable, and they make sure that you notice the progress that you are making. It's not praise that builds confidence, but seeing directly, for oneself, the *progress* in one's own competence.

Carol Dweck's research on mindset says a similar thing about attending to progress. Individuals who believe that their intelligence can be changed under their own control are more academically motivated and perform at higher levels academically (Dweck 2000) and are more likely to hold learning goals that emphasize effort (where the goal of the activity is to improve their ability) versus performance right now (where the goal is to demonstrate current proficiency to others). Middle school students who believe that intelligence grows as you exercise it have higher mathematics achievement than students who believe that intelligence is predetermined by genetics and is static (Blackwell, Trzesniewski, and Dweck 2007). Meghan and many others come to feel that "I am just not good at math" and therefore, *intelligently*, invest their finite energy elsewhere. A different perspective—"I am not *yet* good at math, but *could* be"—would drive greater effort rather than less.

There is evidence that teachers' beliefs about intelligence and learning goals influence these same beliefs in their students. In a study of middle school teachers, Pretzlik and colleagues (2003) found that teachers' judgments of their students' intelligence influenced not only the students' perception of their own intelligence but also their judgments of their peers' intelligence. Dweck's (2006) work suggests that one aspect of effective teachers is that they hold an incremental view of intelligence—a view that it can grow with use—and when teachers hold that view, they are more likely to appreciate and encourage effort. This influences students' behavior: when students' success at some task is attributed to "being smart" (e.g., by some praise from the teacher), they tend to choose their next tasks in ways that do not threaten that image; they choose easy tasks. When their success is attributed to effort, they tend to be more intrepid, choosing harder, but not unreasonably hard, tasks (incidentally, again not threatening the image they have earned, in this case the image as one who puts in effort). Taken together, this research suggests a possible mechanism of development in which teachers' theories about intelligence can influence their students' beliefs about learning, and in turn, their students' mathematics achievement.

Yet another mechanism can explain why these three experiences all aid learning: the surprise discovery of a pattern, the aha! moment of insight in solving a problem, and the recognition of one's own competence that comes from gaining facility with something one had found (or expected to find) difficult. They all produce a strong, positive, alert feeling. That feeling makes the incident salient and aids memory. People like feeling smart, even when their environment, in the many ways it often does, keeps them from feeling smart or limits the situations in which they are comfortable showing that they are (or feel) smart.

One criterion for a good mental mathematics exercise is that it offers many chances to discover pattern and build it into one's "natural" way of thinking: a habit—quite literally, a *habit of mind*.

> The milieu does not change the desire to *be* or *feel* smart, though. Being street-smart or quick-witted or even a good con can be highly prized even where being "school-smart" is socially costly. In a domain that one values, one wants to be smart.

ARITHMETIC, MATHEMATICS, AND EXECUTIVE FUNCTIONS

We will soon give another example of this kind of exercise, but first we should make clearer how this is more than arithmetic.

Unlike standard fact drills, the mental mathematics exercises we describe here do much more than build fast recall memory. These particular exercises are designed to expand capacities that cognitive psychologists refer to as "executive functions"—including working memory and the ability to track one's progress through a multipart process—that are essential infrastructure for doing mathematics. These skills are not themselves mathematics. But the ability to do mathematics, even at a K–12 level, depends on the ability to hold in mind several objects—numbers, constraints, properties, givens, statements, equations, functions, images, geometric objects—and to juggle them in some systematic way. Even when we work by hand on paper, the hand does only what our mind has told it to and the paper just sits there receiving our mind's work. We casually say to kids, "Math is all around us," but it isn't! *Things* are all around us; the mathematics is inside our heads. Squares are things of our imagination, not reality: we can represent them with paper, or drawings, but "real" squares have no thickness and our eyes cannot see them. But our mind can, and it can see infinity and do algebra, too, given training. We need to be playful with mathematics *in our heads* because that's where mathematics happens.

Building a System

These exercises build more than the executive function skills that are part of the essential mathematical infrastructure; they also build a logical system that reflects algebraic ideas, providing a solid foundation for learning algebra. New learning always requires some sort of foundation to anchor it and give it meaning. That could be a context in which the learning is found or applied, or an analogy with familiar ideas, or a framework or system of ideas into which the new learning fits or from which the new learning builds, or, as in this case, a collection of experiences from which the new learning is a generalization. When students have such a solid experiential foundation for learning algebra, they need less explanation of the new ideas of algebra, and they have a better idea how to incorporate and use that new learning; and, when explanation *is* still needed, teachers have that experiential background to refer to and build upon.

There's nothing wrong with committing ten single-digit 9+ facts and another ten single-digit 8+ facts to memory and then learning and using a carrying algorithm to add 9 or 8 to 35 or 47. But what Meghan and her classmates did—and even elementary school students can do, too, if given the opportunity—was the part of mathematics that involves *deriving* a method (in this case, for adding 9 or 8 to anything) based on their own understanding. Moreover, the method they derive explains the "carry"—their method adds the 10 first—and gives them a tool that is, for mental use, easier than the paper algorithm. When they get equally good at subtracting 9 or 8, they've built a logical system that reflects several algebraic ideas.

To add 8 by adding 10 and adjusting can be described this way: to get $n + 8$, we perform $n + 10 - 2$. We *know* in our gut that it works, but what *makes* it work? The actions we are carrying out are $(n + 10) - 2$; the result is $n + (10 - 2)$. That's because addition has the group-it-any-way property (the formal name, *associative* property, has a more restrictive definition), and because we can treat the subtraction in $n + 10 - 2$, which does *not* have the associative property, as addition of the additive inverse: $n + 10 + {}^{-}2$. That new expression is entirely addition, so the additive group-it-any-way property applies. These and other algebraic properties tend to feel arcane to students, because they're nitpicky about things that seem unimportant or obvious, but they have more meaning when they explain a good computational shortcut. This is especially true of the distributive property of multiplication, which really doesn't feel obvious to many students as they first encounter it but gains great meaning when they have developed skill at doubling and halving, as you will shortly see.

Multistep Processes

One mathematical goal of this approach is to increase students' ability to track their way through multistep processes in which they must keep several numbers, placeholders, steps, goals, and/or constraints in mind at once. Being able to start at any number and add or subtract 9 or 8 requires these skills in a small way—one must approximate the result using 10, keep the appropriate complement (1 or 2) in mind to use in refining that result, and keep track of which direction to adjust: "down" if one approximated by adding 10 but intended to add 8 or 9; "up" if one intended to subtract 8 or 9.

See Chapter 3 on the mathematical (not motivational) value of puzzles for more about juggling multiple constraints.

Let's look at another example from Meghan's class that puts even more demands on students' tracking ability.

Doubling and Halving: Getting a Gut Feel for the Distributive Property

On this visit, students were preparing for an upcoming algebraic context that would regularly require them to find half of two-digit numbers. Struggling with the arithmetic would take attention away from the algebraic ideas, so I prepared the students with a three-minute, highly focused drill on halving. As with Meghan's add-9 game, these drills were call-and-response style. The students played the role of a "function" to which I gave an input—deliberately saying no words other than the input number most of the time—and they responded with the output. That day, the function they modeled was "output half." All of them knew, absolutely fluently, half of 2, 4, 6, 8, 10, 12, and 16, and they equally well knew half of 20, 40, 60, 80, and 100. (They were a bit more hesitant with 14 and 18.) But when I gave 48 as input, only a few said 24. Meghan said, "How would I know *that*!" as if it were a fact she'd never been taught and I shouldn't have expected her to know. Imani next to her was just silent.

"Ah, right," I said, "many people don't realize that they can just take half of each part: you know half of 40, and you know half of 8, so half of 48 is . . ."

Meghan said, "24?"

Carefully preceding each compound input like 86 with a known one like 80, I gave more inputs. When the kids were responding confidently, I gave the compound cases without prior scaffolding. For that roughly three-minute session, I stuck strictly to the easiest level—two-digit numbers in which both digits are even. *Everyone* got it! Later that period, as kids were working on their own, I interrupted Meghan and Imani and asked if I could "annoy them with more problems." Meghan tried to ward me off, but Imani was amused by my oddball approach and Meghan gave in, not actually looking all that reluctant.

We briefly played the same halving game that the whole class had played earlier and the examples soon began to feel too easy, so I escalated (without comment or explanation) to a harder sequence that the rest of the class had not yet encountered. I'd say a number (italicized in the dialogue below), and Imani and Meghan would respond (as shown in parentheses).

> *60* (30)
> *40* (20)
> *50* (25?)
> *Yes, of course! Um, 80* (40)
> *60* (30)
> *70* (35?)
> *Yes; 20* (10)
> *30* (15?)
> *Yes! 70* (35)
> *100* (50)
> *80* (40)
> *90* (45!)
> *Yay! Can I give you harder ones?*

Even Meghan said yes. I continued: "*60* (30), *64* (32), *50* (25), *54*." There was a slight pause after I said "54." I think it was Imani who said "29" and then shrieked "No!" Both mumbled "25 . . . 2," and then both shouted, "27!" Most of the class looked up at the outbursts, the three of us giggled, I said, "Oops," and we pressed on, more quietly. At a lively pace, I gave several more, along with a few numbers like 812, and then I said, "OK, enough! Back to work!" Both girls were clearly astonished at what they'd done. Maybe three minutes had gone by.

This exercise gets students "habituated" to the idea that we can find half of a number by partitioning it whatever way we find convenient at the time, separately finding half of each part, and combining the results. That is the mathematics. Once the idea is "natural" to students, they can apply it to any multiplication, and later mental mathematics practices (and other parts of a good curriculum) will give them chances to do that.

Mental Mathematics Versus Written Mathematics

The central algebraic idea involved in halving and doubling is the distributive property. A secondary notion in this exercise is that partitioning by place value is often convenient. And, of course, students build fluency with the numbers, as well.

Commonly, when the distributive property is first taught formally in school, it is presented through a string of symbols, perhaps with purely numerical examples like

$$3 \times (4 + 5) = 3 \times 4 + 3 \times 5 \quad \text{and} \quad 2 \times (50 + 3) = 2 \times 50 + 2 \times 3$$

or with the numbers partially or entirely replaced by letters, like this:

$$2(a + b) = 2a + 2b \quad \text{and} \quad a(b + c) = ab + ac$$

When *writing* is the first way one encounters the distributive property, it may seem totally opaque. In reality, even before children know what multiplication is, they make informal and totally *un*conscious use of logic that they will much later encode as the distributive property. The mental halving exercise described previously lets students make conscious a pattern that they will learn to describe abstractly.

Written formally, the process that Meghan and her classmates (and the second graders the authors have also worked with) went through might look something like this:

$$\frac{48}{2} = \frac{40 + 8}{2} = \frac{40}{2} + \frac{8}{2} = 20 + 4 = 24$$

or

$$48 \div 2 = (40 + 8) \div 2 = (40 \div 2) + (8 \div 2) = 20 + 4 = 24$$

But the teaching activity we have described was very deliberately designed *not* to have such a written component. Here's why.

Long strings of notation, like the ones shown above, cause many readers—even fairly sophisticated ones—to skim over without actually reading closely. Take yourself as an example: did you really look closely enough at those multipart equations to be sure each part was justified and that there were no typos?

Probably not. But for you, that doesn't matter. You already know the full outline of the intent. You know what we should have written, even if we slipped. For a student, the situation is very different. It takes work to decode those statements. At each equal sign, one must pause and see exactly what transformation has taken place from the left to the right and understand why that transformation is legitimate. Otherwise, the string of symbols is either meaningless or arbitrary. If a student skims it, it serves no purpose. If the student does put in the effort to read it, the effort/attention spent on the notation is used up; less is available for the ideas behind the notation.

Let's do it step by step. To read the written form, we must see two things: the first step transforms 48 into a sum of two numbers and the partitioning uses place value.

$$\frac{48}{2} = \frac{40 + 8}{2}$$

The way our language works, we *hear* that partitioning in the name "forty-eight" with no effort at all. Understanding the written form takes more attention.

The second step is the distributive property.

$$\frac{40 + 8}{2} = \frac{40}{2} + \frac{8}{2}$$

Mentally, this feels easy even to end-of-year second graders who have done it a few times and gotten used to holding numbers in their heads. In written form, especially because this is a division example, and especially if we read right to left (seeing "fraction addition"), this easily calls up a host of confusions and misconceptions.

The rest is just arithmetic.

The mental management part—holding several items (in this case, numbers) in one's head and keeping track of where one is in a multistep process—is part of a host of executive skills that are not specifically mathematical, but are essential cognitive infrastructure for success in mathematics. These skills grow naturally with age, and though some of that growth may be neurodevelopmental, some (including the neural development itself) can be improved through experience (Center on the Developing Child at Harvard University 2011; Bierman and Torres 2012).

Another Example: The Any Order, Any Grouping Property of Multiplication

Let's look at another algebraic idea, the associative and commutative properties of multiplication, which, used together, amount to an any order, any grouping property: a sequence of multiplications can be performed in any order and grouped in any way with no change to the result. Mental mathematics practice supports well the building of a gut feel for this essential property. An ideal practice would illustrate the property, building the new idea on skills that are already so well learned that they are not distracting. Combining the well-practiced halving and doubling with the well-practiced multiplication by 10—that is, learning to multiply any two-digit number by 5 mentally by multiplying the number by 10 and then halving the result—is therefore a perfect place to start. Reversing the order, one could halve the input first and *then* multiply by 10.

Using the commutative property as well, and expressing this all in writing, we get

$$(10 \times n) \times \tfrac{1}{2} = 10 \times (n \times \tfrac{1}{2}) = 10 \times (\tfrac{1}{2} \times n) = (10 \times \tfrac{1}{2}) \times n = 5 \times n$$

As is often the case, the written form is a good way to record and examine the entire line of argument, but it is a cumbersome and obfuscating way to encounter the idea in the first place. You can understand that string of symbols because you already know what it is trying to say, but even knowing that, it takes concentration to read it. Try!

But the *idea* feels natural to students when they encounter it mentally. Let's go to another class. The students were already skilled with halving, and all knew (though some had learned just recently) how to multiply by 10 without using paper, so the only new *skill* part was the combining of these two now-familiar operations, tracking of the process and, of course, learning to decide strategically which order felt more convenient for the given problem.

> Students also need to learn what rearrangements they *cannot* make. For example, $420 \div 10 \div 2$ and $420 \div 2 \div 10$, performed left to right, both give the same result: $42 \div 2 = 210 \div 10$. But $420 \div (10 \div 2)$ is $420 \div 5$, a different number. This other learning is more suitable for selected comparison problems than for mental mathematics. It takes explicit understanding, not practice for intuitive feel.

Ashley found this hard work but enjoyed becoming competent at it, taxing herself to multiply 64×5 mentally by thinking $64 \rightarrow 32 \rightarrow 320$, and to do even harder problems like 43×5 by thinking $43 \rightarrow 430 \rightarrow 215$. At first, I could *see* her thinking, her eyes up and to the side as she paused, worked through each step, and then responded, with her eyes darting back to me. But after just a few minutes she had become used to the rhythm of the calculation and was beginning to find it quite natural. When she was clearly pleased with herself, I said, "Enough," and she asked for just one more. I said, "Easy or hard?" and she asked for hard. The 42 that I gave her, though, was actually easy for her by this point. Almost instantly, Ashley responded 105, which is not correct but such a common slip (to be explained in a moment) that I was amused, not dismayed, by it. In fact, this kind of slip is evidence that Ashley really did master the process!

So I explained to her how it's possible for a wrong answer to be proof that she'd become really good at mental math. When she was first learning to multiply by 5 this way, she had to work hard to get from numbers like 42 to the correct answer 210; by now, though, she got there so automatically and quickly that she didn't *feel* "finished," and so applied the last step— divide by 2—again, without noticing that she had already performed that step. (For more on slips of this kind, see Atchley and Lane 2014.) I said that it's the kind of thing that even mathematically competent adults can trip over and that the only thing we really get better at as we gain skill is being aware that we can trip! She found that funny, asked for one last problem, got a hard one, nailed it, and we were done.

This process requires significant working memory and executive oversight. The student must decide whether to halve or to multiply by 10 first. Halving 42 (or 420), as we described earlier, puts five numbers in our heads—42, 40, 2, 20, and 1 (or 420, 400, 20, 200, and 10)—from which we must pick the proper two to make 21 (or 210). And we then need to assess where we are (if we halved first, for example, we must still multiply). And then we must stop, the step that Ashley missed (just once!).

WHY USE THESE EXERCISES IN HIGH SCHOOL?

We have mentioned often that these ninth graders were learning things that second graders can learn. That raises at least three kinds of questions:

- Why wait? If these mental mathematics methods work with young children, wouldn't it be better to use them early, avoiding problems later? And if they are done early, is there any need to repeat?
- Is this an efficient use of older students' time? If they remain arithmetically unskilled at this late age, shouldn't we just hand them a calculator and not waste valuable class time on "old" material when there is so much new material to cover? Is mental calculation valuable enough to devote time to?
- Some students *have* mastered the elementary school facts and are successful at standard paper-and-pencil algorithms. For them, why exercise what seems to be just another way to do things they can already do well on paper? What do they gain from this, especially for algebra, that they are not likely yet to have?

Why Wait?

The vast majority of young students *can* learn to be very good at mental arithmetic through exercises designed according to the principles set out in this chapter, and that does save many students from being seriously disabled by mathematical weaknesses. So we *shouldn't* wait. But the reality is that very few school programs provide such opportunities in a systematic way at any grade level. Though some students achieve with current methods and some don't, achievement shouldn't be equated with *capacity* to achieve. The methods described here tap into a different kind of thinking, much more like what one needs for algebra, and that is part of the reason why these methods are useful even for many students who have gained competence with paper-and-pencil methods.

How Does This Help with Algebra?

The answers to the remaining two questions are intertwined.

Students who arrive in algebra with arithmetic weaknesses should not be counted out prematurely. A student who cannot multiply 7.98 × 6.7 with enough speed or accuracy to get good grades on elementary school tests—whether slowed or flawed by lack of memory of facts or by boredom and inattention or by inaccurate management of the many separate computations involved—may find no difficulty at all with either the concept or the much simpler arithmetic of $2x + 3x$. Success in an algebra class does require arithmetic (generally to complete a problem) as well as the abstraction required of algebra, but learning the new part—the algebraic content that is not taught in elementary school—need not wait for fluency in the old stuff. Putting off algebraic learning while redoing and redoing arithmetic further delays students who are already behind, further convinces them that they are making no progress and are slow learners, and (typically) employs methods that have already failed. In fact, algebraic ideas often help students see previously unnoticed patterns in arithmetic and use those ideas to become successful even at the arithmetic.

> Paying attention takes energy. A lot. And paying attention depletes our supply; the more attention we must pay to calculations, the less attention we will have available for the properties or generalizations or other new learning that these calculations might have led us to see.

If students are successful with paper-and-pencil methods, what do they get from these mental mathematics exercises that could justify even the very small amount of time the exercises take? The standard paper-and-pencil algorithms are optimized for difficult calculations, not for algebraic insight; in fact, part of the virtue of these algorithms is that for people who must regularly do difficult calculations, the algorithms reduce the hard thinking that slows calculation and increases error. So to compute $2(a + b)$, we multiply each term inside the parentheses by 2 and report the sum: $2a + 2b$. That is also what we do when we double 37 mentally (the way we described above): our mind hears "sixty" and "fourteen" and adds them (probably by thinking "sixty plus ten" and then "four more"). By contrast, the standard elementary school method gets us to think: "Seven times two is fourteen, write the four, carry the one, now three times two is six, plus one makes seven, so we write seven." We know about the seventy-four only after we've written it, and *never* did we even mentally hear the numbers thirty or sixty, let alone think $2(30 + 7) = 2 \times 30 + 2 \times 7 = 60 + 14$. The algorithm camouflages the property we need for algebra and gives us less of a foundation for learning algebra.

Our purpose here is not to turn students into calculators; our purpose is to support current algebra students in their learning and/or to prepare young students early so that they have the foundations for that learning. Even the students who were successful in paper-and-pencil algorithms need to relate what they know to the new ways of thinking that must become "natural"—that is, habits of mind—for algebra. And though we want those habits automatic, we also want them conscious, because the new learning requires, at least at the outset, attention to the properties that are being learned. So we want the focus and attention that comes from (mild) struggle: we want *all* our students to be strugglers! Not at all to make them feel the pain or "learn to work hard," but just enough for them to notice what they are doing. The chances are extremely good that students never did really understand why the paper algorithms work. By contrast, they have a strong intuitive understanding of what they're doing and why it works when they do mental mathematics, and that's the disposition we want them to bring to algebra.

Nor do paper-and-pencil skills help much with daily life problems; most daily life calculations are done on the fly, so we rely on mental calculations, not paper, and the more we can do in our heads, the more likely we are to do the arithmetic at all. If the calculations are truly beyond what normal people can learn to do in their heads, we still don't use paper! We estimate (in our heads, using mental mathematics on simpler numbers) or we get a calculator.

So why not hand out calculators and stop teaching arithmetic altogether? There have been strong advocates for this position, and clearly, we're not among them. To make sense of problems, even if one is planning on leaving final calculations to a machine, one has to have some strong sense of how the parts of the problems—in K–12 mathematics, these parts often include numbers—interact. Asked to write an expression that represents "5 less than some number," students (even good ones) often erringly write $5 - n$, vaguely translating the words to symbols in the order they encounter the words. Some also incorrectly write $5 < n$, another "literal translation" that misses the meaning. But many more students can correctly say what *number* is "5 less than 8" or "5 less than 100," and the process of performing that concrete act helps them see that what they are doing in each case is subtracting the 5 from some other number, leading to the correct translation: $n - 5$. Performing such experiments on a calculator is not just slower than one can do in one's head (if, of course, one can do it in one's head); it involves the very translation into print that was the problem to begin with! For calculations that are large or tedious, the calculator is the right tool—better than paper—but we don't know what to ask the calculator to do until we have a sense of the nature of the calculations in the first place.

DESIGNING AND USING MENTAL MATHEMATICS EXERCISES

What distinguishes the three exercises described previously—adding 10 or 9 or 8 to anything, halving anything, multiplying anything by 5—from other familiar kinds of practice, the kind of drill that gets people to invent phrases like "drill and kill"? Properly designed mental mathematics exercises serve three goals: they build mathematical infrastructure; they focus attention on algebraic properties and structure; and they *reduce* the amount of attention that students will need to pay to raw calculations.

Designing Mental Mathematics Exercises That Build Algebraic Habits

You have already seen many of the features of good mental mathematics activities: they are brief, lively, playful, and focused around an algebraic idea (even though they are enacted concretely just through arithmetic); they demand attention and focus, not just recall; and they surprise students with their own competence.

Here is a list of principles to guide your implementation of mental mathematics.

Mathematical Properties Must Form the Core

At the core of these exercises are mathematical (often algebraic) properties: complements or inverses, the distributive or associative property, place value, and so on. Although these exercises give arithmetic practice, they are chosen for and organized around bigger mathematical ideas. Random fact drills—the way flash cards and video games often work—exercise memory alone and focus on speed; the mental mathematics exercises we describe here focus on mathematical structure.

Exercises Should Be Framed as an Input-Output Rule

Students "enact a function." You give them a rule like "add 10" or "divide by 2 (take half)" or "double" and an example (e.g., "Today we're taking half, so, for example, if I say 6, you say 3"). If a rule requires a multistep process, you might let the students work it through once or twice, just to ensure that communication is clear. For example, starting with the logic that if you multiply by 5 you get half of what you get when you multiply by 10, you might have students step through the process once or twice before starting the regular exercise.

Exercises Should Generally Be Oral, Not Written

As explained earlier, the way information is expressed—in mathematical notation or orally in natural language—can influence what features of that information we attend to. For algebra, that is one of the great virtues of mathematical notation—"$x + 5$" is far shorter to write and far easier to work with than "5 more than some quantity." But for the initial building of certain computational ideas, like an early intuitive understanding of the distributive property, the formal notation can be a distraction. Also, a verbal interaction makes it easier for you to adjust pace *watching* the group, keeping it lively enough to build energy without creating pressure that builds anxiety. By contrast, a set of exercises on a worksheet or on the board just sits there being more work and potentially a threat. Therefore, the best mental mathematics exercises are generally call-and-response activities in which one person (often the teacher but, in certain cases, it can be a student) says a number and students respond.

All Students Are Involved

Whole-group and individual answering both have advantages. When the whole class is actively responding, each individual gets the most practice. When students are addressed one at a time in sequence, it can be easy to tune out when it is not your turn. But students can also get lost (or hide deliberately) in the crowd, so from time to time, it makes sense to ask for individual responses, or to vary the texture in other ways, either to spice things up or to give (not force) some students their own space. One way to keep students engaged even while they are waiting for a turn to respond verbally is to have individual responses *use* previous responses. For example, if the exercise is to find half of the input number, give one student 40, the next 6, the next 46, and so on. Or have chain addition of 9, each student saying 9 more than the student before, with *no* further input from you. Or work by rows, rather than individuals or whole group. There's no "rule" here except to maximize the practice per student, which means either being actively responding most of the time or being somehow mentally involved even while not actually speaking.

The Teacher Talks Very Sparingly

After the rule is clear, the teacher gives well-chosen numbers as inputs, with no other words. For example, if the task is halving, then the teacher might say "6, 60, 8, 80, 40, 60, 20, 200, 800," pausing long enough before each new input for students to respond without pressure, but no longer than that. The teacher says just the numbers, not "what is half of 6, what is half of 60," and so on. The reason is to avoid distracting students with words that swamp the numerical pattern that students hear, to keep the interaction lively and maximize the amount of practice within a short exercise, and to increase student focus by limiting redundant words to avoid student fuzz-out.

Number Sequences Are Carefully Chosen

The choice of numbers and their sequence must support the mathematical ideas behind the arithmetic act the students are performing. In halving, for example, two ideas are at play. One idea is that finding half of 8, 80, 800, 8000, and so on requires just one bit of arithmetic knowledge (half of 8 is 4) and place value, a mathematical idea that is built into the language we use to name these numbers. The bigger idea is the distributive property, which allows us to take half of numbers like eighty-six by combining half of eighty and half of six. In that example, we need only to *pronounce* the results we hear in our head: "forty," "three." In a more complicated example, like half of fifty-six, we again combine half of fifty and half of six, but we cannot simply "read off" the results as "twenty-five," "three" as we did before. We must add those results. Recognizing the mathematical and linguistic ideas lets us see that it is easier for beginners to take half of 112 (just say half of one-hundred followed by half of twelve) than half of 56 (which requires adding). Well-chosen numbers let beginners become competent with the steps and with their combinations and build a "gut sense" of the algebraic property by doing the calculations, not by having steps and properties explained and belabored.

- First 6, 60, 8, 80, 800, . . . to get the (linguistic) place-value commonality.
- Then sequences like 40, 48, 60, 64, . . ., in which a "complex" input like 48 is preceded by the opportunity to solve just a part of it (40) to build a "gut feel" for the separateness of the two parts (to which the distributive property is applied) with no extra required arithmetic.
- Then sequences like 60, 40, 60, 40, 50, and 80, 60, 80, 70, . . . to build the logic (and memory) around half of 50 and 70 and extend it to 30, 90, and so on. The back-and-forth between 80 and 60 prepares students with those easy-to-find halves, and the students' logic takes over with the gut feel that half of 70 should be midway between half of 60 and half of 80.
- Then sequences like 50, 58, . . . to apply the logic (distributive property) used earlier to cases where the result requires addition (25 plus 4) and not just "reporting out" (30 + 6 can just be said as "thirty, six" without explicitly noticing the adding that is involved).

The Exercises Are Brief and Lively

Just as with physical exercise, repetitive drill can strengthen or can injure. In the case of mental practice, mere repetition often just puts minds to sleep—not a good state for learning! The best practice is highly focused and lasts a short enough time and is fast enough paced to command riveted attention. It is that *attention*—the alertness that comes from putting one's mind to a situation rather than just repeating a fact or phrase—that builds the kind of learning that restructures and refines students' ways of thinking. That is what builds the foundation for algebra. In fact, becoming "addicted" to the feeling of focus and attention, all by itself, is an important part of the learning.

A vast quantity of research (see Bransford, Brown, and Cocking 2000) backs up the idea that distributed practice—brief intervals separated over time—is more effective than massed practice (the same amount of time all bunched together in one session). Two three- to five-minute practices are better than one longer practice. A pace that is lively keeps students alert; a pace that is not pressured or competitive avoids building tension that impedes learning. The combination—brief and lively—keeps attention and prevents boredom.

The Spirit Is Playful

It is important that the liveliness not be pressured, which diminishes performance. These are exercises, but like aerobics, soccer practice, or piano practice, they can be fun and not just work. Students generally enjoy these practices a lot because they feel competent and because they see their competence grow. Your own demeanor as teacher can add to that. Rather than pushing the students for speed in responding—a pressure that adds tension that can reduce their competence (and increase their reluctance to respond at all)—challenge *yourself* to have a new input ready as soon as they've given their output, and enjoy the funny lapses when you actually have to think for a moment to come up with a new input. Or, deliberately (though rarely, and only for the amusement of surprise or to give yourself a moment more to think of a new input), repeat the very last input. Anything to keep the tone light and quick.

The Exercises Surprise Students with Their Own Progress

The sequencing of mental mathematics exercises must allow students to transition very rapidly from tasks that feel easy to them to ones that look really hard but turn out not to be. For example, we start the activity with "For a moment or two this will feel much too easy for you, but play along and see where it goes," and then we say what the rule is: "We're going to make pairs that add up to 10, so—for example—if I say 8, you'd say 2. Ready?" At a playfully brisk pace, you might give inputs in some order like this: 8, 2, 3, 2, 8, 7, 6, 4, 3, 7, 9, 6, 8, 1, 4, 2, 5, 0, 10 . . . You want the pairs that make 10 to become fully automatic. And when you see that this is too easy, you announce that it is, and that you'll bump it up a bit. But you continue the same game for another few inputs before the change: 8, 6, 7, 6, $6\frac{1}{2}$, 7, 5, $5\frac{1}{2}$, 6, 8, 2, $8\frac{1}{2}$, $9\frac{1}{2}$. When you first say $6\frac{1}{2}$, the chances are that you will hear both $3\frac{1}{2}$, which is correct, and $4\frac{1}{2}$, which is not. If, before going on, you comment that you heard two different answers and that one of them is correct (without even saying which one is correct), students will figure it out anyway, and more will be correct the next time you give as input a number containing $\frac{1}{2}$. Their underlying expectations help them sort it out on their own. First, they have the experience of knowing, from reporting their own age, that $8\frac{1}{2}$ is between 8 and 9. Second, they have the experience that whenever the input number increases or decreases, the output changes in the other direction. Being told that one of the two answers is correct alerts them that there is something to pay attention to, but even in elementary school, they can almost always complete the logic on their own. When students get good at that, switch the game again to pairs that make 100, but give only multiples of 10. So, if you say 80, they say 20. Use the same sequence (but now multiplied by 10) that you used for pairs that make 10. The pairs become even more automatic, and kids quickly catch on that the game is the same, so when they get good at it again, switch it up a bit. After a sequence like 80, 60, 70, 60, try 61. They've just said 40, and they've heard you go up 1, so they must go down 1 to 39. It's not automatic, though, the way the pairs to 10 have become, and because the job is possible but hard (rather than defeating or trivial), it raises students' alertness, both mental and physical. And as long as the growth in complexity is not too fast, students love it, because they recognize their own competence.

> The physical alertness is actually measurable in heart rate increase, pupil dilation, and other responses. This literally wakes students up, and the feeling is positive. *Defeat, or the expectation of defeat, also has physically detectable effects, reduced energy being chief among them* (see, e.g., Kahnemann 2011).

Students Can Learn from Mistakes

Even the mistakes students make in these focused drills can help them learn. The learning environment of these exercises is sometimes all that is necessary to allow students to correct their own mistakes. Beginners (especially young ones) trip on these focused drill problems in very predictable ways: if they err when giving half of 48, they are more likely to say 28 than any other error. Nearly always, this is a difficulty managing the task, not a difficulty with the concept or intent or arithmetic. One piece of evidence that this is a case of tripping rather than misunderstanding is that the error typically diminishes even without feedback. Even in second or third grade, if a class is split roughly down the middle, some answering 24 and others answering 28, we can, without even saying which answer is correct, move on to another two-digit halving problem (e.g., half of 64) and the percentage of correct responses will go up! All students, younger and older, benefit if we periodically scaffold with a known case like 80 immediately before a compound one like 86.

CONCLUSION

The brain is *not* just "a muscle," and the learning processes of mathematics, typing, piano, and soccer are *not* identical, but the analogies, if not pushed too far, are good reminders: exercise is important; more is not always better; exercise should vary; be wary of repetitive stress injuries; refresh old pieces of music from time to time; and be patient. Strength and skill grow over time.

Solving and Building Puzzles

3

To mathematical insiders, mathematics is chock-full of intriguing questions—genuine puzzles not in the sense of something crafted for the sake of entertainment but in the sense that a consulting physician might consider an unfamiliar set of symptoms a puzzle, something that arouses curiosity or that you *want* to solve, even if no one requires you to.

When educators and policy makers talk about mathematics (in fact, all of "STEM"), we often hear phrases like *important* and *essential to success in the twenty-first century*. It is. But those words also carry a level of weight and seriousness that focuses on the risk of failure— the tension that already (in our culture) exists around mathematics. They miss the sense of surprise, curiosity, genuine interest, and satisfaction that mathematics can bring. Books and methods that claim to "make mathematics fun" give the same message: if they had to *make* it fun, it wasn't already.

As is true of any other endeavor, mathematics will not be everyone's *top* interest, but most people have *many* interests and find *many* endeavors appealing. The fact that mathematics is among the common dislikes may be partly because we worry (a deliberately chosen word) more about how to teach it and how to make it fun than about how to let students puzzle some of it out—exploring, seeing its logic, and tapping the surprise and satisfaction of conquering a challenge. We present formality before adequate experience.

In Chapter 1, we looked at habits of mind that especially suit algebra, both as a school subject and as a mathematical field. Other mathematical fields—geometry or probability, for

> Puzzles help students develop some of the habits of mind used by successful algebra students. Without these habits, even students who have the "standard" prerequisites, like fluency in arithmetic calculations, face obstacles as they attempt to learn algebra.

example—involve related but somewhat different habits of mind (Cuoco, Goldenberg, and Mark 1996). We (and see also Cuoco, Goldenberg, and Mark 2010) made the case that these mathematical habits of mind are useful not only in mathematics but also in many fields of human endeavor, even beyond science, technology, and engineering. The reverse is also true. Ongoing research is investigating the conjecture that computer programming helps develop habits of mind quite close to those described in Chapter 1. And in this chapter, we will show how solving and inventing certain kinds of puzzles can help students develop mathematical habits that are useful (even necessary) in making sense of familiar topics in high school algebra: modeling with equations, solving equations and systems of equations, seeking and using algebraic structure, and more.

Puzzles and mathematics have a close and complicated relationship. Many mathematical books and journal articles have been written about how mathematics can be used to analyze puzzles (see, e.g., Benjamin and Brown 2014; Ferland 2014; Berlekamp, Conway, and Guy 1982). And questions that arise from attempts to solve a puzzle have led straight into new areas of mathematical research. In fact, hard mathematical problems are sometimes pursued just out of curiosity and not out of need or initially recognized utility, and the pursuit often turns out to produce valuable mathematical results.

For example, questions about Sudoku led to a new mathematical description of puzzle hardness.

We don't claim that puzzles and mathematics are the same, or that all mathematics can be learned through puzzles. We do claim that the style of thinking that comes from working on certain kinds of puzzles helps students develop some of the mathematical habits they need in elementary algebra and that appropriate puzzle environments are accessible and inviting on-ramps to a sturdy understanding of algebraic ideas and topics.

WHAT MAKES A PUZZLE A PUZZLE?

Something feels like a *puzzle* rather than a forbidding task if you sense that you *can* make some kind of headway and you have the stamina—borne of experience—to try for more than a minute or two. Mathematicians who worked on problems like the Fermat conjecture had to be satisfied with solving smaller problems (generating new mathematical ideas) along the way, because the original problem would take more than a lifetime and require mathematical ideas that weren't yet invented. But the lure to solve any puzzle is a bit like the lure to climb Everest.

You don't even try if you don't believe you have a chance. If you do believe you have a chance, the challenge can be very appealing.

That's true for students, too. Students who lack the skills or the confidence—ones who are (or perceive themselves as) weak—are also typically reluctant to put in the effort that might make them stronger. But that's natural, even smart: no sensible people or businesses would put effort into a venture they think won't succeed. When you do believe you have a chance—when you know your own strength and the task looks accessible—challenge is appealing.

Fermat conjectured that $a^n + b^n = c^n$ has nontrivial solutions only when $n \leq 2$. It took 350 years and the development of a great deal of mathematics that didn't exist in his time to prove, just about two decades ago, that this is true. The work was done not because that answer was needed—the answer itself gives us little—but because the challenge was irresistible and because the route along the way promised, and delivered, developments in mathematics that are, in fact, extremely useful.

Perception: Puzzles Versus Problems

The Fermat conjecture can correctly be called a "problem to solve," or a "theorem to prove," so why also call it a "great puzzle"? The playful name is not intended to sugarcoat or demean but to make clear that the motivation for the mathematician is quite often curiosity, the puzzle of it all, and—fortunately for those who worked on the 350-year-old problem—not dire necessity. Genuine curiosity and the stamina (and other tools) to pursue it are habits of mind that we teachers would like to build in our students. For the curious and intrepid, calling something a *problem* or a *puzzle* really doesn't matter—being called a *puzzle* doesn't improve the problem, and may even feel a bit dismissive. In education, too, it is not the name that matters—there, too, *puzzle* might feel more appealing or might feel dismissive—but regardless of the name, there are very serious reasons to *approach* problems as one approaches puzzles. More about that later.

For now, though, let's just do a puzzle. This mobile has ten objects hanging on it and is perfectly balanced—that is, the two ends of each horizontal beam have the same amount of weight on them. In these puzzles, look-alike objects weigh the same, beams are always suspended at the middle, and the beams and strings weigh nothing. In this example, we are told the combined weight of all the objects on the mobile, and we also know the weight of a single triangle. Take a moment to figure out how much the other two objects weigh.

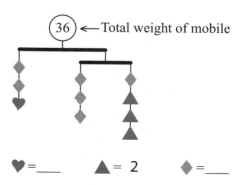

36 ← Total weight of mobile

♥ = ___   ▲ = 2   ◆ = ___

Here is the exact same information presented in the form of a system of equations, instead of a picture.

$$t = 2$$

$$2d + h + 4d + 3t = 36$$

$$2d + h = 4d + 3t$$

$$3d = d + 3t$$

Solving for h and d is the equivalent of what you did with the mobile. You might want to check to see that the equations are, in fact, exact restatements of everything you can see in the mobile, and yet they probably felt quite different.

Why? Perhaps because the puzzle form's *lack* of familiarity says, "You don't need rules and techniques from some course, but can depend just on your own logic," but perhaps even more because the puzzle form highlights the underlying structure, the logical challenge, which is the only part that is actually interesting. People take delight in their own creative conquest, but they feel less personally responsible for the victory when they are merely repeating steps they have learned from others.

How a problem is perceived also depends on one's background. Take, for example, this similar problem: "What numbers must s, d, and h be so that all three equations $s + h = d + s$ and $s = 3d$ and $s + 3d = 12$ are true?" For one who is fluent with algebra, solving this system of equations is not a lot of work, but it's also not a particularly interesting challenge: neither the answer nor the process is interesting! For one who is *not* yet confident with algebra, the equations probably look daunting. Students often experience this more like a test than a puzzle. Only in the middle—neither novice nor expert—could one really have "fun" with the equations, perhaps by looking for the "laziest" possible way to find a solution (using, say, the least computational juggling), or maybe by noticing the structure (like the appearance of s and $3d$ set equal to each other in one equation and added to each other in another).

In fact, "only in the middle" is a general principle: interest peaks when tasks are within our ability to grasp and conquer but hard enough to be fun. The amount of effort we are willing to put in varies with our confidence and stamina, but *everyone* wants at least some challenge: things that are too easy are boring; things that feel inaccessible are forbidding.

WHY DO PEOPLE INVENT PUZZLES, DO THEM, AND LIKE THEM?

Puzzles have been recorded since antiquity. They are clearly motivating, but it's worth asking why. Like all creatures that learn, we are built to seek out and repeat actions that enhance our adaptive advantage. Not surprisingly, a whole network of brain regions is devoted to the motivational "do it again" dopamine jolt we call *pleasure*. The adaptive advantages of cats are their claws, sight, and hunting skills, so kittens get that dopamine reward when they keep those sharp by scratching, stalking, and pouncing. A major evolutionary advantage of humans is our ability to adapt—to solve problems—and so we are impelled to keep our minds agile and sharp. In fact, though it's more common to cite food and sex as the major drives, hunger for mental activity is so strong in humans that even mild deprivation—boredom, the feeling we have when our minds are *not* engaged—is extremely unpleasant. When our minds have nothing to do, we start inventing things—puzzles and games, daydreaming, mischief, *anything*—to stimulate our minds again. Deprivation of mental stimulation is used as punishment; serious deprivation is torture.

The usual informal distinction between games and puzzles is roughly that in games people play "against" each other, whereas in puzzles, you compete with the puzzle itself. But there are also cooperative games in which the players are on the same team battling against the rules of the game, and we will describe "social solving" of puzzles, in which two or more players collaborate to solve the puzzle.

Puzzles entertain not because they are a vacation from the hard work of thinking—they're not—but for precisely the opposite reason: puzzles motivate because they engage our intellect. Of course, not everyone loves puzzles, but puzzles sell so well, even as impulse purchases (like candy!) at supermarket checkout counters, that it is quite apparent that the people who will readily spend more money to challenge themselves with puzzles include a wider market than just those who consider themselves "intellectual."

That raises a new question, important for education. Why is it that people who don't seem to enjoy more "serious" academic pursuits readily take on the intellectual challenge of puzzles?

Perhaps in part because the stakes are not the same. One can, of course, pursue "serious" subjects just out of curiosity or interest, but for many people—at least some of the time and in some areas—the "serious" stuff carries rather heavy baggage, including deadlines, tests, and anxiety about measuring up. This is certainly an issue in school, where testing is such a big part of the experience. Puzzles are essentially tests, too, but they generally don't feel like tests because nobody except you is watching to see if you pass or fail, and nobody is evaluating you and recording the results for posterity.

A piece of research intended for a very different purpose illustrates the importance of this difference. A test called Raven's Advanced Progressive Matrices was designed with no language and no cultural content, specifically to be a culture-free test of general cognitive ability. Yet it produces different results depending on whether the test-taker perceives it as "a set of puzzles" or as "an IQ test" (Brown and Day 2006). Under the normal test conditions, as a test of cognitive ability, African Americans perform worse than whites. Because the difference is presumably not attributable to language or culture, the "obvious implication" is that it must reflect a difference in underlying ability. Dead wrong! It turns out that when the exact same items in the exact same form and order are described to the two groups as a set of puzzles rather than as a test, the difference disappears.

The opposite claim is often argued seriously—get people worked up with a competition or deadline or the threat of a grade and they'll perform better—and general experience makes it seem quite plausible. In many circumstances where people are quite confident that they have a good chance of "winning," it *is* true, but when people have doubts, or when the consequences of loss seem severe, the more common effect is that tension hurts. In fact, raising anxiety even about matters totally irrelevant to the task at hand—like one's age or appearance or financial well-being—diminishes performance (see, e.g., Kahnemann 2011).

The significance of this finding is, of course, enormous, especially in understanding and addressing the achievement gap, and this important fact is not nearly widely enough known in educational circles. Low expectations and heightened anxiety diminish performance; poor performance creates (and confirms) expectation; and the whole cycle continues. But the implications are far broader: *the way a problem is perceived—whether as a puzzle or as a problem or test item—can affect performance even when other bias (e.g., cultural or language) is eliminated.* This particular study focused on race, but anxiety effects raised by the perception of being tested exist even within a single racial, ethnic, cultural, socioeconomic, or gender group. And these effects can follow children throughout their schooling.

Advantages and Risks of Using Puzzles in School

In K–12 curricula, games and puzzles are sometimes treated as a sugarcoating, not "real" work. It's often argued that students must know that not all learning is fun and games. We agree. And there are some serious risks involved in overusing or misusing puzzles and games. For one thing, students themselves—especially those who are most prone to feeling weak or feeling that their strengths are not taken seriously—*can* perceive play in school as a kind of put-down, yet another subtle implication that they are not ready for serious work. Like play, praise also has both value and risk. Praise is great and we all like it, but when "Great job" and other versions of smiley faces are too freely given, they begin to lose their meaning and value—they no longer feel like praise, because they don't distinguish any one performance from any other. Though play is one of the chief ways we learn, even as adults but especially as young people, it is so not part of the expected culture of school that overuse in school often gets students to devalue the learning they're doing, *even if that learning is substantial.*

On the other hand, play *is* powerful, not just because it is a motivator—we all like it!—but because of all the flexible thinking and decision making we need to do to engage in real puzzling and play. That cognitive demand is *why* play is a motivator, and that is the major point of this chapter.

One way to avoid the risks associated with too much play is to be honest about what is *not* play. Just as praise begins to lose its value when students perceive it as completely indiscriminate (when, for example, it is used too often or given for work that the student him- or herself considers a slack-off job), *game* becomes meaningless when it is applied to things that are genuinely not games. In fact, that is pretty common in school, and especially in mathematics classes. Things that are not gamelike—not what students would spontaneously do for fun if given complete freedom—are often called "games" as if the mere renaming makes them more palatable. The implicit message is "You won't like math unless you think it's a game." It's a double insult: to the subject and to the student.

Oddly, the opposite occurs, too. Things that *are* pure inventions get called "real-world problems," perhaps so that they will be taken seriously. Problems like

> If Mary can paint a house in 6 hours and John can paint a house in 9 hours, how long will it take them to paint a house if they work together?

can be extremely useful exercises of particular techniques or ways of thinking about problems, even though neither the scenario they describe nor their mathematical answer is at all realistic.

Students cannot help but see through both of these misnomers. Why not admit that the house-painting problem is a crafted puzzle? Such puzzles are just simplified *models* of reality that serve as stepping stones to harder problems. The puzzles of real life tend to be hard! Likewise, the meanings of *game* and *puzzle* should not be diluted by using them inappropriately: when we do assign pure skill practice and genuine problems, we can say so, and approach them in a pleasant, curious, even playful spirit without claiming that they are actually *play*.

Using Puzzles to Build Mathematical Habits of Mind

As we've said, though puzzles often motivate, that's not their educational value; after all, candy motivates too, but it's hardly intrinsic (or healthy) motivation. The value of well-chosen puzzles is that they naturally foster—motivate, if you like—a mathematical frame of mind that we care about. Well-selected puzzles can help build curiosity; the inclination to scout around, looking for useful information and a smart place to start; the stamina to *keep* looking and see what progress each step makes and what new clues are revealed; the drive to search for interrelationships or structure that simplifies the picture; and an I-can-figure-it-out expectation. These are all dispositions that we are trying to build in our students anyway, dispositions that are essential to proficiency in mathematics. If they are appropriately designed, puzzles can also be very effective contexts for learning content.

For example, consider a genre of puzzles we call Who Am I? puzzles. In a Who Am I? puzzle, some mathematical object—in this case, a number—gives you clues about its identity and you must figure out "who" is speaking. The labeled boxes give h, t, and u a context, making their meaning apparent even to elementary school students.

This genre—and this particular puzzle itself—will be discussed in more detail later. Try the puzzle before reading on.

Who Am I?

h	t	u

- I am an even three-digit number.
- My tens digit is a perfect square.
- $u = h$.
- I am less than 400.
- My tens digit is greater than 4.

What Makes a Puzzle Satisfying?

Finding the answer is satisfying, but that's not what makes this (or any) puzzle appealing. The *answer* to the math "trick" 12,345,679 × 63 may be intriguing and lead to something satisfying, but you get no satisfaction out of *finding* that answer. Multiplying 12,345,679 × 63 involves a preknown method (or just a calculator) and no thinking. By contrast, almost certainly, your path through the Who Am I? puzzle involved moving back and forth among the clues, searching for something useful, revisiting some clues more than once as other clues narrowed the possibilities. It wasn't hard, but it took thought: that is the satisfying part. And it would have been even *more* satisfying to conquer if the struggle had been harder—not more arithmetically tedious, but more logically complex. The harder the puzzle, the more satisfaction you get, up to the point when the puzzle conquers *you*, either because you fail or because the amount of work exceeds your stamina and interest.

Just as puzzles are no fun if they're too easy, they're also not attractive if they feel too hard. The puzzle/problem does not have to *be* too hard to *feel* too hard. Part of learning is developing the confidence and stamina to tackle harder and harder problems, and one advantage of puzzles is that they invite a bit more patience—it's a puzzle, not a test—and can help students develop that stamina.

WHO AM I? PUZZLES

As you've just seen, the instructions for Who Am I? puzzles are simple (a feature of all good puzzles): use the clues to find the suspect. Solving these puzzles requires interpreting constraints (algebraic and/or verbal), coordinating multiple pieces of information, drawing logical conclusions. Who Am I? puzzles also strengthen mathematical language while helping to teach targeted academic and symbolic language.

In early grades, the content of these puzzles can focus on basic operations, comparing numbers, parity (even/odd), and place value. In later grades, the clues can include more advanced topics such as divisibility, primes, squares, roots, magnitude, inequalities, algebraic notation, and so on.

Redundant clues—this puzzle has many—provide alternative entry points, let students check their work, and also allow students to feel clever, announcing they've solved the problem without using all the clues or that some clues are really not needed. Note that some clues are about digits, and others are about the number itself. Even for young students, the context (and the picture that accompanies the puzzle) makes it clear that a clue with very simple algebraic notation, like $u - t = 1$ in the puzzle that follows, means "The units digit minus the tens digit is 1."

Who Am I?

t   *u*

- I am an even number.
- I am more than 12.
- My units digit is even.
- I am less than 16.
- I am equal to 5 + 9.
- My tens digit is odd.
- My units digit is not 5.

For algebra students, clues can be written with an even wider variety and greater number of algebraic statements. These puzzles could be solved as systems of equations, but the fact that *digits* are a highly constrained set makes it possible, and often logically more interesting, to examine and record possibilities while reasoning out the clues.

For example, the puzzler may use the second clue in the second Who Am I? puzzle ($h = 2u$) to identify four coordinated possibilities for the hundreds and units digits and record them as shown here. These are the only possibilities because h must be a single digit and cannot be 0 ("I am a three-digit number"). The puzzler may then look to other clues to isolate the answer.

With simpler puzzles, such as the two-digit puzzle shown earlier, it may be possible to juggle the constraints mentally, but with more complex puzzles, keeping notes often feels necessary, and *so* natural that puzzlers don't need to be told to do it. They often invent their own systems, and even improve their systems over time, a skill

that translates well to broader mathematical problem-solving contexts. The notes are also a good example of slowing down and thinking, accepting partial results as real progress, and expecting that these partial results will lead somewhere.

Who Am I? puzzles aren't restricted to integers. Extensions for decimals and fractions are easy to design, limited only by the qualities of any good puzzle: easy enough to solve, hard enough to be fun.

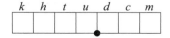

Who Am I?

h	t	u

- I am a three-digit number.
- $h = 2u$.
- $h = 1 + t + u$.
- $ut > h$.
- $u - t = 1$.
- $u + 4t = 2h$.

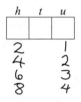

h	t	u
2		1
4		2
6		3
8		4

Who Am I?

$$\frac{\text{numerator}}{\text{denominator}} = \frac{\Box}{\Box}$$

- I am less than $\frac{1}{2}$.
- I am not 0.
- My numerator and my denominator both have one digit.
- My denominator is 3 more than my numerator.
- Neither my numerator nor my denominator is a square number.

Depending on the learning goals, one might even omit the place-value labels entirely. For example, one might want students to use logic to determine not only the digits but also the location of the decimal point, as in the example to the right.

Ultimately, conventionally structured problems can also come to feel more like puzzles (of course, until they are too easy and mechanical to be interesting at all). After all,

> Find the coefficients a, b, and c in the quadratic $y = ax^2 + bx + c$ so that the roots are $-\frac{2}{3}$ and $-\frac{1}{2}$ and the maximum value y can attain is $8\frac{1}{8}$.

Who Am I?

- I am less than $1\frac{1}{2}$.
- I'm greater than 1.45.
- Three of my digits are even.
- None of my digits are prime.
- My hundredths digit minus my thousandths digit is 2.
- The product of my hundredths digit and my thousandths digit is 48.

gives clues and asks for numbers, just like the previous Who Am I? puzzles. But before we feel confident about mathematics, such a problem may feel like a test to fail, not a puzzle to conquer.

In the Who Am I? puzzles you just played, the hidden suspect was a number, but Who Am I? puzzles can be crafted about any mathematical objects and for any topic. For example, "I am a polyhedron. I have the same number of vertices as faces. At least one of my faces is a triangle. At least one of my faces is a pentagon. Who am I?" Or, as made up by a particularly tricky student once: "I am a polyhedron. Six of my faces are rectangles. Two of my faces are squares. I have no other faces. Who am I?"

After students have solved several Who Am I? puzzles (at any difficulty level and with any content), they can benefit from (and enjoy!) inventing their own. In general, a way to start is to write the solution, then invent clues that fit the solution, and continue until there appear to be just the right clues to determine that answer uniquely. Erase the answer and the puzzle's done. Uniqueness, of course, isn't essential—one could, instead of "Who Am I?" ask, "What numbers could I be?"—but puzzle solvers need that warning, or they feel stuck when they've correctly used all the clues and have not arrived at a solution. As you invent puzzles for your students, or as you encourage them to invent puzzles for each other, you can draw from (or suggest to them) a wide variety of clue types. Clues can involve parity, sign, multiples, factors, squares, primes, algebraic notation and/or solving, inequalities, substitution, order of operations, distribution, factoring, systematic listing (e.g., the sum of my three digits is 11), maxima, and so on. The end of this chapter will have more to say about inventing puzzles.

MOBILES AND MYSTERY NUMBER PUZZLES

Mobile Puzzles

Mobile puzzles, as you've seen, ask the puzzler to figure out unknown weights. Identical shapes represent the same weight; nonmatching shapes may have the same weight or may have different weights (just as different variables in algebra *may* have the same value); and, as was said before, the beams are suspended at their midpoints and the strings and beams are treated as weightless.

You've also seen that mobile puzzles are analogues of systems of equations. Used thoughtfully, the transition to algebraic notation and the logic of solving systems of equations can be smooth. In fact, students can *induce* the conventional "rules" for solving—ideas, for example, about substitution—from their actions on the mobiles and then apply them to standard algebra.

One step in that transition to algebra is learning to translate the information presented in a mobile into algebraic notation, in part just to make explicit what information is given in a mobile, and how efficient algebraic notation is in recording that information. So, for example, students may be given a puzzle, like the one here, and a key like

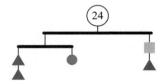

■ = s, ▲ = t, and ● = c, and asked to translate the puzzle into equations. The fact that the mobile is balanced suggests two equations: $2t = c$ (the short lower beam on the left) and $2t + c = s + t$ (the main beam on the top). To solve the mobile puzzle, we must also use the weight at the top.

Students typically use that total weight just in passing, without writing the equation it represents: $3t + c + s = 24$. It is enough for them to note that the entire left side of the top beam weighed 12 and then move directly to the next step, seeing $c = 6$ and $2t = 6$. But in a translation assignment, students do sometimes write the equation $2t + c = 12$.

The system of three equations, as shown at right, describes the structure of the mobile: the total weight of all stuff and the two balanced beams. It contains all the information given in the mobile puzzle (though other equations, like $s + t = 12$, can be written). Of course, many other equivalent sets of equations—sets that provide the same information in some other form and thus have the same solution—can be written.

$$\begin{cases} 3t + c + s = 24 \\ 2t + c = s + t \\ c = 2t \end{cases}$$

Another step in the transition to algebra is making the logic explicit. In the previous puzzle, one might find a solution without noticing the various steps one has taken, so, at some point, more attention might need to be drawn to that logic.

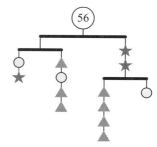

Before reading on, play with the much more difficult puzzle on the right. Give it some time and *notice* what you try (both what works and what doesn't).

Pure experimentation may solve the problem, but if you solved it deductively, you probably, at some point, used the fact that the short beam on the left has a ◯ on each side of it. Because those circles *must* balance each other, the remaining objects show that ★ exactly balances three ▲s. This logical deduction from the mobile is the equivalent of the "subtract from both sides" in algebra, but it arises from insight based on experience, not as an arbitrary given rule.

This new piece of information, ★ = ▲▲▲, can be substituted into the short beam on the right, the one that currently says ★ + ▲ = ◯, to get ▲▲▲▲ = ◯, yet another new piece of information. We still can't figure out any weights directly, but we are getting closer to a situation (only one kind of object, in this case a ▲, on a string whose weight is known) that allows us to deduce, directly and without guesswork, the weight of one ▲.

At no time did we think in terms of following a set of rules handed down by an outside authority, a book or a teacher—isolate variables, subtract from both sides, substitute, divide by a common factor. But those are exactly the steps we took as we made sense of this mobile. With more experience, we see the same reasoning repeating often, and naming the steps becomes worthwhile. The terms used in algebra class now name logic we own; they don't have be imposed and memorized.

The Utility and Limitations of Mobiles

The weights on mobile puzzles can have any value at all—whole number, fractional, and (with some imagination) even negative—but the *coefficients* in equations that can be represented with mobiles are pretty much limited to positive integers: we cannot put −3.1 stars on a string. Moreover, two unknown values cannot be multiplied: a mobile can represent 3*t*, but cannot represent *st*. So mobiles are not as versatile and flexible

> Visit http://solveme.edc.org for hundreds of puzzles to solve. You can also build and share your own puzzles.

as equations and are neither a substitute for algebra nor a method for solving equations. But the mobile imagery can be a powerful tool for thinking about how we solve equations and for generating and understanding the logic behind solution strategies. Though not all linear equations translate well into mobiles, the variety of solving steps that mobiles can require is close to a complete introduction to (or refresher of) the logic of solving systems of linear equations. Mobile puzzles' informality—in particular, the pull to develop one's own logic—forms a solid foundation of experience on which to build the formal rules.

Referring to the logic of the mobile can also help straighten out common algebraic slips like subtracting something from one side of an equation and adding it to the other: "If you subtract something from one side of a mobile and add it to the other, will the mobile stay balanced?" You can also ask students to determine whether a given mobile *must* be balanced regardless of the weights of the objects, *can't* ever balance regardless of the weights of the objects, or balances *only for specific choices* of the weights. And you can ask them to make simple examples of each of these cases. The analysis they must go through to create the examples can be of great benefit.

Mystery Number Puzzles

Like mobile puzzles, Mystery Number puzzles present sets of constraints equivalent to systems of equations. The Mystery Number puzzles are presented directly in the form of equations—possibly with shapes, even with letters—and can represent multiplication and division of unknowns as well as sums and differences. Unlike the mobile puzzles, the purpose is not to reason about "algebraic solving moves" but to notice and use some properties of numbers and operations (like additive and multiplicative identity). Alone or in combination, the clues place restrictions on the values of the variables to help focus on these properties. Like the Who Am I? puzzles, Mystery Number puzzles build working memory and the ability to coordinate multiple pieces of information, as this example—essentially a system of simultaneous equations—shows.

Lucky you! In your backyard, you found several fragments of pottery—maybe a secret code, or from a spaceship or an ancient ruin, or just from some country whose language you don't know.

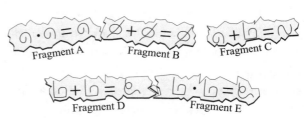

From other fragments, you already figured out that the "•" and "+" and "=" mean exactly what they mean in your language, and it turns out that the other symbols are digits, so

they must be different digits and only 0 through 9. But what digits are they?!

What number(s) could that jelly roll-shaped figure be in Fragment A? Something times itself equals itself? The only possibilities (for different reasons) are 0 and 1. The squiggles in Fragment B are more certain: the only thing that can be added without changing the result is 0, so the jelly roll in A must be 1.

The focus on properties is possibly more obvious in this puzzle. Because the operations are normal addition and multiplication (and their inverses), the symbol that behaves like the additive identity is 0; the symbol that behaves like a multiplicative identity is 1; and so on. For the same reason that redundant information is useful in Who Am I? puzzles—alternative entry points, checks on work, and the opportunity to say,

"I've solved it without even using all the clues!"—it is often useful here. Which equations in this set don't you need to consult at all? How do you figure out ♣ ?

Depending on our purposes, we might want to specify, in advance, that all symbols represent whole numbers and that different symbols represent different numbers. (And we might want to call special attention to the fact that this is *not* how we standardly interpret variables in algebra.) If we allow different symbols to have the same value, this set of equations has more than one solution. A student who comes up with a second solution is definitely clever! Are there *more* than two solutions? What if the variables need not have integer values?

Since these are letterlike anyway, why not actual letters? Why, in fact, not use letters on the mobiles right from the start, getting students used to "letters standing for numbers"? Observation with students suggests that the psychology is very different. Elementary school students see 2 + 3 not just as a record of a calculation but as a "call for action." They must *perform* it, not just acknowledge it. In fact, in Chapter 1 we spoke of helping them to *not* jump straight to calculation when they are asked to write >, =, or < in the circle to make 7 + 5 ◯ 7 + 4 true.

For children in early grades, the expression 2 + 3 fairly screams out 5. The written form $x + y$ is incomputable; there is no action we can take. Being told about letters standing for numbers feels mysterious. If x is 2, why do we write x instead? But children seem much more open to the idea that shapes are "containers" in which numbers might be placed. We don't claim that 🪣 + 🪣 is immediately obvious, but given a context, it *becomes* obvious very quickly.

But the strange symbols on the fragments of pottery are not containers, so why are *they* "better" than letters? We are less sure, but again it seems that the psychology is different. The symbols themselves don't especially help, but the *setting*—ancient ruin, spaceship, secret code, foreign country—makes it clear that these *are* numbers, not "letters standing for numbers," and our problem is merely that we don't (yet) know what numbers they are.

Finding a Place to Start

We'll return to the focus on properties in a moment, but in a sense, they're almost incidental learning—practice (through use) of something important, but a by-product of something even more important. The key mathematical habit of mind exercised in nearly all puzzles is the habit of scanning the whole situation—all clues—to look for some key piece of information that serves as a good (often meaning relatively easy) place to start.

That's a habit of mind we want students to have when they approach a problem like figuring out the solution to a system of equations like this:

$$\begin{cases} 3x - 4y + z = 2 \\ x + y - 2z = 3 \\ 2x - 3y + 5z = 9 \end{cases}$$

An introduction to solving systems would likely start with a simpler set of equations, but the simpler it is—for example, juggling just $x + y = 27$ and $x - y = 5$—the less opportunity there is to "scan the whole situation"; there just isn't much situation to scan! But in a problem like this, students will likely need to scan to find a starting step (such as adding the second and third equations and then subtracting the result from the first equation to eliminate x).

Emphasizing Properties

The equations represented by mobile puzzles are necessarily all linear. Because Mystery Number puzzles focus on algebraic properties of both multiplication and addition—including, for example, properties that are sometimes called the "zero property," the "identity property," and so on—some equations must not be linear. Unlike mobile puzzles, in which students work from known values to discover unknown values, these problems generally do not offer any known values as clues. Students reason purely from the structure of the equations and the algebraic properties involved. If distinct shapes *can* assume the same value, there are more options in the solutions and it is good practice for students to consider how many solutions are possible. Some clue types are particularly rich. Each one of these, by itself, is a separate micro-puzzle. Thinking through these four will give you a sense of the underlying logic in Mystery Number puzzles.

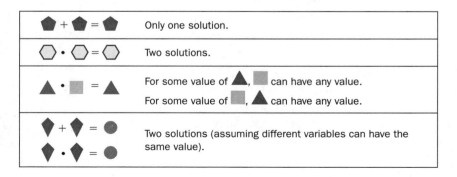

The goal, of course, is for students to reason through Mystery Number puzzles and build the logic for themselves, not to learn a bunch of facts for solving the puzzles. The latter would be silly, because solving this particular kind of puzzle isn't a life skill and serves neither for schooling nor even for recreation (these, unlike Sudoku and crossword puzzles, don't appear in newspapers and on airplane magazines). Nor are the answers at all important: only the ability and stamina to puzzle through, and the knowledge about mathematical properties that one gains along the way, are useful.

Experimentation alone should suffice for nearly all students, and many will be, or will quickly learn to be, more strategic than that. In class discussions, you'd like to hear students give some of the reasoning, explaining, for example, that ◆ + ◆ = ● says the same thing as 2 · ◆ = ●, and so ◆ · ◆ = ● tells us that ◆ · ◆ = 2 · ◆, which means that the kite must stand for 2 or 0. And if the kite and circle *must* be different, then….

To help students who seem stuck, you may wish to offer one or two of the relevant equations above without revealing its implications (e.g., $h \cdot h = h$, without even saying that there are two solutions). In other words, treat the micro-puzzles, if you use them at all, as a way to focus or summarize or give just-in-time support rather than as a default way to prepare students. The value of a puzzle is in puzzling it out.

You can, of course, make up your own puzzles, and make them as elaborate as you like. The following puzzle is an example of a more elaborate one.

The ten letters $a, b, c, d, e, p, q, r, s$, and t stand for the ten single-digit numbers, 0 through 9. Replace each letter with one of those numbers so that every clue remains true.

Use all ten numbers; a number that replaces a letter in one clue must replace that same letter wherever that letter appears in other clues.

You may use clues in any order.

For an extra challenge, prove that you don't need all the clues! What is the smallest number of clues you can get by with?

1.	$e > r$
2.	$p \times t = t$
3.	$s \times a = a$
4.	$p \times r = r$
5.	$p + b = q$
6.	$b \times b = c$
7.	$r = c \times b - p$
8.	$t > e$
9.	$b + b = c$
10.	$q + q = d$
11.	$s - b = q$
12.	$b + b = b \times b$

Student-Constructed Puzzles

Your students can make up puzzles, too. To keep the puzzles "tame" so that students don't invent totally arbitrary equations with unwieldy numbers, it can be useful to limit the numbers to some simple set, like 0 through 9 or, at the outset, an even narrower set. Then invent some "giveaway clues" that use properties of 0 (e.g., $x - x = y$) or of 1 (e.g., $ab = a$, which also is a property of 0), or the distributive property (e.g., $m + m + m = rm$), or camouflage some of these by saying, for example, $c + c = d$, and $d + d = pd$, which tells us nothing about c or d (unless we know a maximum size of the numbers we may use), but does tell us what number p is. Then, based on the earlier clues, invent clues for any remaining numbers, plus optional redundant clues just for fun. Finally, except for rank beginners, *arrange* the clues so that the "giveaways" don't all come at the beginning.

With all puzzles, having students construct their own engages them in analysis that can often be deeper than the thinking they must devote to solving such a puzzle. Having students construct a puzzle is also useful formative assessment. When students follow the dictum that "a good puzzle is just easy enough to solve, but hard enough to be fun," you get a good picture of what they consider easy and hard.

LATIN SQUARE-BASED PUZZLES

The goals of searching for a starting place and developing solving stamina are particularly well served by this genre of puzzles, in part because the sheer number of clues and elements of the solution can get large, yet the problems themselves can be as easy (or super challenging!) as one desires.

Latin Square *a, b, c, d*

c	a	d	b
b	d	c	a
a	c	b	d
d	b	a	c

An $n \times n$ Latin square is defined as a square array of numbers in which each number from 1 to n appears exactly once in each row and each column. More generally, *any* elements (not just numbers) arranged so that they appear exactly once in each row and column are said to be arranged in a Latin square. For example, here is one way (of many) to arrange the letters a, b, c, and d in a Latin square.

Latin square structure is used in the design of experiments that involve multiple variables, in error-correcting codes (ways of encoding information to account for interference in transmission), and other mathematical, statistical, and computer science applications.

The same structure is also the basis of many puzzles. One puzzle type fills in some of the elements of a Latin square and tasks the puzzler with filling in the remaining cells to complete the Latin square. In each of these puzzles, the title tells you what elements must be used.

Latin Square *x, y, z*

	x	
z		

Latin Square **1, 2, 3, 4**

	4		3
		2	
	2		
1			

By adding further constraints to a Latin square, or changing the nature of the clues, one can create other puzzles of interest. For example, one might require that certain specially outlined regions within the square also contain each of the square's distinct elements with no repeats.

Special Latin Square **1, 2, 3, 4**

	4		3
		2	
	3		

At right is a 4 × 4 version of such a puzzle: in each cell, you must write one of the numbers 1, 2, 3, or 4. As in all Latin squares, each row and column must contain all four numbers; and in this special puzzle, the same is true for each 2 × 2 bold-outlined box.

This is the structure on which Sudoku puzzles are based. The solution to a Sudoku puzzle is a 9 × 9 Latin square, with the additional constraint that all elements must also appear in each of the nine 3 × 3 tiles that cover the puzzle. To create the puzzle, one might start with the "answer"—the arrangement of numbers in this special Latin square—and erase most of the elements, leaving only a few as clues.

> A good mathematical meta-puzzle (a puzzle *about* puzzles) is to make a Latin square of some size and then figure out how many of its elements you can erase and still leave just enough information for a person to be able to complete the Latin square in exactly one way.

Futoshiki Puzzles

The Latin square-based puzzles we have shown so far all use some elements of the solution as clues, but it's possible to give clues that are of a different kind altogether. For example, a Futoshiki puzzle uses clues that indicate which of two adjacent cells has the greater number (and sometimes also includes one or more of the numbers as additional clues). A good first strategy for a puzzle like this is to look for places in which the highest or lowest number (in this example, 4 or 1) *cannot* go to help decide where it *must* go. In this puzzle, inspection of the bottom two rows reveals a location for a 4 and a location for a 1.

This kind of puzzle also encourages if–then thinking: if I put a 3 here, then the consequences for these spaces are. . . . Constructing and keeping track of trains of such consequences is one small example of the kind of multistep logical argument that we want students to develop and that is described in the Common Core State Standards for Mathematical Practice.

Futoshiki **1, 2, 3, 4**

MysteryGrid Puzzles

Another type of Latin square puzzle provides clues that require, along with the logical reasoning, flexible thinking about calculations, giving them great versatility and application in the classroom. One version of this puzzle type is best known under the registered name of KenKen, and the KenKen website offers an essentially unlimited number of these, with the player choosing the size (from 3×3 to 9×9) and difficulty of the puzzle. (Their site also offers wonderful resources for teachers.)

The name is owned, but the idea is not, and many such puzzles under various names can be found on the Internet. Importantly, you and your students can make up puzzles of this kind. We have found this kind of puzzle so appealing to students that we have adapted it to serve other learning goals. We call the ones we make up *MysteryGrid puzzles.*

As with the other Latin square-based puzzles, the only numbers you are allowed to write are the ones indicated in the title of the puzzle. In the puzzle on the right, only the numbers 1, 2, 3, and 4 may be written, and all (as always) must appear in each row and each column. Each specially outlined region, called a "cage," contains a target number and, if the cage encloses more than one cell, an operation. The numbers you write in the cells of the cage must make the target using the required operation. The easiest cages to fill in are the single-cell cages, each of which (in this puzzle) has a target of 4. Just write in 4, and you're done! The "3,+"

MysteryGrid **1, 2, 3, 4**

cage is tempting, too: we know for sure that it must contain 2 and 1, but we don't yet know in which order. For now, we can just pencil in [3,+ 1 2] to remind us of what we do know without making guesses about what we don't know. But even that is useful information: it tells us that the number in the top cell of the "9,+" cage is 3, the only number left for that row.

Alternatively, we might have started with the "9,×" cage, in which we must write three numbers (from among the permitted 1, 2, 3, 4) whose product is 9. That can only be 1, 3, and 3, and because the two threes cannot appear in the same row or column, we know exactly which cells to write them in. Now we have enough information to sort out the order of the two entries in the "3,+" cage. Note that in the two "2,−" cages, we can write either 1 and 3 (in either order) or 2 and 4 (in either order), so those are not convenient places to start. They are much better to fill in after other clues have given us more information. Also, in the "2,÷" cage (bottom right), the order of the two entries will depend on clues outside that cage.

In a 4 × 4 puzzle, easy or hard, one must fill in sixteen entries. A 6 × 6 puzzle can be just as easy (or hard) but takes more stamina, requiring over twice the number of entries, and requiring a scan of more potential starting places. Students who get hooked on 4 × 4 puzzles and progress to larger ones—as nearly all do—get enormous amounts of computational practice looking for various ways to decompose sums and various factorings of target numbers and various pairs of numbers with a given ratio. When we make up our own puzzles, we will often vary the sets of elements to vary the targets without increasing the stamina required. For example, we might make up a MysteryGrid 2, 3, 5, 6 puzzle, allowing some of the combinations and facts that a 6 × 6 would afford but without increasing the number of entries a student must write. Students have also enjoyed the MysteryGrids we've made in which the allowed entries include fractions. And they've made up their own!

> There are more than a dozen ways to fill in this cage using only the numbers 1 through 6. How many can you find?
>

For all students, the incidental gains in computational fluency are noticeable. For some students, those gains are so great and such a contribution to the rest of their mathematical work that for that value alone, the puzzles are great. And the students themselves notice their increased strength and are choosing the practice, not being pushed into it. The real utility of a puzzle (as opposed to a drill motivated by, for example, rewards) goes far beyond computational practice. What students really learn from a puzzle of this kind is search, logic, perseverance, tracking and managing multiple constraints, the habit of shifting strategies (sometimes factoring, sometimes using process of elimination, sometimes making an organized list and checking other constraints against the list to rule out some of the items), reasoning strategically rather than guessing, and, not incidentally, that solving something truly hard can be fun.

Like the Who Am I? puzzles, MysteryGrid puzzles can be adapted to suit algebra as well as arithmetic. In this example, the title indicates that one may write only the expressions 1, x, $x + 1$, and x^2 in the cells in order to reach the targets using the given operations. As pure exercise, this form has the added benefit of being largely self-checking, because the responses must fit not only the clues but also the Latin square constraints.

MysteryGrid **1, x, $x + 1$, x^2**

$x^2, \bullet$		x	$2x+1, +$
$x^2+x+1, +$	$x+1, +$	$x+2, +$	
			$x^4, \bullet$
$x^2+x, \bullet$			

Constructing MysteryGrid Puzzles

Like all other puzzles, students can construct these themselves after they have had some experience solving them. A general rule: construct the solution (a Latin square of the desired elements) first; then group cells into cages and write clues in them. Larger cages provide harder clues—for example, a cage that contains all the cells in a column provides no information at all because you already know what must go in that column and the "clue" doesn't help you with the order—and may make the puzzle unsolvable. It is important to test, even when all cages are small, to see whether the clues are sufficient to find one and only one solution. The construction of a good puzzle can stimulate a lot of good logical thinking (not to mention a lot of computational practice).

TEACHING WITH PUZZLES

We close this chapter with three elements of teaching with puzzles: a way to introduce puzzles, a way to help focus students' thinking, and the intellectual opportunity you provide to students (and the assessment value you gain) when you encourage students to *build* their own puzzles.

Focus on Introduction: Brevity, Clarity, and Social Solving

Puzzles (and games) have rules, and because those rules are essentially arbitrary, students cannot be expected to know or guess them. They cannot (and should not be asked to) answer "How do you think this is played?" Such questions are asked with good intentions—to get students thinking—but the rules have to be *given*, not guessed at. On the other hand, there are ways to minimize instructions before starting the puzzle and that, too, is important.

Brevity and Clarity

For some puzzles, startup is easy. Puzzles like Who Am I? almost explain themselves. Some students do ask about the ⊞ box, but for most students, the context is sufficient to explain both the box and the letters above it.

On the other hand, the rules for a puzzle like MysteryGrid are not immediately obvious to a new player. Explaining *all* the rules abstractly before doing any part of the puzzle is way too hard to remember, so it is useful to introduce and play socially (the entire class) at the same time.

> The title tells you what numbers you can write. So, in this puzzle, the only numbers you can write are 1, 2, 3, and 4. Each row [point] and each column [point] must have all four numbers. Each of these special regions called "cages" has a target number [point at it] and an operation [point]. What they tell you is that the numbers you write in that cage must *make that target,* using **only that operation.** So, for example, what numbers must go in this cage? [Pick a two-cell cage, like "3,+" in which only one possible pair of numbers can be used.] Because we don't yet know which order to write those numbers, we will do this ⊞ for now. Now, what might we do next?

Extra clarifications—for example, that in a single-cell cage that has no operation, we can just write that number, or that even in a subtraction or division cage we may write the numbers in either order—can wait and come up during play. Giving just enough instructions to start, and then more as needed, makes the instructions easier to understand.

Social Solving

Projecting a puzzle so all can see and letting the entire class contribute both reduces the pressure on an individual and also multiplies the variety of approaches. If students don't know what to do next, they can wait and see what someone else picks. Students get the feeling "Oh, I could have done that." And they have more clues now to work with and still have time to contribute at the next step. Social solving, especially on larger puzzles, also reduces the stamina that an individual alone needs to have to complete the puzzle, but makes it clear that such "big" puzzles really can be solved and is encouragement to try one alone some time.

The following example using a particularly elaborate Who Am I? puzzle illustrates the power of social solving. The setting was a relatively small ninth-grade class, seventeen students on that particular day, all enrolled in algebra but deemed at risk of failing and given a concurrent course to help them make the transition to algebra successfully. That parallel course focused on building mathematical habits of mind, rather than on remedial topics or instruction, and made liberal use of puzzles of the kind described in this chapter to help draw out students' expectation that everything in mathematics should fit together and make sense.

At first glance, the students—who were branded as "weak" and thought of themselves that way—saw this problem as daunting, too much to solve alone. But the group as a whole kept feeding each other ideas.

One student said that even numbers end with 2, 4, 6, or 8. Another included 0 as well. Another commented, redundantly except to clarify the language, that even numbers had even units digits. Another said, "But it's not 4," using the bottom clue. Acting merely as scribe, the teacher held a marker poised below the "u" box, and some students said to write 0, 2, 6, and 8.

A student combined two clues to state that the hundreds digit was an odd number less than seven. "So . . . 1, 3, or 5," said another. The teacher wrote it and then handed the marker to a student to take over being the scribe.

A quiet voice from the back said, "But [the units digit] can't be 2 or 6, right?" because "It says that the units digit is 1 more than the hundreds digit, and it also says the hundreds digit has to be less than 7." Several students got excited by the new clue she had called attention to, but corrected her at once, saying 2 and 6 were actually the *only* possibilities for the units digit. The new scribe didn't move, so the quiet voice from the back said, "Erase the 0 and 8."

Who Am I?

h t u

- I am even.
- My digits are all different.
- I am greater than 319.
- My hundreds digit is less than 7.
- $u = 1 + h$.
- My tens digit is my largest digit.
- My hundreds digit is my only odd digit.
- My units digit is one more than my hundreds digit.
- The sum of all three of my digits is 19.
- My units digit is not 4.

Silence. Then a confident voice, "The hundreds is 5."

Someone asked, "How do you know?" "Because the number has to be greater than 319. So you can cross out 1 and 3." The scribe erased them.

An explosion of talk and then, "No, you can't erase 3!" The student who had suggested it corrected himself: "Oh, right. It could be like, 320, or something."

One student mentioned the clue that stated that the sum of the digits was 19. "The tens is 8," he said confidently, "Because 5 + 8 + 6 is 19."

Momentary silence, then a dissenting voice, "No. Because it could be 7 + 8 + 4 and still make 19."

"But the hundreds is less than 7."

"And it can't end in 4."

The actual classroom dialogue was more complex, with unfinished sentence fragments like "If that's true . . ." or "But I thought someone said . . ." or "That *can't* be true because. . . ." Though not very systematically—even with the "scribe" there—the students were keeping rough track of what was known, what was said, and what *could be said.* Importantly, no one asked the teacher for the answer, or how to find the answer, or whether their claims (or final answer) were correct. Students decided on their own which of their mathematical ideas were valid, without referring to an external authority.

Though all of the students in this class had the knowledge to solve the puzzle, few, if any, would have had the confidence and stamina to do it alone. But the excitement of "beating" the puzzle socially was contagious. And even "wrong" contributions helped: for example, the student who claimed that the units digit could not be 2 or 6 was wrong, but calling attention to the "less than 7" clue launched other student thinking and contributed to finding new information.

In this example, the teacher initially served as recorder of mathematical ideas, and also asked students to share just one thought at a time to prevent runaway thinking that stole thinking opportunities from other students.

Focus on Thinking: Start, Strategy, Stamina

A lot of strategic thinking goes into the solving of all puzzles, and you, as teacher, can play an important role in setting the tone from the outset. Here are a few places to focus attention.

Where Can We Start?

A good place to start is a place where you know *something,* even if you don't know *everything.* Finding such a place involves scanning the whole puzzle before diving in. Often there are several possibilities for a good place to start. In the MysteryGrid 1, 2, 3, 4 puzzle example, we could start with the easy "4" cages. Or we might notice that only 1 and 2 can work in the "3,+" cage, and though we don't yet know the order they go in, we could at least write them down. Or, we could start with the 3, 3, 1 that must go in the "9,×" cage. It is far more strategic to start in these easy places than to list all of the possibilities for the "2,−" cages.

MysteryGrid **1, 2, 3, 4**

2, −		2, −	
3, +		9, +	4
9, ×			2, ÷
4			

In the Mystery Number and Who Am I? puzzles, one similarly scans all the clues first, looking for "easy" ones to start with. And if no clue is easy by itself, one then looks for pairs of clues that work together. For example, if *h*, *t*, and *u* are known to be different digits, then neither

$t^2 = t$ nor $h + t = u$ tells us any of the digits, but the two clues together tell us what t must be (though we still don't know much about h and u). This is the same kind of thinking we use in a crossword puzzle: when wondering where to start, we first look for easy clues, and if we don't find a clue that gives us easy certainty, we look for pairs of across and down clues that, together, give us the certainty we need.

Strategy and Stamina

What do I know now? What do I not yet know? MysteryGrid puzzles are a particularly good venue for helping students distinguish what they do know from what they don't yet know. For example, in the previous puzzle, the "3,+" cage must contain the numbers 1 and 2, but we don't (without other information) know what order to write them in. So we find some convenient way to record what we know without guessing the order, because everything we write becomes a new clue, and a *wrong* clue will lead us astray. Even such partial information can be important; for example, in this case it tells us what goes in the top cell of the "9,+" cage. A similar recording technique can be used for the vertical "2,÷" cage at the bottom right. The only possibilities are 1, 2 and 2, 4. Even if we did not yet know which possibility is correct, we would know that either way a 2 must go in one of those cells. In this case, we *do* know that a 4 can't be in there (because it already appears in that column), so we can write 1, 2 in that cage, to be sorted out later.

In a similar way, in a Mystery Number puzzle, the clue $\bigcirc \cdot \bigcirc = \bigcirc$ gives us only partial information, but if we jot down what we know—that only 0 and 1 are possible values—we can narrow the possibilities later.

What is *not* a solution? Look at the second column in the above MysteryGrid and ask yourself where the number 4 can be placed. It is not a factor of 9, so it can't be in either of the bottom two cells, and it's too large to go in the "3,+" cell, so it must go in the top cell. To use this approach, one must at first be strategic. You would have ruled nothing out if you had chosen first to ask yourself where the number 1 could be placed. Over time, one develops some intuitions that let one be more strategic, and one begins to understand that eliminating possibilities can be just as valuable as finding them. Finding counterexamples and proving that something can't be a solution is valuable mathematical thinking.

What can we do next? After finding where to start, we have more information. Clues that we rejected as starting places may now have become more useful so, again, we scan for "easy" places to go next. Puzzlers may try a few cages in a MysteryGrid or a few clues in a Who Am I? or Mystery Number puzzle before finding a next one to work with. This feature of puzzles supports students in trying something else when they get stuck rather than giving up.

Encourage students to look over the whole puzzle and try to identify a good next place to work where they know something even if they don't know everything.

Many students are amused at the advice to be strategically lazy. This is not at all the same as being just plain lazy! It is encouragement to put the effort into the search for a convenient (easy) next step, rather than putting the effort into brute force computations.

Focus on Construction: Problem Posing and Problem Solving

Many of the benefits of having students construct their own puzzles have already been mentioned: it gives practice; it requires deep analysis of the logical constraints of the puzzle; it provides the teacher with a window into the student's sense of easy and hard, and into the student's logic; it is mathematically creative.

There's another element as well: posing problems is a key part of solving problems. Pólya's 1957 analysis of how to be a good problem solver, *How to Solve It*, was so clear, brilliant, and influential that it has been cited, adapted, and used in a vast number of books and articles. In mathematics education, a shorthand version is so common that it is a cliché: understand the problem, devise a plan, carry out the plan, and look back (often recast, incorrectly, as "check your work"). Unfortunately, that so vastly oversimplifies the idea that it is nearly useless. If problem solving were so simple, all the world's problems would be solved!

Pólya's thinking was much deeper, and he was careful to say that the ideas he presented were heuristics—approaches that were likely to move one along toward a solution and to suggest new approaches—not a formula or method. *How to Solve It* is a small book, but a book, not a list of steps. Elaborations in Pólya's *Mathematical Discovery: On Understanding, Learning, and Teaching Problem Solving* (1981) originally took two volumes, again short and clear, but not formulaic. And he regarded teaching with the same respect: he would not reduce it to right or wrong "moves" but thought of it as attitudes toward mathematics, learning, and the student.

Pólya regarded "devise a plan," of course, as the hardest part. One heuristic in devising the plan is thinking of a related problem. This is too often trivialized as if it meant something like "Try to remember what we did earlier in this chapter." That certainly *is* a useful step, but it doesn't help in the real world. You aren't in a chapter in the real world, and a real problem isn't a mere example of a problem type that you have learned. Pólya (1957) suggests specific ways to "vary the problem, as generalization, specialization, use of analogy, dropping a part of the condition," and so on. These related problems are created by the solver as steps toward insight into the original unsolved problem.

Steve Brown and Marion Walter's 2005 classic *The Art of Problem Posing* elaborates on that generative step. Their focus on how to *pose* new problems involves, among other methods, analysis and systematic variation of the attributes of the problem. They analyze, for example, the familiar Pythagorean relation $a^2 + b^2 = c^2$ and consider what features can be varied. The question could be about geometry: What is implied about a triangle if $a^2 + b^2 < c^2$? Or, what relation describes the three sides of a triangle in which one angle is required to be 60° instead of 90°? Or the question could be about number theory: Can $a^2 + b^2 = c^2$ have integer solutions other than (0, 0, 0) and (3, 4, 5), and if so, what restrictions, if any, are there on the values of c? Or, can integer solutions be found if the exponent is greater than 2? That latter was Fermat's question, mentioned at the start of this chapter. Goldenberg and Walter (2003) choose problems familiar in some high school curricula and describe specific approaches to problem posing that allow students to create productive modifications of these problems in service of learning to be good problem solvers.

As these examples show, building a puzzle is not at all the only way to learn the art of problem posing, but it is a way that is accessible even to beginners. It requires thought and analysis. And the results, with a little effort, feel genuinely like one's own unique creation and not just a change of wording or numbers from an essentially familiar form.

CONCLUSION

Puzzles are, of course, not a cure for all ills, nor can puzzles and games be a complete curriculum. But the role of thoughtfully selected or crafted puzzles in mathematics learning and teaching can go well beyond motivational breaks from (or sugarcoatings for) the real work. They can *be* a significant part of the real work.

And some of the kinds of puzzles that often get treated in K–12 classrooms as amusing time sponges for a rainy day when all the real work is done are taken quite seriously in higher education. Here's a good example. Try it!

- Six people—Benjamin, Gabriela, Patrick, Rose, Sam, and Yolanda—are standing in a row.
- There are exactly two people between Rose and Patrick.
- There is exactly one person between Yolanda and Patrick.
- Rose and Yolanda are not next to each other.
- Gabriela is to the left of Benjamin (but we don't know how far).
- Rose is to the left of Sam (but we don't know how far).
- Who *must* be standing next to Patrick?

The Law School Admission Test devotes a major section to what it calls "logic games." This puzzle was lightly adapted from a respected practice book for that serious test. Want to prepare your students with the logic it takes to go to law school? Want to prepare them with the logic of algebra? In both cases, the right puzzles can help.

Extended Investigations for Students

. . . a question posed by a student: "Why is [π] almost 3.14 and not almost something else, such as 3.13 or 3.15?"

If the question had remained unanswered, this would have left students with the impression that the discovery of important mathematical ideas such as this one are the products of the instant insights of an extraordinary mind, rather than the product of systematic investigation open to anyone willing to acquire necessary skills and do the systematic work of mathematical investigation. Moreover, if the concept is presented as a fact isolated from its original context, students are deprived of the important insight into how a person can figure out that mysterious number.

—(Papadopoulos 2013)

E xercises to apply specific content knowledge or to rehearse skills or procedures are typically short: solve the following equations; simplify and write in standard form; find the greatest common divisor of the terms in each polynomial and factor the polynomial; make a table for each function, evaluating that function for integer values of x from -2 through $+5$; identify each exponential function as either growth or decay. Exercises give useful practice and take knowledge and perhaps thought, but have no exploratory phase and typically don't require problem-solving perseverance.

Puzzles of the types we've described require more stamina—usually offering multiple clues to scan and requiring multiple steps (and perhaps multiple numbers or other objects to find) before a solution is complete—but even good puzzles rarely require much experimentation.

The world's real problems, however, require not just the stamina to apply methods and knowledge one already has but also the disposition (and skill) to investigate and gather new knowledge and develop new methods. For students to learn to think like problem solvers, they need regular experience doing such investigative work in which one must think, experiment, organize information, follow hunches, interact, take wrong turns, discover, think more, and synthesize one's findings as a conclusion. That is, they need age- and knowledge-appropriate research experiences. How extended the research can be, of course, depends on students' prior experience. Less experienced researchers are likely to need more support and shorter investigations. But for the purpose to be realized, genuine challenge must remain: problems that are too short or too scaffolded don't increase students' investigation skills or stamina.

Put simply, the point of such research is to learn how to be a good investigator. Although that clearly requires getting to some kind of defensible answer—productive investigation is more than poking around in the dark and describing random things one bumps into—the *answer* is not the classroom goal. It is at best one indicator, among others, of having productively investigated.

> By definition, including problems that are *not* short will take time. The curriculum is already crowded. Where does that time come from? Some of it gets paid for by greater retention—insights gained from direct experience make the ideas of mathematics more stable and better connected to other mathematics one has learned. And some of it gets paid for by teaching students how to figure out what they have forgotten or never learned. Of course, some investigations are more likely to be profitable than others. This chapter will help you choose good ones or design your own.

Building the particular mental habits that lead to productive investigation is one educational role for the extended projects we describe here. Investigations can also reveal some of the appealing surprises that lurk just beneath mathematics' surface, the product of its deep underlying structure and logic. In fact, using, imposing, finding, and expressing structure are the core of investigation, teaching how to investigate as well as the habit of seeking and using structure.

This chapter identifies some features of investigatory problems, examines some mathematical themes well suited to research by students making the transition to algebra, and shares ways in which such investigations can help students develop valuable mathematical habits over time.

EXPERIENCE BEFORE FORMALITY: TRY IT YOURSELF

Before we present theory, try these two investigations on your own to build a background of experience. Pay particular attention to your own process of experimentation and to when and how you make discoveries. What are *your* habits of mind as you approach these problems?

Investigations can be highly structured or can pose problems and leave the approach up to the explorer. Our examples here are structured to accommodate both options. The big picture question comes first, along with a clarifying example of some kind, and the remaining sections—warming up, a starting place, further investigation—are provided only as one possible structure for explorers who want more guidance. So, if you like, feel free to start your own investigation as soon as you understand the big question.

Investigation 1: Two-Color Towers

The big picture problem: Assume you have a specific number of blocks—two gray and all the rest white. How many *different* ways can you arrange the blocks in a tower? Describe one possible way of organizing drawings of those towers so that you could be absolutely sure you had every one, with no duplication.

A clarifying example: If you have exactly three blocks—two gray, as always, and the remaining one white—exactly three arrangements are possible.

Warming up: With four blocks, two of which are gray, you will have two whites. Exactly six different towers can be built. Three are shown here. Draw the last three.

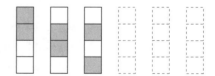

A starting place: You have *six* blocks—two gray and the rest white. How many different towers can you make? Organize your solutions and describe how your method of organization helps to show that you have found all possible solutions.

Further investigation: How many different ways can you arrange *seven* blocks (with two gray, as always, and five white)? What if you had *eight* blocks?

Back to the big picture: If you had 100 blocks, you could build 4950 different towers. Imagine drawing them all! Describe one possible way of organizing those drawings so that you could be absolutely sure you had every one, and no duplicates.

Investigation 2: Staircase Pattern

The big picture problem: These staircases are two steps tall and four steps tall. The shorter one is built from three square tiles; the taller required ten tiles. Other heights can be made. Describe a general method you can use to figure out exactly how many tiles are needed for a staircase of a specified height.

Warming up: Here are some staircases of increasing height. Fill in the missing drawings.

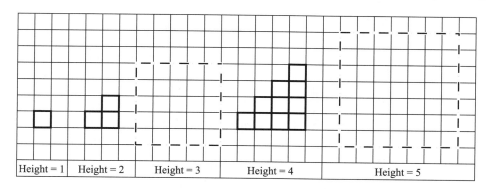

| Height = 1 | Height = 2 | Height = 3 | Height = 4 | Height = 5 |

A starting place: Without actually drawing a staircase of height 6, *describe* how to draw it.

Further investigation: How would you figure out the number of square tiles in a staircase of height 11?

Back to the big picture: If you are given the height, describe a general method for finding the number of square tiles it would take to build that staircase.

Reflect on the thinking you did when you were working. Which mathematical habits of mind did you use? Which of these habits of mind do you feel your students would naturally apply? Which might your students most need to develop?

Both of these investigations, by the way, generate the sequence of numbers 1, 3, 6, 10, 15. . . . See if you can find some convincing reason why that *should* be and is not just a coincidence.

PRINCIPLES: WHAT MAKES A GOOD INVESTIGATION?

Keep your experience with those examples of investigations in mind as a context and foundation for the analysis that follows, the "formal" part. Other investigations will later expand the picture. Investigation can be a part of almost any mathematical task, not just fancy ones (of which there are many sources). Investigation is in the *approach*, not the task, and almost any problem can be approached in an exploratory way. Take, for example, this straightforward problem:

$$\text{Solve for } x: 3x + 4 = 29$$

We can use this problem to launch any number of investigations. For example, as teachers, we might pose the following questions. Or, given time and opportunity and encouragement, students might learn to pose such extensions themselves:

> While this investigation seems, on the surface, to switch to a completely different topic from the original "solve for x," it continues to require students to solve equations of this form. If practice is needed, this investigation certainly supplies plenty of it!

- What number(s) could we replace 29 with to get integer solutions for x? What number(s) could we replace 4 with to get integer solutions for x? What can you say about those sets of numbers?
- How does the solution to $3x + 4 = 29$ compare to the solution of $4x + 4 = 29$? What happens to the value of x as we increase its coefficient?
- What if $3x + 4 > 29$? What number(s) can replace x as a solution in this case?
- What happens if we square both sides of the equation to get $(3x + 4)^2 = 29^2$? Does this equation have the same solution?

As described in Chapters 1 and 3, problem posing is itself an act of investigation.

The activities we describe in this chapter are not special in themselves; their value is in the opportunities they present. Investigation takes extended time, giving teachers a setting for focusing on student thinking. The extended time devoted to one problem also gives students time to investigate an idea in greater than usual depth.

Stand-Alone Investigations

Our examples, like the Two-Color Towers and Staircase Pattern you worked on, are purposely stand-alone activities that do not depend on a curriculum sequence. Investigations can, of course, be integrated into a curriculum and, as you saw, can be inspired by any mathematics task (e.g., solve for x), but there are reasons one may choose to make investigations stand-alone activities anyway. One reason is to help both the teacher and students focus on mathematical thinking rather than focusing on the content they do or don't know. Another reason for stand-alone investigations is to give students the experience of pursuing a problem without the expectation that the current topic dictates what they are "supposed" to do. Having independent investigations helps students make connections beyond the content and strategies of the current lesson topic. A goal in every classroom is to prepare students for further study and learning. Explicitly practicing the skill of making connections outside of the current topic helps students build a habit of drawing from all their experience, including remembering to use this year's learning in next year's mathematics.

In this next section, we describe some key features of good investigations. They include:

> Why deliberately put an investigation *out* of sequence instead of inside a chapter that deals with that topic? Because that's more realistic. Life's real problems arrive at any time, not just when you are conveniently studying how to solve them. We investigate when we *don't* know how to solve a problem. We must not start out by thinking, "Oh, I'm supposed to factor because that's what we're studying now."

- Core mathematical themes are central.
- The explorer *experiences* the mathematics before *formalizing* the ideas.
- The explorer builds connections between different ideas in mathematics and starts forming additional questions (posing new problems).
- The investigation has a low threshold for entry but a high ceiling of mathematical ideas to be investigated.
- The explorer *experiments*. This could involve just calculations and/or sketches on paper, or might use manipulatives and other tools. Explorers should be free (and encouraged!) to choose the mode and tools they think will best support their investigation. They should also be encouraged to be flexible in their thinking and free (and encouraged!) to discuss their experiments and ideas with others.
- The experiments have visible enough components to give *you*, as teacher, insight into the student's thinking.

We aim to show why it is valuable to make extended investigation a regular part of mathematics learning. Of course, we do not claim it should be the only part, or that all activities should have its key features. Though these features can help you design investigations, that is not the primary purpose of listing them here and describing them below. The primary purpose is to give you useful heuristics for drawing the most out of any mathematical task and to help you orchestrate an investigation in effective ways to ensure that your students' investigative experience is productive. After describing these features in a bit more detail below, we will present some examples and themes for building investigations, as well as some ideas for how to structure discussions of these investigations in a whole-class setting.

We avoid the common terminology "big mathematical ideas." Mathematics is so interconnected that it's hard to make a consistent statement about what makes a mathematical idea "big" (or even "important") or, for that matter, what exactly we mean by *idea* rather than *fact* or *habit of mind*. Depending on the context, 4 + 3 or the Pythagorean theorem or looking for structure can be the most important idea to come to mind. Context matters. In elementary school, understanding addition as putting together is an important idea. In high school, even a student who can't add fluently certainly has the idea, and so it is not a big idea at that point.

Low-level stuff can be important, even for high-level investigation. We *can* think mathematically without having an extensive mathematical vocabulary or familiarity with the conventions of mathematical notation (e.g., order of operations, how to name points on a coordinate grid, algebraic conventions like writing the coefficient before the variable), or even basic facts, but a lack of those will limit what we can do.

Core Mathematical Themes

Just about any content, no matter how basic, can be presented in a way that contains or foreshadows core mathematical themes. Consider, for example, the following table from *Math Workshop*, a K–6 curriculum from half a century ago (Wirtz et al. 1964). On the surface, this problem for second graders (a bit before midyear) is pure computational practice arranged in a somewhat routine form—a table. Its design, however, introduces a core mathematical theme, requires thought, and invites investigation. The last six "exercises"—especially the last two—pick up a theme that runs throughout mathematics. With none of the notation and no learning of "rules of algebra," second graders use and stretch their understanding of the relationship of addition and subtraction, building more robust and flexible connections between these two operations and beginning, informally, to make the logic of solving equations feel intuitively obvious rather than waiting seven more years to learn it as a potentially arbitrary-feeling set of rules. All this while "just" practicing arithmetic.

◇+○	7	10			29				20	26
◇	4	8	9	10	20		16			
○	3	2	4	5		7		20		
◇−○	1	6				0	8	40	6	8

Even the organization of the information in this table reflected the authors' understanding of *how* children learn. Talking to 7-year-olds about "variables" could be almost guaranteed to mystify them, so instead, the authors took advantage of the fact that children, especially when they are young, are superb language learners. The authors made use of the way children figure out the meanings of new words when they hear them in use: not by definitions and explanations, but by use in context. First, earlier in the year, before students see this table, they've had lots of experience puzzling out simpler tables and are quite used to "pattern indicators," as *Math Workshop* (Wirtz et al. 1964) called the expressions in the left-hand column. Why that name? Because the pattern itself can be inferred by the children from the numbers alone, ignoring the column with symbols. The very first time children encounter pattern indicators, they are not explained either, but children infer the pattern and *assign* the meaning to the symbolic expressions.

Goldenberg, Mark, and Cuoco (2010) give this example (adapted from the article):

The following kind of exercise, without the leftmost column, is familiar enough in many curricula. Children look for a pattern in the inputs and outputs, figure out a rule, and complete the table. A later curriculum, *Think Math!* (EDC 2008), building on ideas from *Math Workshop*, often adds a "pattern indicator" to problems of this kind.

n	10	8	28	18	17			58	57
$n - 8$	2	0	20			3	4		

When Michelle, a second grader in a *Think Math!* classroom, finished filling out this table before I had finished handing out copies to all the children, I asked her how she had done it so *fast*. She said, "Well, I saw it was take away 8 because I looked at the 28 and the 20, and then I saw that 10 and 2 was take away 8 again, and then I saw 8 and 0."

And then she paused, grinned, as if I had made some mistake on the paper, pointed to the leftmost column, and added, "Besides, it *says* that right here!" How did Michelle know that? Though the algebraic symbols are there on the page, they are not an explicit part of the lesson—there is no discussion with the children of variables or letters standing for numbers or the fact that in algebra, "this means subtract 8." In fact, if Michelle had seen *just* the following table, with no examples to infer from,

n	18	17			58	57
$n - 8$			3	4		

she most likely would *not* have known what the symbols meant, and the symbols would not have helped her solve the puzzle.

Michelle's description of what she did was accurate: after she figured out the "take away 8" pattern from the numbers alone, she *assigned* that meaning to the symbols, which looked "close enough" to the meaning she already understood. That is the language-learning trick that little children excel at: she inferred, from context, the meaning of the new expression.

By midyear, the 1964 *Math Workshop* presented the table you first saw, involving two "rules," $\diamondsuit + \bigcirc$ and $\diamondsuit - \bigcirc$, to get from from the middle two rows to the top and bottom rows. The last six problems involved multistep reasoning to fill in the missing numbers, but the authors still provided the redundancy from which children could continue establishing the language, the meaning of the "pattern indicators" $\diamondsuit + \bigcirc$ and $\diamondsuit - \bigcirc$. The details of notation are just details, but the idea that a precise, convenient notation gives great power is a core mathematical theme, and so is the notion of figuring out unknown numbers.

Choosing Themes

The mathematical theme(s) to highlight in an investigation will depend both on the goals of your course and on the avenue a student chooses to explore. For example, in Two-Color Towers, one student might spend time puzzling over knowing whether he has found all of the combinations of towers. The central theme in his work might be how to structure the search (establish an order for the list). Or it might be to establish a formula, and the logic behind it, for finding the number of towers of a specified height, a topic from combinatorics. Another student may notice that she has made 5 towers with the gray blocks adjacent (0 white blocks between them), 4 towers with the gray blocks separated by 1 white, 3 towers with the grays separated by 2 whites, 2 towers with them separated by 3 whites, and 1 tower with them separated by 4 whites. She might conjecture that this pattern of consecutive integers will apply to towers of any height. That might lead her in one of at least two directions. The core theme for her might then be researching the possible sums of various-length sequences of consecutive integers. Or she might try formulating a proof of her conjecture or some other regularity she notices in her explorations. Yet another student might try to express the sum of consecutive integers using algebra. Core themes for this student might be in finding a way to express this sum recursively, or in being able to generalize a pattern.

The mathematical themes can be content as in the previous examples, but they can also be mathematical habits of mind. The process of investigating involves reasoning, abstracting, encoding, revising, and communicating. Because investigations are not straightforward problems, they should lead students to ask more questions, try ideas, develop and test conjectures, and draw conclusions. Just as students may not recognize the value of their work related to mathematical content, students also often overlook ways in which they use mathematical habits of mind. One student might show great strides in puzzling and persevering; another student might develop and demonstrate the disposition to seek and use structure. You, as teacher, bring added value to the process of investigation for students by calling attention to the ways they are developing mathematical thinking.

Not everything that is useful to know is a core mathematical theme. Without knowing certain terms (e.g., *absolute value*), definitions (e.g., the symbol $\sqrt{4}$ refers *only* to +2, even though both +2 and −2 squared equal 4), and conventions (e.g., order of operations), students are limited in what they can do. It also helps a lot to have a well-stocked mental library of commonly occurring sets of numbers (like 1, 2, 4, 8, 16 . . . and 0, 3, 6, 9 . . . and 0, 1, 4, 9, 16 . . . and 1, 3, 6, 10, 15 . . . and primes, and so on) *and* the core structures that they illustrate, because these support investigation by helping us recognize features of a new territory that we wander into. These *are* important, but none of these—not the terms and definitions or conventions or sets of numbers or particular procedures—are themselves core mathematical themes. By treating everything as equally big and important, nothing stands out: the curriculum is flat.

> Getting to know numbers and sets of numbers very well is so useful that we refer to it playfully as "making friends with numbers."

Experience Before Formality

This is a general principle not just for research-like problems but for all mathematical learning because it faithfully represents the way the discipline is practiced. The job of mathematicians is to figure out how to solve problems for which methods (or theory) are not already known (including finding connections among results that are already known); after all, why pay Ph.D.s to work on problems that need little more than existing recipes and a calculator? So, what do mathematicians *do* when they encounter these new problems? They experiment, play with them, think, build experience, generate hunches—guesses, as Pólya liked to say—and *then* try to organize and formalize what they've learned and, eventually, prove their conjectures.

Mathematical play is crucial to investigation. By *play*, we don't mean games (though we also don't mean to rule them out). We mean tinkering, trying things out, playing with ideas, following curiosity, posing new closely related problems by what-if-ing and what-if-not-ing and by other means (Brown and Walter 2005). Through investigations, teachers and students can discover that although some avenues of mathematical play can lead to dead ends or relatively light discoveries, many, especially with a bit of steering, lead to core themes. A central role for you, as teacher, is to be alert for mathematical gems that students can easily stumble across without noticing, or without realizing the value of what they've found.

Calling attention to these ideas identifies the content and makes it salient, legitimizes the mathematical play and the process of investigation, and may also help develop your students' eye for mathematical significance. When students make discoveries that anticipate topics covered later in the year, naming the discovery after the student and then bringing it back by name when that topic is introduced enriches the study of the topic and also makes clear the objective value of a student's work.

> The branch of mathematics called *game theory* is, despite its name, only partially about what we usually call *games*. But combinatorial game theory, a blend of mathematics and computer science, is very much about games like chess, checkers, dots-and-boxes, and so on. Serious (actually quite playful!) mathematical tomes have been written about games. For one, see Berlekamp, Conway, and Guy's *Winning Ways for Your Mathematical Plays* (1982).

Why Experience First?

Not only is the "experience before formality" approach faithful to mathematics, it also makes sense for education. The formal parts—our words, definitions, symbols, and formulas—are the organization and codification of our experience. For a mathematician working in unknown territory, formality *can't* come first: without experience, there is nothing to codify. Because a student learns mathematics that already exists, formality *can* be taught first, but at a sacrifice: if the formality is unsupported by experience, it refers to nothing and is unlikely to have much meaning. For example, one can imagine completely bypassing the investigative part of the Two-Color Towers and just teaching students how to solve the problem: "The number of distinct 6-story towers that can be built with 2 gray blocks is called '6 choose 2.' It is notated as $\binom{6}{2}$ or $_6C_2$ and can be calculated as $\frac{6!}{2!4!}$. More generally, the number of distinct towers n blocks tall with k gray blocks is $\frac{n!}{k!(n-k)!}$." But with no experience counting and organizing towers, no experience thinking about how the numbers of towers change as the height changes, and no other background in combinatorics to draw upon, expressions like $\frac{6!}{2!4!}$ are essentially magic. The student might surmise where the 6 and 2 come from in that expression, but why factorial, why is one divided by the other, and why did 4! also get into the act? The problem is solved, but without insight or the exercise of curiosity. It's over. Not only are the opportunities for insights bypassed, but students have had no chance to learn how to grapple with an unfamiliar problem and make even a little progress.

Of course, even with the exploration, students may not completely solve the problem, but they'll have some experiences on which to build. Those who do solve the problem are hardly likely to connect it with factorials and are much more likely to connect the number of towers with the sequence $1, 1 + 2, 1 + 2 + 3, 1 + 2 + 3 + 4, \ldots$ and look for ways to express those values succinctly and precisely. Further experimentation with the sums might well lead to the generalization $\frac{n(n-1)}{2}$, with the form $\frac{n!}{2!(n-2)!}$ still unlikely to appear. But even if we were to stop the investigation at that point and move on to teaching a general method, the investigation has created a perfect foundation for comparing $\frac{n(n-1)}{2}$ with $\frac{n!}{2!(n-2)!}$ by evaluating, in particular, $\frac{n!}{(n-2)!}$. We now have some background for looking for and making sense of a generalization to n choose k.

How Much Experience Before Formality?

The amount of experience that is needed before you introduce formality is a matter of clinical judgment. There is no formula and you just need to watch. But some things are known that can help you know what to watch for and assist your clinical judgment.

Sometimes students have built enough background from prior learning to enter new territory using their old knowledge as the experience, and they can make sense of new facts and methods without a new investigation. At other times, what seems like a lot of experience turns out not to be enough. Listening for the connections students make between their investigations and the formality and listening for how they might generalize beyond the formality will give you useful data.

Research on how people learn also tells us that a little calendar time between investigation and formality allows us to do the (not necessarily conscious) cognitive work of reflecting on, processing, connecting, and integrating our experiences and ideas before they are all crystallized by a packaging that is done for us. Also, having our experience in the *back* of our mind—not as an assignment to write about the investigation, not the focus of attention—is important to learning. Educators often fear that breaks lead to forgetting, but what scientists know about cognition and learning, and what creative artists know about "putting the work aside for a bit," is that giving the brain some gestation time *and then coming back to it* helps rather than hurts. Cognitively, that is just as much part of the investigation as the active experimenting. Waiting a day or two from the end of the investigation to the introduction of more formality allows students to do that work.

Building Connections

Investigations can be used to help students become more aware of the underlying structure of patterns in numbers and of mathematics in general, often unearthing a surprising fact or satisfying pattern that connects students' current and previous experiences. For instance, students may find that similar number patterns show up in seemingly unrelated contexts, or they may encounter a situation where they don't expect a rule and are surprised when one exists.

Investigation 3: UpDown Towers

The big picture problem: These two pictures show UpDown Towers that are three steps tall and four steps tall. Give a general method for finding the number of square tiles it would take to build a tower of some other specified height. Also, write instructions that tell exactly how to draw an UpDown Tower of any given height. Make your instructions clear enough for someone who has never seen these towers.

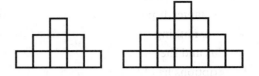

Warming up: Here are some towers of increasing height. Fill in the missing drawings.

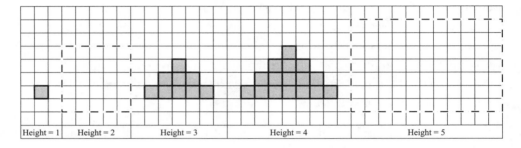

| Height = 1 | Height = 2 | Height = 3 | Height = 4 | Height = 5 |

A starting place: To draw the missing figures, you might notice the number of tiles in each vertical column or each horizontal row in the three figures that are drawn for you.

Further investigation: Without actually *drawing* a tower of height 6, *describe how* to draw it. How would you figure out the number of square tiles in a tower that is 11 tiles tall?

Back to the big picture: Describe precisely how to draw a tower of any given height, and say how many square tiles are in it.

People recognize an overall shape right away. But as you'll see later in this chapter, grasping its structure does not happen so automatically, and (unless we call attention to counting tiles in each column or row) many students do not draw the missing UpDown Towers correctly themselves, let alone describe a clear method to others. Some algebra texts expect students to start from a geometric growing pattern such as this and write an algebraic description of one of its features, but clearly a first step is for them to learn even to *see* the features with precision. They need first to learn to *analyze* what they see. Often, though not always, that requires analyzing from more than one perspective.

Look at the tallest (height = 4) tower drawing. In the columns, we see $1 + 2 + 3 + 4 + 3 + 2 + 1$ tiles; in the layers, top to bottom, we see $1 + 3 + 5 + 7$ tiles. Remember "deferred evaluation" (see Chapter 1, page 26)? These descriptions show structure, not just the total number of tiles. In fact, nothing special is noticeable about the total 16 until we look at the totals for other towers and the *collection* of numbers happens to ring a bell for us. All of these quantitative descriptions help us draw the two other towers and ultimately help us describe how to draw towers of any height. Students who have played with the earlier two investigations, Two-Color Towers and Staircase Pattern, are ready to notice the triangular numbers (sums of consecutive integers starting at 1). Seeing them here connected with odd numbers, sums of odd numbers, and square numbers is likely to provoke at least a little surprise, and some curiosity. Although the purpose of investigation *in the classroom* is to learn how to investigate, the reason to learn to investigate is that it is a powerful problem-solving technique: it gives data to work from and leads to connections that may be clues to the solution of the problem.

Investigations and Problem Posing

Investigations also create opportunities for students to pose new problems, a habit of mind worth developing because it naturally increases the number of built (and noticed) connections. For example, after finding that odd, triangular, and square numbers are all related, a student might try to color or otherwise annotate the drawings to make the relationship more evident. Or a student might wonder what would happen if the lengths of the layers of the tower were consecutive even numbers instead of odd. Or what if the structure were three-dimensional instead of two-dimensional? Both you and your students can adapt or expand an investigation by asking a related question or modifying the starting conditions. Depending on your class and your own goals, you might want to encourage such modification throughout students' work, perhaps arranging for different groups in class to pursue different avenues of research.

There isn't enough time for all students to investigate all possibilities, nor is that important. What *is* important is the opportunity to investigate, share ideas with others, and build connections.

Low Threshold, High Ceiling

The recommendation is familiar and the language almost cliché, but the principle is important. Whether you are choosing or designing investigations for your classes, you want to be sure that all learners, regardless of prior mathematical performance, can enter. Even the layout may matter: for example, placing the big picture question first, as we did in our preceding examples, may be a poor strategy until students feel free to read ahead or skip

Some teachers have had success getting students to look through, say, a section of a textbook before reading it and pick out a few things they think it's getting to, or asking a few questions ahead of reading. Making a habit of asking, "What's familiar, stuff that you already know well?" and "What's the new part, the unfamiliar?" also helps students structure their look-ahead. That can be a very effective start for an exploration and can, over time, help students make that their own habitual approach. Although to some extent you can, just by watching what students do, tell when they feel free to skip around, students arrive at that sense of liberty at different rates, and some—at all levels of success— seem to resist for a very long time. Crafting your materials with a big picture question before the step-by-step scaffolding and just being mindful of who might need extra encouragement to look ahead might help your students learn to do that.

around when they are puzzled. The threshold, if they stop at the big picture and don't look further, could be too high.

But some will appreciate having the big goal come first and will like knowing that they can pursue it in their own way without filling in blanks and answering specific questions before getting started. Although you want to ensure a low threshold, it is equally important to ensure a *high ceiling*—opportunities for deeper investigation and richer mathematics using the kind of thinking we want students to develop. As accessible as the "warming up" and "starting place" are, the big picture problem shows the enormous height of the ceiling.

In part, what distinguishes a high ceiling is the nature of the answer. In a warm-up or starting place problem, the answer might well be a single number, expression, or picture. But when the answer is found, *that* problem is done. A high ceiling problem generally needs to ask for some form of generalization. The generalization could be a method or process; it could be explaining a connection among seemingly unrelated problems; it could be written, spoken, notated in algebraic language (if appropriate), or illustrated by a sequence of pictures with a caption that describes the structure and how the sequence will continue. Instead of "How many tiles in *this* tower?" (low threshold if the height is small, but also low ceiling), the question becomes "If you're given the height of a tower, how can you figure out how many different towers can be made without actually making them all?" (high threshold, but high ceiling).

We always want to acknowledge and appreciate the work of students who are at the single-answer-all-done stage—the ones who say, "There are 15 different Two-Color Towers," and feel finished. But we also want to notice when they've had enough success at that level and are really ready to be nudged further. With a problem of this kind, one kind of effective nudge is "How can you show that you got them all?" which calls for a review of the process and then an explanation, not just a number. There are several sensible methods. One student might say, "Because you can keep a blue block on the bottom, then put the other blue block in 5 different places, so that's the first 5 towers. Then if you move the bottom blue block up. . . ." Another might explain, "Because there are 5 ways that the blue blocks can be side by side, and then you have to have 1 white block between them, and then. . . ." Each response is rich and indicative of the thinking process, and ultimately draws students into more interesting mathematics. Without giving a sense of doubting the result, other potentially useful nudges include "Why?" or "What makes you sure?" or even "How could you teach someone to do that?" All of these hint at generalization, but concretely—just justifying *this* case, without asking for the full-blown thing. Answering such questions is not simple; students are often not able, at first, to articulate their method so clearly.

A good problem solver can receive the high ceiling version, particularize it into a few low threshold examples to investigate, and then work back to the original high ceiling problem. To help students *become* good problem solvers, you first supply the low threshold steps, calling attention to what they are—just special and small versions of the original problem. Later, you might present only the big picture (high ceiling) problem, but still *ask* students, as a first step, to brainstorm in a class discussion (that you can help support, if necessary) to help invent their own special, small versions. Still later, you might ask students to work in small groups, figuring out how to turn a big complicated problem into smaller ones they can handle. The goal, of course, is that they eventually learn how to tell themselves to take such steps entirely on their own.

Experimenting: Choosing Tools and Approaches

Mathematicians often perform thought experiments, picturing geometric structures, images of objects or symbols being rearranged. Sometimes they build and manipulate physical models to help them perform thought experiments. When the burden on memory is high, they keep notes, making rough sketches on paper or writing out calculations. Or they use other technologies.

The tools extend our reach and memory, but it remains *our* job to figure out what solution path might work, to organize useful experiments, and to choose appropriate calculations to perform. Even when we calculate on paper, we organize that calculation in our head: what we write must be in our head before our fingers can set it down. Our mental work is always central.

But the physical can help. For learners, the tools we call "experimentation aids" (see Chapter 1, page 29) help not only to *perform* the kinds of experiments that lead to a solution but also to exercise the part of our mind that *directs* such experiments. In at least some cases, manipulatives can help us internalize the experiments. From experiments that we first perform with physical manipulatives and watch with our physical eyes, we learn to perform mental experiments and watch with our mind's eye.

In high school, physical manipulatives are often stigmatized as aids for students who aren't quite making it on their own: ones who "need" concrete hands-on activities to learn what others can do more abstractly, or who are unmotivated and need things to be "fun," or need remedial support. Students may resist them as "babyish." This may be a holdover from early grades where children count blocks until they can add and are praised when they can do without them. Subtle messages like "Use manipulatives if you need them" can contribute to this perception. *Need* suggests weakness.

At some point, of course, we *must* move beyond manipulatives in at least some domains. That's not because they're "crutches" nor because we won't always have them—we can always count on our fingers, for example—but because our ideas and thinking can grow beyond what the manipulatives can represent. Blocks are a fine model for counting numbers, awkward but adaptable for negative integers, very limited for fractions, and useless for irrational numbers.

Of course, computers allow us to invent new manipulatives. Geometer's Sketchpad and Geometry Expressions, for example, are tools that allow, in very different ways, concrete experiments that model a world that we can see but cannot readily experiment on with physical objects. Other computational media allow us to model mathematical objects that have no physical counterpart at all. And objects that are "abstract" can, with experience, become so familiar that they feel quite concrete: as integers begin to feel concrete, so can complex numbers, and polynomials and vectors and spaces become objects we manipulate casually to understand "more abstract" things.

But where appropriate, they can support both experimentation and *learning* to experiment. In the Two-Color Towers problem, for example, though drawing and shading squares is technically sufficient, moving actual objects very much changes what one sees. Building with blocks can make more obvious the transformation that takes place as one rearranges the blocks.

And just as manipulatives can make a student's actions visible enough for the student to see, adjust, and analyze, the visibility also gives you, as teacher, clues about the student's thinking, clues that can help you guide instruction or guide discussion—for example, selecting students who solved a problem with different correct approaches to share their varied ideas.

Making Students' Thinking Visible

When we introduced the UpDown Tower Investigation (page 100), we said that not all students see the structure with enough precision to draw the patterns correctly. It may seem surprising that this can be the case even in high school, but the following examples are all from ninth-grade algebra students. As you look at the students' work, try to characterize as clearly as possible what they *are* seeing clearly and what they are not. That is, ask yourself, even in the worst messes, what is right about the drawing as well as what misperception or inaccuracy or missed detail might have caused the particular ways in which the drawing is wrong. And where drawings are correct, what evidence in the drawing helps show what structure the student might have been using to get it correct?

Example 1

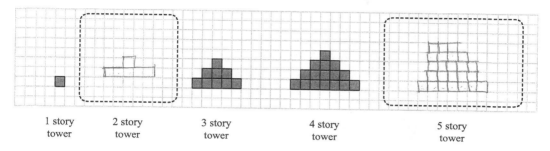

In each case, we see that the students attended to at least some features of the figures that had been drawn for them. The student's drawings in Example 1 both carefully use the grid lines, but the 2-story tower, though the correct height, uses the base of the 3-story tower rather than being the width suggested by the pattern of other towers. The dots inside the tiles in the 4- and 5-story towers might indicate that the student was counting, but, again, we see a *copy* of the base of the nearest tower rather than systematic change. The 5-story tower shows the diminishing width of each layer of the building, but it, too, is not systematic.

Example 2

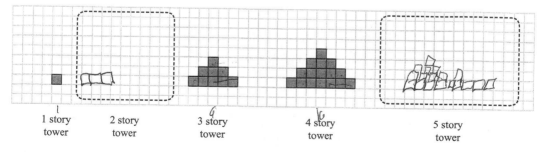

In Example 2, the drawing is far more crude, and the appearance of the 5-story structure makes it seem as if the student is not even seeing the scaffold of the grid, let alone the structure of the completed drawings, but this student does seem to have noticed the pattern of growth of the bottom layer, which is correct in both the incomplete 2-story tower and the highly disorganized 5-story tower. All we can tell for sure about the student's perception of the rest of the figure is that it gets narrower at each level until the top, which is 1 tile. Why is that missing in the 2-story tower? In both of these cases, a follow-up question might be "How did you decide what the figure should look like?"

Example 3

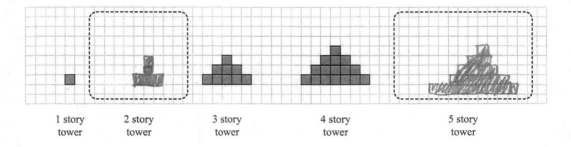

| 1 story tower | 2 story tower | 3 story tower | 4 story tower | 5 story tower |

Example 4

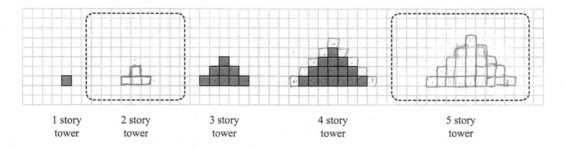

| 1 story tower | 2 story tower | 3 story tower | 4 story tower | 5 story tower |

Example 4 is particularly interesting. Though we'd have to talk with the student to know what she was thinking, we can see just by looking at the drawing of the 5-story tower that this student noticed the columns. We might presume that after setting out the bottom row as a kind of floor plan, she drew, on the left-hand side, vertical rectangles of the appropriate heights 1×1, 1×2, 1×3, and 1×4. Though we don't know whether she started at the center and worked out, or started at the side and worked in, we do know that she attended to the limits. The right side looks a bit less structured, 1 tile at a time rather than columns. Perhaps that came first? And note how the difference between the 4-story tower and the 5-story tower was sketched in on the 4-story tower. She seemed to be indicating (or discovering) *how* each new tower differed from the last.

Example 5

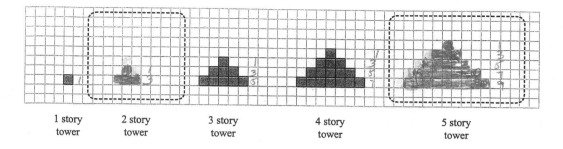

1 story tower	2 story tower	3 story tower	4 story tower	5 story tower

The fifth student seems to view the tower in rows rather than columns and shows that attention not only through the numbers written systematically on all the pictures but also with the direction of the coloring of each row. Note, in that regard, that student 3 colored diagonally, suggesting attention to the sloping up, but not to the structure of either the rows or the columns.

Why might we care about any of this? Focusing on the logic of student work can help students see their work as a process to be refined (either by them or by their work partners) rather than a mistake to be discarded. Noticing how differently students 4 and 5 approached the problem lets us choose them, in particular, to spark a good discussion following the investigation, explaining how they drew their UpDown Towers. Seeing that very different approaches can lead to correct results can be liberating for some students. Also, where some students are likely to toss off their poor productions with "I'm just not very good at drawing," both students 4 and 5 are likely to illustrate how tracing directly on the background structure (the grid) using counting, not art talent, guided their work. Noticing what the students have done helps *us* teach them better. We might direct students 1, 2, and 3 more to the scaffolding questions in the investigation—the starting place and possibly the further investigation. Even for students 4 and 5, seeing the alternative structure may well be novel to them and suggest new insights.

ASPECTS OF INVESTIGATION: ENTERING, SHAPING, AND EXTENDING INVESTIGATIONS

At the beginning of this chapter, we wrote that "using, imposing, finding, and expressing structure are the core of investigation." For students just learning to investigate, the "using, imposing, finding, and expressing" are rough approximations of stages in their development.

Though there are many ways to start an excellent investigation or to raise the ceiling in an ongoing investigation, just about any mathematical topic can be treated in an investigative way, and just about any ongoing investigations can be extended using these four strategies:

- connecting the visual and numeric: presenting structure, starting with a relatively low threshold, calling on students to *use* the structure they see
- asking, "Have you found all the solutions?": raising the ceiling, challenging students to *impose* structure on their work
- making friends with numbers: extending students' repertoire of structures, and calling on them to seek hidden structures
- representing general patterns with algebra: generalizing and abstracting, describing structure in precise language.

Connecting the Visual and Numeric: Making Structure Visible

It is not mathematically honest to present a sequence of numbers like 1, 2, 4 and ask what the next three numbers are. A student who recognizes the powers of 2 (who is "friends" with that set) might well be tempted to say 8, 16, and 32, seeing each number as twice the previous one. Having a hunch is extremely valuable in mathematics as elsewhere, but in mathematics, the next step requires checking the hunch and proving it. The reason we cannot honestly ask what follows 1, 2, 4 is that after we come up with a hunch, we have *no more data* (nothing else given) by which we can check that hunch or prove it correct (or wrong). In fact, infinitely many other continuations are possible. For example, if instead of looking at what we multiply by to get from 1 to 2 to 4, we look at what we *add*, we'd develop a different hunch. We'd see that first we add 1 (to get from 1 to 2), then we add 2, so we might reasonably continue by adding 3 and then 4 and then 5 to get 7, 11, and 16. The expression $\frac{n(n+1)}{2} + 1$ takes on the values 1, 2, 4, 7, 11, and 16 as we vary n from 0 through 5, and in fact, this sequence of numbers is just a very slightly disguised version of a sequence we've seen before: 1, 3, 6, 10, 15 . . . . A sequence of numbers, by itself, does not reveal what structure lies behind it.

Students who can evaluate algebraic expressions might enjoy evaluating $\frac{n^3 + 5n}{6} + 1$ for values of n from 0 through 4. Again, the sequence is a bit fickle! It seems to make one promise and then it proves that hunches, although really useful and well worth jumping to, must then be checked.

But physical arrangements of objects and various geometric patterns do reveal their structure and help students look for structure. They can therefore be a fertile basis for investigations in which the question "What comes next?" is legitimate.

Investigation 4: Milk Chocolates

The situation: A company packages chocolates in boxes of various sizes, in arrangements like the ones shown here.

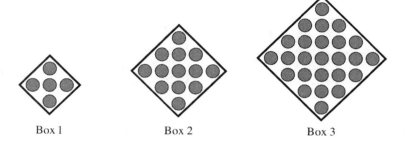

Box 1   Box 2   Box 3

The company also has a Box 4 and Box 5 and so on, arranged the same way.

The big picture problem: If you are told which box (for example, Box 10), how can you figure out how many chocolates they will have in that box?

> *Reality often bends quite a lot for problems of this sort. Box 3 is plausible enough, but by Box 10, no sane company would keep packaging their chocolates in the same arrangement. Still, "What if?" is always a fine question to ask, and the structure of this progression is completely unambiguous.*

Students who examine what they already see, just by counting, will see 5, 13, 25. If they then start working only with the numbers, what they guess for the next number is (and should be, as we said earlier) entirely up for grabs. Lots of patterns will work.

But students who have become more skilled at investigation may try looking at the organization of the candies in the boxes to see if that gives them more information than numbers alone; they may try drawing at least part of Box 4, though this is, as we've seen with the UpDown Towers, not easy for all of them; and they may experiment a bit with different ways of counting the candies in each of these boxes. These might well be listed as warming up or a starting place or further investigation steps for less experienced students.

By looking at the arrangement in the box and not just the total, they may see why the numbers of chocolates at the perimeters of the boxes are 4, 8, and 12 and must be 16, 20, and so on in the next boxes. A student who recognizes these as consecutive multiples of 4—a student for whom that set is familiar or who knows to look for multiplicative patterns—is ready to make predictions even about Box 10, though it might well take figuring out all the boxes that come before it.

Investigation 5: White and Dark Chocolates

The situation: The same company sells boxes with chocolates arranged exactly the same way, but in alternating rows of white and dark chocolate, like this.

Box 1   Box 2   Box 3

The big picture problem: If you are told which box (for example, Box 10), how can you figure out how many chocolates they will have in that box?

By counting the number of white and dark chocolates separately, students see a very different pattern. They generally find it a bit easier to see the structure and to draw Box 4. Students who are "friends" with the square numbers will recognize the 1, 4, and 9 white chocolates in successive boxes, and the 4, 9, and 16 dark chocolates. They may be tempted to *guess* that the numbers will always be squares, but it's possible to be sure about that. The arrangement of the chocolates of each type is a square array, so the square numbers are no coincidence. The next step is to relate those numbers to the box number. The pattern is clearer if we describe the numbers we see rather than giving the actual count. That is, when we see the square arrays of white chocolates, we defer evaluation and write 1^2, 2^2, and 3^2 instead of writing 1, 4, and 9.

Box number	1	2	3	
White chocolates	1^2	2^2	3^2	
Dark chocolates	2^2	3^2	4^2	

From this, students readily make claims not only about Box 10 but about Box 100 (a fatteningly large 100^2 white and 101^2 dark) and Box b as well, writing the algebraic expression $b^2 + (b + 1)^2$.

Pairing these two investigations might lead some students to wonder how the multiples of 4 that we saw in the first investigation relate to the squares that we saw in the second.

Investigation 6: Toothpick Squares

Here is another low threshold visually/geometrically based investigation. Again, the geometry of the situation guarantees that the sequence of numbers we are looking for is unambiguous: only one sequence fits the situation, though that sequence can be expressed in many ways.

The situation: Here is a row of two squares ▢▢ constructed using 7 toothpicks. Longer rows, like ▢▢▢, naturally need more toothpicks.

The big picture problem: If you are told how many squares in a row, explain how you can figure out, without building or drawing the row, how many toothpicks the row will need.

A starting place: How many toothpicks are required to build a row of 4 squares?

Further investigation: How many toothpicks are needed for a row of 1000 squares?

The question itself is not daunting: toothpicks are fun to move around, making four squares is easy enough, and counting the toothpicks is trivial. It's possible to do this by just drawing, but having and encouraging students to *use* physical materials really helps. Students immediately guess answers without even touching the toothpicks. But those who start without investigation are quite often tempted to answer the starting place question with "14 'cause it's twice as many; see, 2 squares took 7 toothpicks, so 4 squares will need 14," which is not correct. Some will answer, "16, because there are 4 squares" (also not correct).

Investigation changes that. The further investigation question introduces the need for a general method, an abstraction, because the row itself is impractical to build. It is, for all practical purposes, the same as the big picture problem, except posed with a specific number. Here, investigation serves the purpose of gathering enough sense with the small numbers to generate the needed abstraction. The challenge of 1000 may feel daunting to some students, but *beginning* the investigation has a low threshold; once it is begun, 1000 is far less intimidating. This is the same way "real" mathematicians work. They begin with a concrete task or question, then one concrete task follows another in hopes of elucidating just what the task *is,* to eventually form new insights for concise, neat packaging.

As for describing the abstraction—the actual big picture "How can you figure out . . ." questions—different groups of students might see this pattern in different ways. One might see "4 toothpicks in the first square, and then 3 more for each additional square" and write $4 + 3(n - 1)$ toothpicks for a row of n squares. Another might see that "a row of n squares has n toothpicks on top, n on bottom, $n - 1$ separating them, and 1 at each end of the row" and write $n + n + (n - 1) + 2$. And one might explain, "If we remove the toothpick at the [right] end, the rest of the squares are just a row of C's made of 3 toothpicks each [one top, one left, one bottom]" and write $3n + 1$. These are, of course, all equivalent.

Have You Found All the Solutions?

Asking students to find concrete examples of some situation, such as numbers between 4 and 5, Two-Color Towers with 5 blocks (2 of which are gray and the rest white), multiples of 2, prime numbers, or rational numbers, is a way to begin an investigation with a low threshold: most students can find some examples. If a student stops after one or two, raise the ceiling by encouraging her to keep going. When a student is generating examples, she might discover patterns that allow her to create more examples quickly: this is an important beginning to understanding in a more general way what makes a number rational, or located between 4 and 5, or prime, and so on. Other students may decide to look at numbers in a related but distinct set, such as numbers between 7 and 8 or irrational numbers. If a student has made a collection of examples but has not yet found a pattern or a question to investigate, you might want to again raise the ceiling by asking if he has found all of the possible examples.

> Try, yourself, to come up with a list of, say, 30 numbers that you are sure are irrational. Be creative! After all, there are infinitely many that look like the first example that's likely to pop into your mind, and it's boring to get all of your 30 just by taking that first example and using it as a model for the next 29. Can you come up with two "kinds" of examples? Three? More?

For example, a student is writing numbers between 4 and 5. He has a large collection, including $4\frac{1}{2}$, $4\frac{3}{4}$, 4.27, 4.99995, 4.3278, and 4.3279. It is likely that he already has a sense that there are too many possibilities to write, but he might not yet have the sense that the list has no end at all. Asking if he has found all possible numbers between 4 and 5 may encourage him to focus on these numbers in a more organized way. Or pointing to two numbers on his list and asking, "Are there any numbers between those two?" may lead to a new understanding of the gaps and might be enough to help him conclude that there is no limit to the number of examples. Of course, it's also fair game for you, as teacher, to toss in new ideas if you think a student is ready. "What about $\sqrt{43}$? Is *that* a number between 4 and 5?" If the student decides that it is not, "Can you think of an example that is sort of like that one, but *is* between 4 and 5?" And you might also tame the problem in a way that does make it possible to find all the examples: "Can you find all numbers of the form $\frac{n}{7}$ (with n an integer) that are between 4 and 5? What about all numbers with two digits to the right of the decimal point?"

> Wait! Don't reach for the calculator! You can figure this out in your head.

Investigation 7: All Gray/White Towers

In arrangements of a finite number of physical objects in a finite number of fixed locations, it's always theoretically possible to find all the cases, but it usually takes some organization—imposing a structure—to find them.

> **The big picture problem:** You are making towers of a specific height, using only blocks that are gray or white. (They may all be one color, or any mix of just those two colors.) How many *different* towers can you make of that height?

> **A clarifying example:** If you have exactly 3 blocks in each tower, these arrangements and more are possible.

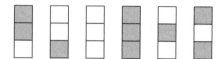

For example, how many *different* towers can be created that are exactly 5 blocks tall, using only gray blocks and/or white blocks? Students can generate *many* towers; the challenge is to know when they have found *all* of them. To figure this out, students must organize their solutions in a way that allows them to justify logically that they have found *all* possible solutions. Often, students find that organizing solutions in a logical manner also reveals an underlying mathematical structure that lends support to their conclusion. They use this structure, as any mathematician would, to defend their argument and extend their reasoning.

> This is a slight variation on the Two-Color Towers investigation. In that investigation, exactly 2 gray blocks had to be used in each tower, and the remaining blocks had to be white. In this investigation, *any number of gray blocks (including 0) can be used, and the rest must be white.*

Students who have had little experience with problems of this kind are typically haphazard about the way they experiment at first. When Jacob, for example, first tackled the Two-Color Towers problem, he started by making a tower 6 blocks tall using exactly 2 gray blocks and the remaining white. As many students would do, Jacob built a few towers, realized he couldn't keep track of the combinations in his mind, and started sketching the different towers he made. Because this was early in the year and investigation was still new to the students, they had all been given a sheet that suggests recording solutions, and has a place for them to keep notes. They had also been given blocks that snap together to experiment with. At first, Jacob generated new towers fairly randomly, breaking off bits of an existing tower, reattaching them, and looking through his list to see if the result was new or a tower he had already made. At this point in his work, Jacob was not yet systematic, but he had no trouble understanding, approaching, and engaging in the task of finding tower combinations. His initial work looked like the picture below:

After one or two more, Jacob looks like he thinks he's done, and so the teacher asks, "Do you think you've found all of the towers?" Jacob affirms that he thinks he has but then notices that Emma has a few more towers. He is surprised and gets ready to draw the new towers, but the teacher changes the question. "Maybe you do have them all, Jacob. Emma, have you checked

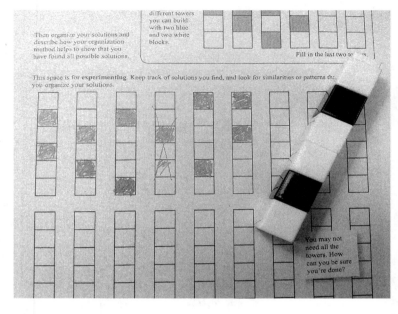

to be sure you have no repeats? And how *can* you check to see if you have them all?" Jacob has not yet developed the *habit* of seeking an underlying structure or approaching the problem in a systematic way, but this question already sets him up to look for a way to organize his drawings.

After he has found all of the towers that are 6 blocks tall, Jacob is then asked to do the same problem for a 7-block-tall tower, with 5 white blocks instead of 4. Though he starts out again generating towers as they occur to him, he quickly switches to a more systematic approach.

Becoming Systematic

For third- or fourth-grade students, the *idea* of being systematic comes fairly quickly, in just a few experiences, but learning to *be* systematic develops over time. Students in middle school and beyond generally *can* build the orderliness, with some example or prompt, even if it is not yet their habit to do so, but the amount of time it takes seems to depend mostly on the investment and confidence of the student.

The more successful students are often already systematic, or become so quickly with a good question and a little experience. Because being systematic means figuring out what will bring order to each particular situation, it is always a puzzle, but one that the more successful students are already inclined to solve.

Students whose experience of mathematics has been discouraging often expect there to be one right way but don't yet see themselves capable of finding it. One consequence is that they either give up early or go for the "effort" grade, just looking for answers to put on paper, rather than giving themselves time to find order: they don't expect mathematics to make sense, and don't see themselves as sense makers. Experience with investigation can help to change this perception.

The teacher's question ("How can you check to see if you have them all?") is essentially a question about proof: How do you prove that you have found every tower? This is generally not a familiar question, and many students even in high school don't know how a response to such a question should sound or look. When finding towers, Jacob's initial focus was on looking to see if he had made a new tower, not on devising a systematic method for generating towers. Regular experience with investigations of this kind and questions of this kind help students develop the skill of system building and also change the search for organization into a habit.

Making Friends with Numbers: Seeking Hidden Structure

By the end of this chapter, more than one of the "how many ways" investigations will have turned up the numbers 1, 3, 6, 10, 15. . . , more than one will have turned up the numbers 1, 2, 3, 5, 8, 13 . . . , and the numbers 1, 2, 4, 8, 16 . . . will also have turned up more than once. But there's nothing particularly interesting about a number or a set of numbers unless it rings some kind of bell, unless it has turned up before and is back again, an old friend in a new place. To a mathematics teacher, 1, 4, 9, 16, 25 is a familiar family; we know them well and they've been close friends for a while. To a first grader who does not yet multiply, this is just a list of numbers no more special or interesting than any other list of numbers, and far *less* interesting than, say 2, 4, 6, 8, 10. . . .

"Making friends with numbers" is a playful metaphor for the serious idea of getting to know numbers—specific ones and also sets and sequences of them—and their characteristics. The number 36 isn't just any old number: it's a square; it's in the thirties; it's a multiple of 12; it has some familiar factors; it's a tenth of the number of degrees in a full rotation; it's even; it's the sum of the first eight counting numbers; it's the sum of the first six odd numbers; and so on. It has a personality and we know some of the circles it hangs out in; we have various associations when we see it. Fairly early, certain numbers have lots of family associations: 5 is the number of fingers on a hand, the number of cents in a nickel, the number of minutes between the marked numbers on a clock, and so on. And fingers and nickels also relate 5 to 10 (two hands or a dime).

As we showed earlier, a partial sequence of numbers like 1, 2, 4, 8 can be continued in more than one way, reflecting more than one possible structure that could generate it. Though those four numbers are insufficient to determine *the* structure behind them, it is still a useful exercise to look for *a* structure, one possible rule that could explain the set or sequence we see. The honest question would not be "What's the next number?" but "What *could* my rule be?"

The numbers 1, 2, 4, 8, . . . do not reveal their structure. Whatever structure led to these numbers is hidden from us, and we need to find one that makes sense in the current situation and declare it. The most obvious is probably 1, 2, 4, 8, . . . , 2^n, . . . , but there are others as well, like 1, 2, 4, 8, . . . , $\frac{n^3 + 5n}{6}$, . . . Looking for a structure behind 1, 3, 4, 7, 11, 18, 29, . . . requires some experimentation and thought: it is very much a case of looking for a hidden structure.

Representing General Patterns with Algebra: Describing Structure in Precise Language

Successful investigations often involve students first in gathering data, reasoning with specific numerical examples. After they have worked with enough numbers to get a sense of the rhythm of the calculations, students express the general relationship in algebra: a "pattern indicator." Deliberately building in this progression can help students develop the habit of describing repeated reasoning using algebraic language. For example, in Toothpick Squares, students first build a row of squares using toothpicks, recording in a table the number of toothpicks it takes to build up to 6 squares. Then they describe how they might figure out the number of toothpicks it would take to build a row of 10, then 20, then 100 squares without building the actual row. The purpose of these intermediate problems is to help students figure out a way to express the reasoning behind their calculations. Too often, students think that writing an algebraic expression is a separate skill from reasoning about numbers, rather than an extension. Asking students about larger numbers helps them to see the repetition in their reasoning. By the time they are asked to write an expression for the number of toothpicks it would take to build *s* squares, students know they can apply the pattern of calculation to any number, even when that number is expressed as a variable.

TEACHING THROUGH INVESTIGATION

Some curricula contain investigations, and there are good resources on the Web. There are also many books, for example, *Discovering Mathematics: The Art of Investigation* (Gardiner 2007). With work, you can make, collect, or invent your own investigations and tailor them in ways that particularly suit your goals and your students. You also want to think about how to help your class discuss their investigations once they are under way (or complete) and consider when and how to use individual or group investigation.

The *Making Mathematics* project (http://www2.edc.org/makingmath/) describes in detail a number of mathematical investigations. In addition to providing a printable version of each project, the site lists prerequisites, warm-up problems, hints, resources, teaching notes, extension problems, and some results. Five of these problems are excellent for students making the transition to algebra, because no algebra is required to enter the problems, but elementary algebra can be used well. The site is open to students. To access teaching notes, use the password *mathisfun*. Searching for "mathematical investigations for high school students" on the Web will turn up many other resources from which ideas can be selected.

Inventing Investigations

You might also want to invent your own investigations, perhaps giving specific attention to investigations that build the ideas of imposing structure and seeking hidden structure. Here are suggestions for developing new investigations of those two kinds.

Have You Found Them All? Learning to Impose Structure

Here are several problems that involve the "Have you found them all? How can you *know* you have found them all?" question. In each case, you see that you can make up a new problem just by changing the constraints, the setup, slightly.

Problems Involving Money

- In how many ways can you make 48¢ using no dimes?
- In how many ways can you make 48¢ using no quarters or nickels?
- How many different amounts of money can you make using exactly 6 coins?

Problems Involving Cuisenaire Rods

Cuisenaire rods are of lengths 1, 2, and so on through 10. A train of rods can be 1 rod or a collection of rods laid end to end. A train of length 3 could be made of 3 rods of length 1, or of 2 rods of the right length, or just of a single rod. ▮▯ is different from ▯▮. We could, of course, just play with the numbers, representing ▮▯ as 2 + 1, and representing ▯▮ as 1 + 2, but at least initially, one gets different and worthwhile insights actually moving the rods around.

- *Using any rods, alone or in combination*, there are exactly two different ways to make a train of length 2: ▯▯ or ▮. How many *different* trains of length 3 can be made? How many for lengths 4, 5, *n*?
- *Using only rods of length 1 or 2*, how many different trains of length 3 can you make? How many for lengths 4, 5, 6, 7, 8?
- *Using exactly 3 rods (same or different and any length)*, there is only one way to make a train of length 3: ▯▯▯. How many trains of length 4 are there? 5? 6? 7? *n*?
- This time you may use any number of rods, but they must be of exactly 2 different lengths. There are no such trains of length 2 and only 2 ways to make trains of length 3. How many different trains of length 4 are there? 5? 6? 7? What regularity could help you find all the possibilities for 8?

> The fourth rod problem requires perseverance and careful work. Not much jumps out at the beginning. Part of learning to be a good investigator is recognizing that an investigation does not have to produce all possible results. Finding *some* reportable results—methods for working, patterns in numbers, numbers of trains for *certain* combinations of rods—is good enough!

Problems Involving Arrangements

- Given a specific number of stories tall, how many different towers can you build using only blue or white blocks (any number, including 0, of either color)?
- Same problem, but restricted to exactly *1* blue block and the rest white.
- Same problem, restricted to exactly *2* blue and the rest white (Jacob's Two-Color Tower problem).
- Same problem, but with exactly 1 red, 1 blue, and the rest white.

Problems Involving Paths

- How many ways can you get from start to the station labeled *B* if you are allowed *only* to go north (up) and east (right) in any order, with no backtracking by going south or west? How many for each of the other lettered stations?

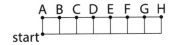

• How many ways can you get from start to each of the stations *J* through *R* if you are allowed *only* to go north and east? How do those relate to the number of ways you got to *A* through *H*?

• How many ways can you get from start to *C* if you must always be farther to the east at each move? (That is, you may move directly east, or southeast, or northeast, but never back toward the west.) How many ways to each of the other lettered stations?

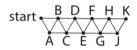

Making Friends with Numbers—Seeking Hidden Structure

Meghan, described in Chapter 2, was stumped at the idea of taking half of the number 48 because, for her at that moment, it was just a number that followed 47, and not a 40 + 8 that could be halved to make 20 + 4. She needed to get to know that number in a new way. Similarly, when we ask students to factor $405ab + 320xy$, students for whom the multiples of 5 don't just jump out as familiar friends might be stymied. For features of numbers to jump out at us, we have to have a kind of familiarity with them, much more than the ability to figure things out with effort. For this reason, we often want to increase not only the kinds of associations that students have with numbers but also the ease with which they make these associations, their familiarity, all so that students can more readily learn to use these associations in their computations and in their investigations. Here are some ways to help students build more associations with numbers and build up the habit of looking for the characteristics of numbers or what families they might belong to.

The reappearing set. One strategy, of course, is to present investigations that keep turning up the same set of numbers. Powers of 2; square numbers; the triangular numbers 1, 3, 6, 10, 15 . . . $\frac{n(n + 1)}{2}$; multiples of some number; and so on are sets that pop up often.

One of these numbers is not like the others. Encourage students to approach collections of numbers by *looking* for what binds them and to think about numbers that don't seem to belong. Giving students collections of numbers that come close to following a few different rules, but don't quite fit any, can both help students learn about new kinds of numbers and encourage them to practice the important investigative skill of looking for more than one way in which a collection of numbers might be associated. Consider these two groups of numbers.

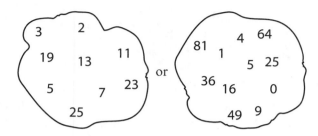

These collections may lead students to feel some disquiet when they notice that the numbers don't seem internally quite consistent. In each, there appears to be a number that does not belong. In fact, in each there are a few different sensible choices of which number doesn't belong. Discussion is often a particularly good way to help students see more than one of these choices. Even though we've given a perfectly good example earlier in this chapter (page 116) of a sequence that grows 1, 2, 4, 8, *15*, students *should* feel a bit of disquiet when they see what looked like a pattern of doubling suddenly go astray. At that point, we check to make sure we are getting things right. It could be that the 15 was a miscalculation. Or it could be correct, and we invent a new theory.

The "one of these numbers doesn't belong" exercise lays the groundwork for knowing how to respond when an investigation turns up collections like these. It helps prepare you to consider a variety of possible associations—extending the investigation into related territories, going back and rechecking the one or two numbers that don't seem to fit. If you see every number as arbitrary and indistinguishable from any other number—if you have too limited a set of associations with a number—you wouldn't be inclined to perform any such check. And if you see the exercise as mere practice in taxonomy, you would also not be inclined to use the pattern you see to further an investigation. But if you recognize a set of numbers as having a meaning, you might well look into the investigation to figure out why *that* set appears in *that* place.

Looking at numbers more than one way. Give students investigations that involve looking at more than one kind of number grouping. A person who is friends with numbers has a more interesting and less disorienting experience of numbers. If she encounters 12, her mind may automatically associate it with its factors, 1, 2, 3, 4, 6, and 12. If she encounters 49, she might recall that it is a square number. Perhaps the number 23 is linked with the knowledge that it is prime. Such connections are important to algebraic thinking. If we encounter the sequence 0, 1, 4, 9, 16, 25, 36, . . . and know only to take differences between consecutive elements, we'll find a very interesting pattern, but it will be easier to write an expression that generates these numbers if the numbers in that set are already familiar friends. Faced with the sequence 2, 6, 10, 14, 18, 22, 26 . . . and told that it continues growing by 4 at each new step, a person who sees the "personality" of the numbers would likely feel certain, even without formal proof, that 20567 will not appear anywhere in that sequence. It might take longer to decide whether 40000 will appear in the sequence, but again, even without the machinery of a number theory course, knowing what clubs 2, 6, 10, 14, etc., do and don't belong to is likely—with some thought, experimentation, and time—to lead to a conjecture. Like 40000, the sequence is made up of even numbers. However, the sequence also skips over all the multiples of 4, so it'll skip over 40000.

Keep a record of sets. Encourage students to keep track of sets of numbers that they or you notice in their problem solving. They should record both the set and a brief description of how it was found.

It's likely that your students will recognize some common sets of numbers, for example, even and odd and multiples of 5 and 10. Some may recognize square numbers and powers of 2. Some may even recognize triangular numbers (0, 1, 3, 6, 10, 15, 21, 28, our friend 36, and so on). If you see a student generating a set of numbers that your student has some familiarity with, you may decide to wonder out loud why he is finding only those numbers.

The mystery set. For sets that your students find in an investigation but are not yet familiar with, you might encourage them to see if they can find a relationship among the numbers. It's fine to leave this question unanswered and for the students to simply add the sequence to their list. When they encounter the same set in a different context, the question can be raised again. After the set has been rediscovered in a variety of contexts, your students will have more information to use in figuring out what the relationship is among these numbers.

> You or your students may be interested to know that it is possible to look up sequences to learn more about them. Go to https://oeis.org/ and type in the sequence you have. You might want enjoy looking up 1, 2, 4, 8, 16, 31 to see what investigations can generate that sequence.

Foreshadowing. If you know that a topic is approaching where your students are likely to see sets of certain kinds of numbers, you might want to make those numbers the focus of a quick (two- or three-minute) whole-class mental mathematics activity. For example, when a situation that will involve square numbers is coming up, you might do a call-and-response activity in which you say a "reasonable" number—generally integers 0 through 10 or 12, and small multiples of 10—and students respond with the square of that number. Or if students will soon be doing some of the problems involving paths (page 118), you might have students generate the Fibonacci sequence by writing 0, 1 and then telling students that each new number will be the sum of the previous two, and letting them go. And, also for the path problems (and many others listed in this chapter), you might have students generate triangular numbers by telling them that each number they say will be the last number they said plus a new number you will give them. Start them at 1 and then say "plus 2," and when they've responded, you say "plus 3," and then "plus 4" and so on, up to, say, 10. If possible, do this a week or two before the topic. This gives students the experience of recognizing the sequence from previous study.

Structuring Whole-Class Discussions of Investigations

Pursue One of the Directions
The teacher's goals may determine which path is worth the time to explore further. In the discussion of the Two-Color Towers investigation (page 96), each of three students took a different investigative direction. The teacher has many decisions to make about how a whole-class discussion of this investigation should proceed. The teacher might draw attention to the work of the student who wrote a recursive function for the number of possible towers with 2 gray blocks out of n blocks. In this case, it may turn out that the first student (whose investigation was in finding combinations) is not able to relate to the discussion because of the path of his play. A very useful practice is to have the kids report and explain their results. Chapter 6 will say more about helping students speak in class.

Highlight Mathematical Practice
A teacher may decide to conduct a whole-class discussion focusing on an element of mathematical practice, perhaps having students reflect on their use of multiple solution strategies or perhaps sharing ways in which some other student's critique of their work helped to advance their thinking.

Focus on a Common Finding
The teacher might choose to organize the investigations into some coherent finding or statement. After both Two-Color Towers and Staircase Pattern, the teacher might call attention to the 1, 3, 6, 10, 15 . . . that appeared in both and invite discussion of whether that's just random coincidence or what might be going on beneath the surface that makes the numbers turn out the same.

Highlight a Variety of Possible Investigations and Discoveries

The teacher might decide to focus on the variety of discoveries that can be made. If students are given time to diverge in their investigations, variety will come up. Orchestrating discussions can help students appreciate the wide variety of directions of study. This discussion allows students to share in the benefits of investigations done by others and the ideas that those investigations generated.

Collaboration and Individual Work

Individual Work: Jacob

Let's return to Jacob, a student we met earlier in the chapter, as he tackles a further investigation later in the year.

Tiling Patterns

The "big picture" problem: How many *different* ways can you completely fill a $2 \times n$ space with 1×2 tiles?

A clarifying example: There are exactly *five* different ways you can completely fill a 2×4 space with 1×2 tiles. Here are three. Find the last two.

Warming up: How many different ways can you fill a 2×6 space with 1×2 tiles?

Later in the year, Jacob still starts new investigations in what appears to be a nonsystematic way, but it is clear now that this start-up phase is his way of playing with the task to make some sense of it. This is good strategy. It's also clear that Jacob has changed since he first began the Two-Color Towers investigation, as he now moves spontaneously from the initial exploratory play to imposing structure in his work. In fact, because Jacob's first two trials to fill up a 2×6 space were ⬚⬚⬚⬚⬚ and ▭▭▭, it may be that even the start-up phase in Jacob's work was not random, but checking the extremes—all vertical, all horizontal. Checking extreme cases is also very good strategy.

Jacob was, at this point in this investigation, working entirely alone. In the beginning of the year, Jacob tended to work alone and really didn't know how to work collaboratively. At the same time, he also depended on collaboration more than he does now, because back then he didn't really know how to investigate independently. He tried things but saw little order, was "done" before he was done, and needed interaction with others both to notice that they had different things on their papers and also to be challenged to decide whether that meant that *they* or *he* or *both* were right. Or wrong, for that matter! His default was to assume that the other was right, and he needed to learn to evaluate, to figure out how to assume more authority himself.

At this stage of the year, he still defaults to working alone but works quite well with others. He also has less immediate need for external ideas to challenge his own because he is more able to pursue an investigation independently, but interaction often brings good ideas and is sometimes its own goal. And, frankly, most students need more than a few minutes to make sense of investigative problems like this and may need at least some initial stretch of that time alone. So, Jacob's teacher thinks a lot about when to leave him working on his own and when to engineer more interaction.

When Jacob was still poor at working with others but poor working without them, the decision was, in a way, easier: put him in a pair or group, but stop back by that group often, while attending to others in class, to help the group collaborate. Recall the interaction with Emma at the beginning of the year, when Jacob noticed that Emma had a few more towers:

> *He is surprised and gets ready to draw the new towers, but the teacher changes the question. "Maybe you do have them all, Jacob. Emma, have you checked, to be sure you have no repeats? And how* can *you check to see if you have them all?"*

Jacob did *not* have all the towers, but the teacher's response was to have Emma check for repeats. This gives no right or wrong information to either student but gives them a strategy for deciding on their own. Emma had no repeats but hadn't already checked and therefore got the opportunity to prove herself right. What Jacob learned—almost certainly not from this event alone—was that it was possible to get real ideas from working with someone else, but their ideas were not necessarily confirmation that *his* ideas were not good. He had a way of checking.

Now, Jacob works pretty well both alone and with others, so the decision is more complicated. Why push him to collaborate? But isn't it good to interact? At this point, his teacher monitors to make sure that he doesn't *only* work alone, but otherwise lets him choose.

Collaboration: Yolanda and David

Although Jacob's search for structure was independent, students also benefit from collaborating and sharing their thinking about a problem to build a structure for solving it.

When Yolanda and David discussed how many toothpicks (see Investigation 6: Toothpick Squares, page 111) will be in a row of 4 or 1000 squares, Yolanda is daunted by the idea of making a row with 1000 squares and she looks ready to give up. David has been carefully making a row of 10, quietly engaged. He says to her, "You just add 3 more toothpicks every time you make a square."

"So, what, it's 300 then?"

David's not sure. He wants the problem to be that simple, but he knows it isn't. He shrugs.

In the absence of anything else to do, Yolanda makes a square out of toothpicks. She says simply, "Well, the first time you use 4."

This is clearly the missing piece for David and he says, "Yeah. Yeah, it's 4, and then 3 every time. So with 100 squares it would be . . ." He squints, and loses confidence.

Yolanda says, "Yeah, 4 plus whatever 99 times 3 is."

Without full awareness of doing so, the students combined their recognition of a pattern and their understanding of the one exception to that pattern and thus uncovered the information they will need to generalize their rudimentary formula to any number of squares. Not only were they able to recognize an underlying structure, but they did so by reasoning collaboratively through several steps of the problem.

CONCLUSION

Investigations help to develop students' mathematical habits of mind over the course of the school year. They are engaging, approachable, mathematically significant problems that encourage creativity and perseverance. They invite students to draw connections, make generalizations, and reveal underlying mathematical structures. They elicit multiple solutions and reward experimentation, organization, and logical thinking. As students progress through them, they make mathematical discoveries and develop their own identities as mathematicians. And investigations take time. It's too easy to get stuck on the disadvantage of taking time; the advantage is that investigations help build stamina. And, far from taking up time with digressions, extended investigations help build mathematical habits that actually save time.

The investigation strategy of beginning with concrete examples and moving to more general understanding is valuable. It is part of learning that complicated problems can be broken down into pieces to be more easily understood, and that finding a strategy that works for small numbers or a simpler problem can help one find a strategy for larger or more complicated numbers. For students making the transition to algebra, this kind of work demonstrates that the language of algebra is accessible and is used to express patterns that can be found almost anywhere.

A Geometric Look at Algebra

5

G eometric notions—in particular, location, distance, and area—can help us understand and reason about arithmetic operations and can help us organize algebraic calculations as well. In this chapter, we discuss two tools for building mental models that are useful in both pre-algebra and algebra classrooms: number lines, primarily for order, addition, and subtraction; and the area model, primarily for multiplication, division, and (in algebra) factoring. Both of these are mental model builders that give students a visual lens through which to look at mathematical ideas—subtracting negative numbers or factoring algebraic expressions—helping them to clarify what they already know and to extend and deepen their understanding.

Mathematicians and teachers may see how subtraction of negative numbers is a logical extension of subtraction of positive integers, but the similarities are notoriously hard for students to understand, and they often end up relying on mantras like "two negatives make a positive," which can get misapplied or distorted because they don't come from logic. Using visual models, students can extend understandings that they have spent years developing, rather than starting all over again at the beginning, and they can extend their considerable logic about positive integers to include new sets of numbers, and their thinking about algebra.

THE NUMBER LINE: NUMBERS AS LOCATIONS AND DISTANCES

The number line is a coherent representation for making sense of the real number system— particularly integers, fractions, and decimal representations—and for building understanding of the properties of operations on integers and rational numbers. The Common Core State Standards for Mathematics promote the number line as an integral tool for student learning and understanding. The number line can help students see the relationships between numbers, the commonalities shared by all real numbers, and the meaning of operations such as addition and subtraction, including addition and subtraction of rational numbers and algebraic expressions. Notions of distance on the number line are particularly valuable in helping students make sense of the arithmetic of signed numbers and avoid common mistakes like this:

$$-12 - 5 = \underline{7}$$

which was explained by the student as "two negatives make a positive."

A visual mental model can help students sort out perennial questions like "Which is bigger, -80 or -81?" "Why isn't $3.6 + 3.6$ just 6.12?" "How can 6.4 and 6.40 be the same number?" and "Which is bigger, $\frac{99}{98}$ or $\frac{51}{50}$?" More advanced students can literally *see* why $3 + n$ is always bigger than n, but $3n$ is sometimes larger than n, sometimes the same, and sometimes smaller, and why $-2n$ can be positive.

To build a versatile number line image that is robust enough to help both beginner and advanced students see a structure in number that they can port to algebra, it helps to begin by thinking about the "geography" of the number line, and where the numbers they know fit in. We start with stories from two classrooms, and then we discuss the mathematics and pedagogy behind these examples.

Two Classrooms

These stories show how students learn to place on the number line—negative numbers, decimals, and fractions, numbers that can remain somewhat muddled to many students even in high school. By systematizing their understanding of the placement of these numbers relative to each other, students build a structure that lets them extend what they already know about operations on positive integers to all real numbers and to generalize to algebraic expressions. The first step is to help students see how all of these numbers fit, in order, along the number line.

A Ninth-Grade Algebra Support Class

We were working with an algebra support class for high school freshmen. They were finding terms in a descending arithmetic sequence and had no difficulty while the sequence remained positive integers but some were shaky when they reached zero. What came next? Negatives? Decimals? Fractions? And how did the order then continue? They had no real sense of the "geography" of the number line except for positive integers. For the next class, I arranged an activity that I hoped would get them started sorting out at least some of this on their own.

I drew a rough sketch of the following number line on a blackboard.

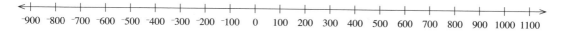

I said only, "I have a bunch of sticky notes with numbers. I'll give each of you a sticky, and as soon as I do, go to the board and stick it where you think it should go." From then on, I said nothing, but moved from student to student as quickly as I could, sometimes handing them a sticky and sometimes just pasting it on them (which amused them), and they trooped off. Four or five were typically at the board at one time. With thirty-six sticky notes and seventeen students, each student got to the board more than once. The thirty-six stickies included numbers ranging from $-800\frac{1}{2}$ to 1000, but the set was deliberately designed so that two thirds of the numbers fell between -100 and 100 and most of that cluster were within 40 of each other, so when the kids stuck them on the board, most of the stickies were crowded into what the kids described as "a big mess."

As in earlier chapters, the "I" here refers to one of the authors, E.P.G., who was working with these students.

After all the stickies were placed, I pointed to the sticky that said "1000" (placed correctly at the farthest right) and asked, "Is this correct?" No controversy. I then moved to the left, to the next sticky, just pointed without repeating my question, and let the kids respond. The 743 was between 700 and 800 and slightly off center, closer to 700 than to 800, but some kids argued that it was too much off center to be accurate. I spoke up and said my whole sketch was pretty rough; as a group they then agreed that "approximately right" should be good enough. Even after agreeing to that, the class wanted to indicate, by placement, that 295.5 was less than 304.5, but any noticeable separation was too much; their positions no longer seemed approximately right.

When we got near the "big mess," I just skipped over it and went to the far left. Questions came up immediately. Whoever posted $-800\frac{1}{2}$ put it between -800 and -900. Joseph argued that the number is "Eight hundred and a half, so it should be bigger," by which he meant farther to the right, but Chiara argued back. "No! It goes seven hundred, eight hundred, nine hundred," she said as she pointed at -700, -800, and -900, "so bigger goes on that side," between what she called "eight hundred" and "nine hundred," where it had already been correctly placed. Chiara knew that the numbers she was pointing to were "negative seven hundred" and so on, but omitting the word *negative* (or *minus*) called attention to the increasing magnitude, which was her point. She convinced the class, but they ultimately decided that the sticky should be at the ⁻800, "because ⁻800$\frac{1}{2}$ is so close to ⁻800."

The order of ⁻555.5 and ⁻552 raised the same question about order and was settled in the same way: ⁻555.5 should be left of ⁻552, but like 295.5 and 304.5, they were too close to worry about.

Then we tackled the "big mess" between ⁻100 and 100. I removed all those stickies and "zoomed in" on that region. First, I named the numbers we needed: ⁻100, ⁻90, ⁻80, and so on up through 70, 80, 90, 100. Then I erased zeros at the end of each number on the line that was already drawn.

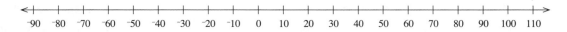

I ran around again, giving kids stickies from that region to post. The placement of 31, 50, and 80 was straightforward. When people noticed that the sticky with ⁻55 was placed to the right of ⁻50, they objected, and the class corrected it on their own as they had earlier.

The class was deeply concerned about ⁻8.5 and ⁻8$\frac{1}{2}$. Which order did they go in? Were they the same? Some kids were sure enough that 8.5 = 8$\frac{1}{2}$, but less sure about the negative ones. I asked what they thought *should* be the case. One student argued that if 8.5 and 8$\frac{1}{2}$ are the same, then the negatives should be the same, too. The class readily agreed that was the only sensible thing, but it was also clear that most, maybe all, of the students were still unhappy with the numbers being "in the same place." That idea would take some getting used to.

There was still a "big mess," this time between 0 and 20, so I took the stickies off again, enlarged that part of the line to fill the board, and gave out those stickies for us to start over.

This time there was no "big mess." Mostly everything had its own place, but we still had to discuss 11$\frac{1}{2}$ and 11.5 and 14$\frac{1}{2}$ and 14.5. Nobody doubted that the numbers were equal, but being in the same place still felt weird! Would they always sit on top of each other, or were they a kind of "little mess" that we could separate if only we drew the right line?

At some point we would need to make explicit some ideas that they had already handled implicitly; they would need to learn/relearn to perform arithmetic sensibly with these numbers; and they still needed to learn for the first time the algebraic extensions of those ideas. But they now had a sense-making experience upon which we could build a formal structure. What they had "learned" prior to this was apparently muddled, not made fully sensible in a way that they could "rework it out" if they forgot some rule or another.

Though I spoke very little and the class figured out a lot, the class's discoveries weren't pure accident: the structure of the task made a lot of information available and, though mostly silent, actually taught quite a lot. It's worth taking a moment to see what ideas came up and where they came from.

The symmetry of the number line, for one thing, allowed students to reason that $^-610$ should go between $^-600$ and $^-700$, just as positive 610 goes between 600 and 700. In places where some of the students were less certain, the pure "reasonableness" of other students' arguments was convincing. Placing $^-610$ to the right of $^-600$ would "mess up the order," as one student put it. The class was not yet secure about what all this meant. It would take more learning to sort out all the parts, but they had begun the work, and in a way that supported a deep goal: getting the students to expect mathematics to make sense. Students now had a framework that gave them a way to check and incorporate new ideas.

Early on, when the teacher dismissed the entire sketch as "pretty rough," the class seemed to take that as a kind of relief: we won't be nit-picking about precision. At least for now, the goal is sensible reasoning. Later, when the students were worried about -8.5 and $-8\frac{1}{2}$, the teacher gave the same message by asking what they thought *should* be the case, reaffirming the goal of seeing mathematics as making consistent sense.

And without any mention at all by the teacher, two other important ideas came up: distance and scale. Kids explicitly referred to the distance between numbers, noting that some were too close to each other to set in order. But that implicitly used the idea of scale, because given more space, they could be more precise about placement. In later lessons, these students will

In higher mathematics, we sometimes do encounter results that initially feel counterintuitive—like many notions about infinity. When we accept those results, it is so that we don't create an even more unsettling inconsistency.

Students in high school algebra can use a keep-it-consistent argument to show why we'd want to define 2^0, 2^{-1}, and 2^{-2} the way we do.

We invent the notation 2^n to mean that we are multiplying together a string of n 2's. Using that consistently tells us (for positive integer exponents) that 2^3 means $2 \times 2 \times 2$ and 2^4 means $2 \times 2 \times 2 \times 2$, so $2^3 \times 2^4 = 2^7$. More generally $2^a \times 2^b = 2^{(a+b)}$. But we have no meaning for "multiplying together a string of one-and-a-half 2's" or of "negative two 2's" or even of "zero 2's." So we *define* them, looking for a structure to preserve that lets us avoid troubling inconsistencies. In the sequence

$$2^5 = 32$$
$$2^4 = 16$$
$$2^3 = 8$$
$$2^2 = 4$$

we divide by 2 each time. So we *want* 2^1 to be 2. That still fits (awkwardly) with our n 2's idea (in this case only one 2). We still have no "intuitive" meaning for 2^0, 2^{-1}, and so on, but dividing by 2 again gives 1 and then $\frac{1}{2}$, so we now have reason to want to define exponents so that

$$2^0 = 1$$
$$2^{-1} = \frac{1}{2}$$
$$2^{-2} = \frac{1}{4}$$

That is consistent with our idea that $2^a \times 2^b = 2^{(a+b)}$ because $2^{-2} \times 2^5$ should then be 2^3, and that's what we get when we multiply $32 \times \frac{1}{4}$. Now we have a system that works.

build on the ideas they generated in this lesson. They will use both distance and scale *explicitly* to make sense of decimal and fraction notation and to understand subtraction of signed numbers. We will say more about that mathematics and those lessons later in this chapter.

A Fourth-Grade Beginning the Study of Decimals

Several years earlier, we had used the same kind of activity with a different set of numbers in a fourth-grade class that had begun studying decimals. These students already had been introduced to some ways of looking at the order of decimals, but they were still beginners. This activity was practice and refinement rather than introduction.

For the fourth graders, the goal was to get a visual idea of decimal order, largely to solidify decimal order (e.g., making clear why 3.6 > 3.12), and also to make sense of decimal addition (e.g., 3.2 + 3.2 = 6.4, but 3.6 + 3.6 ≠ 6.12). So, for this group, we included many more decimal numbers, and not just ones that ended in .5, as we had for the ninth graders. A very few numbers would wind up in the same place, like 3.5 and $3\frac{1}{2}$, but most of the focus would be on another deliberately created big mess, all around 120 and requiring more zooming in on the number line, enough to distinguish a few numbers that had three digits to the right of the decimal point.

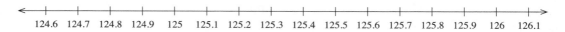

124.6 124.7 124.8 124.9 125 125.1 125.2 125.3 125.4 125.5 125.6 125.7 125.8 125.9 126 126.1

The culminating challenge was to understand that 125.325 was larger than 125.32, but that 125.4 was even larger.

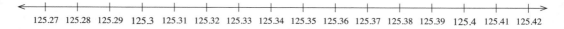

125.27 125.28 125.29 125.3 125.31 125.32 125.33 125.34 125.35 125.36 125.37 125.38 125.39 125.4 125.41 125.42

Though the content and purpose were different, the dynamic in class was much the same. We drew the original number line from ⁻200 to 1000. The task was introduced the same way, with brief instructions and then nothing from the teacher except a stream of sticky notes. When all the notes were placed on the number line, we again started at the far right. One or two notes had been placed incorrectly, but there was no controversy at all about them, and the class even treated them as if they were just slips. After skipping over the big mess, there was a brief discussion of 3.5 and $3\frac{1}{2}$, but all the children seemed perfectly comfortable that those went in the same place because they were the same, although a couple of the children quibbled that they were not the same number, by which they meant not the same *written* symbol (i.e., not the same *numeral*, but they didn't apparently have the vocabulary to make that distinction).

The real work came when they were trying to place numbers like 125.325 correctly, and when they encountered 125.30 and 125.300. They were not nearly as comfortable with the idea that 125.3 and 125.30 belonged in the same place or even were the same number. They agreed, but could not yet be happy to put 125.300 in the same place though they tolerated putting 125.32 and 125.320 in the same place. It took a few more lessons for the equivalence of these written forms to stop feeling weird to the students.

The fourth graders were also just as argumentative and cogent, though not quite as articulate, as the ninth graders about defending their placement of numbers. With the negative numbers, they used the increasing-magnitude-as-we-go-left argument as Chiara did in the ninth-grade class as a way of saying where the stickies go. Though not all their initial statements were correct, their defenses were attempts to be logical, not just stubborn, with the result that the discussions ended with consensus and correct placements. The teacher sometimes asked questions like, "Would you say more? I didn't quite understand" where statements seemed incomplete, whether or not they were correct, and never weighed in on the correctness or incorrectness of statements.

Location and Order: Mapping the Geography of the Number Line

The number line is common in the early elementary grades, but then it sometimes vanishes until students analyze the real line in college or graduate school. Let's revisit for a minute what a number line—our imagination's superidealization of a ruler—really is. The essential feature of a ruler is that it has a starting place—a *0*, whether it is labeled on the ruler or not—and regular markings in some unit indicating the mark's distance from 0. The number line has essentially the same features, with some simplifications and some extras. On the number line, we no longer care about inches or centimeters, but we still need the origin—a point labeled 0—and marks indicating distance from the origin. Because the number line is a creation of our mind, it can, unlike rulers, stretch infinitely in both directions from its origin. Furthermore, we can imagine zooming in or zooming out infinitely to explore numbers of any magnitude and precision.

Distance from 0 Goes Both Ways

When students work only with positive numbers, greater magnitude means a larger number. When students begin to work with negative numbers, this focus on magnitude often leads them to see numbers like −81 as larger than −80. The number line image helps students rework the intuitions they've built around positive numbers, so that they can work successfully with negative numbers. Where magnitude is no longer sufficient to say which number is greater, students refocus on another relationship that does remain the same: a number that is farther to the left on the number line is smaller.

The statement "[one number] is . . . to the left of [another number]" is a statement about points, not numbers, but is much less cumbersome than "the point labeled with the number −81 is to the left of the point labeled with the number −80." Precise language is important because it avoids ambiguities and confusion, but once we understand what we are talking about, more casual language can sometimes be clearer.

Numbers all name distances of points from 0, and the *sign* of the number indicates which side of 0, which *direction* from 0. So the number 40 labels the point that is 40 units from 0 and to the right of 0; −80 labels the point that is precisely twice as far from 0 and to the left of 0; though it is twice as far from 0, we call −80 "less than" 40 because we define *less than* to mean what it meant when we looked only at positive numbers, "to the left of." Using distance from 0 and reminding students that the convention of being to the left means the number is smaller helps students sort out order and magnitude of negative numbers using logic they have already developed. This is exactly what students need anyway to work with the coordinate plane.

Students often jump quickly (and in error) to decide that −81 is bigger than −80 because they are thinking only about magnitude. The number line allows the teacher to use a consistent image: −81 is farther to the left than −80, which students have long known with *positive* numbers to mean that it is actually smaller. Students generally also have a difficult time ordering mixed numbers that are to the left of 0. The number $-4\frac{1}{2}$ is four and one half units from 0, and it is on the left-hand side, exactly halfway between −4 and −5, so it is to the *left* of −4, and thus $-4\frac{1}{2} < -4$. This is exactly what Joseph and Chiara were able to work out with the placement of $-800\frac{1}{2}$ earlier in this chapter. And it's a kind of making sense that many students need. Students generally find the number line easy to understand and compelling, because it helps them see how to reason about negative numbers using many of the same ideas that they have long used for positive numbers. Framing the discussion this way makes it sense-bound rather than rule-bound.

Zooming In

On a number line that is marked off by thousands, we can zoom in on the interval between any two marks—"magnifying" it so that we can see more detail, more precision—and subdivide it into 10 intervals of 100 each.

So, we explicitly introduce the notion of zooming in on the thousands, complete with a magnifying glass, and see 10 new intervals of 100 each. Separating those smaller intervals are 9 new marks. We label the marks using 1 through 9. In this case, the 1 through 9 indicate hundreds: 3**1**00, 3**2**00, 3**3**00, 3**4**00, 3**5**00, 3**6**00, 3**7**00, 3**8**00, 3**9**00.

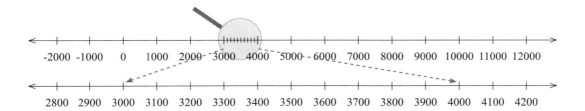

We can zoom in on, say, the interval 3500 to 3600 and see 10 new intervals of 10 each, again separated by 9 new marks, which we label using 1 through 9: 35**1**0, 35**2**0, 35**3**0, 35**4**0, and so on. If we zoom in on, say, 3520 to 3530, we see 352**1**, 352**2**, 352**3**, 352**4**, 352**5**, and so on.

People designed decimal notation in such a way that that the next step—magnifying the interval between any two consecutive marks on a number line that is marked off by ones—is done in the exact same way. We subdivide the interval into 10 intervals separated by 9 new marks labeled using 1 through 9. This time, the 1 through 9 indicate tenths: 3.**1**, 3.**2**, 3.**3**, 3.**4**, and so on, which we pronounce "three point one, three point two, . . ."

Why emphasize the language "three point five nine, three point six"? Using the language of fractions to name *those* numbers—*reading* them as "three and fifty-nine hundredths" and "three and six tenths"—makes the smaller one sound larger in every way. The other common alternative, "three point fifty-nine," definitely makes "three point six" sound smaller. The string to the right of the decimal point is not an integer (unless we see it as shorthand for the numerator of a fraction), so treating it like an integer is fodder for misconceptions. "Three point five nine" literally spells out the numeral, emphasizing the "three point five"-ness of the number, with an appendage that specifies a bit more precision. Like our use of the number line, we have taken this from the way mathematicians talk about numbers. Our experience has been that students more readily build a strong understanding of decimal notation using this terminology, and can then come quickly to understand the equivalence of decimals with tenths, hundredths, and so on. This "spelling pronunciation" is also the one used mathematics, engineering, physics, and medicine, essentially everywhere outside of school.

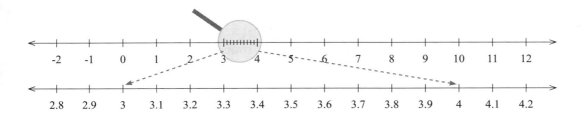

If we need more precision, we do it again, getting 10 contiguous intervals separated by 9 marks, which we number 1 through 9, this time counting hundredths: 3.5<u>1</u>, 3.5<u>2</u>, 3.5<u>3</u>, 3.5<u>4</u>, 3.5<u>5</u>, 3.5<u>6</u>, 3.5<u>7</u>, 3.5<u>8</u>, 3.5<u>9</u>. We pronounce these "three point five one, three point five two," and so on.

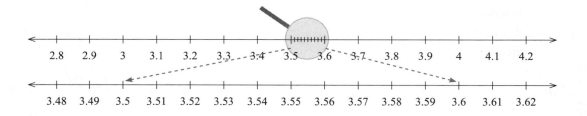

A Consistent System

The image that we want for students is that the system is always the same, and we can make it as precise as we like. Instead, as Victoria Steinle's research[1] shows, students often get very inconsistent images of decimals, some perhaps by having pedagogy tie decimal notation too closely with notation for money, which always has exactly two digits to the right of the decimal point. Tying decimals to students' fragile fraction knowledge might be one source of treating the digits to the right of the decimal place as if they were independent integers, making 3.256 sound much larger than 3.9 because 256 > 9 and because two hundred fifty-six thousandths gets us thinking about and comparing the integer two hundred fifty-six to the integer nine.

By contrast, using the zooming-in image shows that each new digit is simply the result of refining a coarser view, so 3.256 is a "3.25 with some extra," but not enough extra to make it 3.26—that is, it is between 3.25 and 3.26. The act of zooming in on the interval between 0 and 1 to find 0.1, 0.2, 0.3, and so on, and then zooming in on the interval between 0.1 and 0.2 to find, for example, 0.14, also helps students see why 0.7 + 0.7 *can't* sensibly be 0.14. The number 0.14 comes between 0.1 and 0.2, which are both less than 0.7.

Building Understanding: A Seventh-Grade Example

This is exactly how seventh graders in a class that had struggled with decimals in previous years managed finally to sort out their understanding. They were reintroduced to decimals

[1] See, e.g., http://smartvic.com/test1/feed/explain/smart_diagnosis_advice/1ebb_understanding_decimals_shorter_diagnosis_advice.html and http://www.mav.vic.edu.au/files/conferences/2004/Steinle-formatted.pdf

using the notion of "zooming in" on the number line. In preparation for recording the number exactly halfway between .006 and .007, the students consolidated what they already knew from looking at number lines by recording numbers exactly halfway between 600 and 700, then 60 and 70, then 6 and 7, then .6 and .7, and then .06 and .07. Liza, like her classmates, quickly and accurately completed all of those tasks. However, when she was asked, without all of the scaffolding, what number is exactly halfway between 5.246 and 5.247, she incorrectly wrote 5.255. Her teacher encouraged her to put the numbers on a number line. She sketched a line and

first placed 5 and 6. Then she placed 5.1 and paused, clearly thinking. No more detail was required. She said with a smile, "Oh, I see." She erased the 5.255 and carefully wrote 5.2465, adding that "the number has to be between the 6 and the 7."

Zooming In with Fractions

Fraction and decimal notation serve us in different ways. Some reasoning is much easier with fractions, some is much easier with decimals, and that's why we have both. (Compare, for example, adding $3.\overline{285714} + 5.\overline{571428}$ with adding $3\frac{2}{7} + 5\frac{4}{7}$.) But even for the task of comparing *magnitudes*—generally hard with fractions—the same imagery of zooming in on a number line can also help students' reasoning.

Let's imagine, as before, a magnifying glass that lets us look more closely at a unit interval (the space between 0 and 1, say), but this time, instead of seeing 10 subintervals with 9 new numbers to separate them, we might see 2 intervals with 1 new number between them, or 3 intervals with 2 new numbers between them. If we're zooming in on the interval from 0 to 1, we might see something like this.

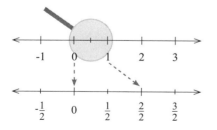
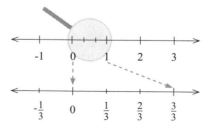

But, of course, we can zoom in anywhere and see new numbers.

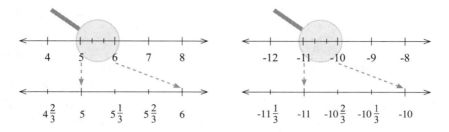

These images show something else. Not only are we seeing new numbers; we are also seeing new names for "old" numbers. With whole numbers, there seems to be only one written form for each number: thirty-seven is just 37, and that's all. With decimals, there are more forms—2.5 and 2.50 are two names for the exact same number—but they begin to feel a lot alike. With fractions, the story is quite different, as the previous pictures suggest. The number listed after $\frac{2}{3}$ can, of course, be $\frac{3}{3}$, but we already know it well by the name 1 and, in the picture on the preceding page, it is named $\frac{2}{2}$. A major part of understanding fractions is knowing that the number we befriended first as $\frac{1}{2}$ can also be called by many other names. A number line that "counts by" fourths will show $\frac{1}{2}$ as $\frac{2}{4}$. And that means we were wrong about our friend 37. It, too, has more names, including $\frac{74}{2}, \frac{111}{3}$, and $\frac{222}{6}$.

> Even in scientific and engineering contexts, where 2.5 and 2.50 are distinguished by the amount of precision they imply, the *number* is known to be the same; only the precision you attach to that number differs.

Recognizing the equivalence of many forms becomes especially important in algebra, where we choose when to "simplify" and when to defer evaluation to preserve structure.

These images also allow us to compare some fractions by thinking about their locations. Our geometric view of number locates them according to their distance from 0. So, for example, $\frac{7}{8}$ and $\frac{10}{11}$ are both to the right of 0 and the left of 1. If we think about each number's distance from 1 on a number line, we see that $\frac{7}{8}$ is $\frac{1}{8}$ away, and $\frac{10}{11}$ is $\frac{1}{11}$ away. We know how to compare those distances from 1, because we have an image of chopping up the unit interval to help us see that $\frac{1}{8}$ is greater than $\frac{1}{11}$. Because $\frac{10}{11}$ is closer to 1, it will be to the right of $\frac{7}{8}$. With practice, that mental image lets us see that $\frac{10}{11} > \frac{7}{8}$. The value of this number line visualization is not primarily in its ability to compare the magnitude of fractions, however, but in the increased insight it gives about fractions.

Distance and Movement: Subtraction and Addition

Though distance is at its core a geometric idea, we routinely apply it, by analogy, in nonspatial contexts that are "pathlike." On the path from 0 to 5000 signatures on a petition, we want to know how far we have to go if we're now at 2537; if we've found $5.49 tucked under the couch cushions, we might want to know how far that is from $10. Using distance and movement on the number line can help students reason about how to perform computations like $^-7 - 12$, $^-12 - {}^-7$, $-3.5 - 16.8$, and $5\frac{3}{8} - 2\frac{7}{8}$ or $^-4 + 5\frac{3}{5}$. It can also give meaning to "5 less than m."

Subtraction and Sense Making

When students learn about signed numbers, some texts teach what feel like several different cases—some for addition and some for subtraction—each with a rule. Relying only on memory rather than sense making is *hard*, because we must remember not only the rules but what cases they go with. One high school text gives two rules for addition—a rule for adding numbers with the same sign and a rule for adding numbers with different signs—and one rule for subtraction that says, in effect, "to subtract a number, add its opposite." The chain of steps and decisions becomes daunting and makes the procedure opaque, especially when we must be able to use it with all eight of the following possibilities:

$$8 - 5 \qquad\qquad 5 - 8$$
$$^-8 - 5 \qquad\qquad 5 - {}^-8$$
$$8 - {}^-5 \qquad\qquad ^-5 - 8$$
$$^-8 - {}^-5 \qquad\qquad ^-5 - {}^-8$$

Alternatively, using the number line strategically as a tool, and thinking of subtraction as finding distance, we can treat all these as *one* case with no extra rules to remember. We sketch a rough number line and place $^-8$, $^-5$, 0, 5, and 8 on it, paying strict attention to order but little attention to precision and scale.

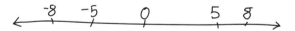

Even this crude drawing helps us *see*, roughly, the distance between any two numbers. The distance between "some kind of 8" (that is, a positive or negative 8) and "some kind of 5" depends on whether the two are on the same side of zero or on opposite sides. The model helps organize and orient our thinking. The drawing tells us what question to ask; arithmetic then tells us the answer: the distance is "some kind of 3" (positive or negative) or "some kind of 13."

The remaining step is to figure out *which* "kind" of 3 or 13. Computing 8 − 5 and 5 − 8 is easy enough: 3 and −3. What about −8 − −5 and −5 − −8? On a (paper or mental) number line, we see them close to each other; arithmetic tells us that the *distance* between them is 3. Visualization also shows which number is smaller: −5 − −8 subtracts smaller (−8) from larger (−5), so the result should be positive (3) just as subtracting smaller from larger has always been; by contrast −8 − −5 is negative (−3) because it subtracts larger from smaller. With 8 − −5 and −5 − 8 the *distance* is 13, because one number is a distance of 8 from 0 and the other is a distance of 5 *on the other side* of 0; the distance between them combines those two distances. As for sign, 8 − −5 subtracts smaller from larger, so it's positive (13); and −5 − 8 subtracts larger from smaller, so it's negative (−13).

This is far too dense to teach by explaining—teaching the previous paragraph would be terrible—but when students work a few examples, sorting out the "how far" and "which is smaller" themselves on the number line, it makes sense to them. And it sticks.

Addition

Addition uses the geometric image with a slightly different interpretation. Adding is continuing a journey, and so we use knowledge of where we've started and how far the continuation is (and in what direction) to determine where we end.

Subtraction as distance: −8 − −5

How far from −5 to −8?

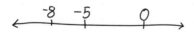

The *distance* between them is 3.

We're subtracting larger (−5) from smaller (−8), so
−8 − −5 = −3.

Addition as movement: $-4 + 5\frac{3}{5}$

Start at −4 and move $5\frac{3}{5}$ to the right.

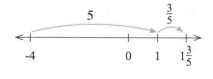

or

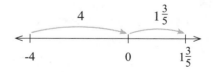

Because we cross 0, the sum is positive.

The second move lands us on $1\frac{3}{5}$.

When we extend to 4 + ⁻7, the endpoint should move beyond 0 and look like this.

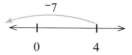

We still aren't using the image to *get* an answer—we're not drawing to scale, we're not marking intervals and counting. We're using the image only to gain intuition about what kind of result would be consistent with the system we've built. Our diagram tells us the result is negative. Our everyday experience traversing distances now tells us what we must do to figure out how far beyond 0 we have gone.

How can a student use a diagram to puzzle out the meaning of ⁻41 + ⁻27? The expression says that we start at ⁻41 and then go ⁻27, so we make a sketch. As always, we are strict about order but don't care at all about accurate scale.

The result is farther from 0, so we are *adding* the two distances—0 to −41 and then 27 more—for a total distance of 68. The endpoint location is negative, so we conclude: ⁻41 + ⁻27 = ⁻68.

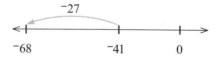

As we often teach students, ⁻41 + ⁻27 is like ⁻41 − 27. The subtraction form suggests distance: how far is it from 27 to ⁻41? We had better get the same answer!

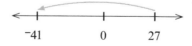

It's comforting to see that the ways we've been thinking are consistent! Again ⁻41 − 27 represents the *sum* of the two distances, 27 to the right of 0 and 41 to the left. Because the change from 27 to ⁻41 is in a negative direction, we get what we expect to get, ⁻68.

When students rely on memorized rules to compute ⁻41 + ⁻27 (or the equivalent ⁻41 − 27), they sometimes dredge up "two negatives make a positive," which is inappropriate for this computation. On the other hand, when students picture even a very rough image of *placement and movement* (or distance) along a one-dimensional coordinate system—a number line—they are well set to figure out what computations to perform.

Teaching Decisions: Which Approach Should I Use?

The history of attempts to teach arithmetic with negative numbers is full of very clever, very mathematically sound ideas, and *all* of them have virtue but none of them make the teaching job trivial. We have found the distance image—thinking of subtraction as asking how far—*very* clarifying for students, easy for them to use in reasoning, and with payoffs also for thinking about absolute value (not discussed in this chapter), but they don't make *addition* easy.

Having different interpretations for addition and subtraction increases complexity. For yourself or your students you might want to view *both* operations as movement or both as distance. Thinking of addition as movement requires two directions of movement (depending on the sign of the number you are adding). Thinking of *subtraction* as movement requires another embellishment. We face right for addition and move forward or backward depending on the sign of the number. We face left for subtraction and move forward or backward depending on the number. It all makes complete sense, but it, too, is complex for students.

In Action: An Accelerated Sixth-Grade

Students in this class were able to find a logical way to solve algebraic equations like $84 - 37 = n - 43$, but their teacher's goal was to get them to look beyond the simple arithmetic and think about the whole equation—in particular, what the equality of the two expressions $84 - 37$ and $n - 43$ must mean—and to exercise their emerging ideas about how the *difference* of two numbers (the result of subtraction) relates to *distance* between the numbers.

The teacher put $23{,}578{,}463 - 26 = m - 27$ and this numberless line on an interactive whiteboard.

Students were invited to explain their reasoning to the class. Alia came up and marked the line like this:

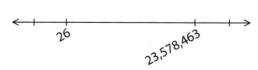

Annie didn't think that was right because "the two lines had to cross." There were no crossing lines anywhere to be seen, so she elaborated: "Subtraction finds the distance and these two distances [she pointed to the equation to indicate the distance between 23,578,463 and 26 and the distance between the tick marks to be used for the *m* and 27] have to be the same." Eva added that "You know the distances have to stay the same because of the equal sign" in the equation. Annie came to the board and slid the 26 to the left, wrote in *m* and *27*, and then sketched lines to show which distances were the same.

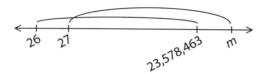

Noah said that to keep the distances the same, the missing number had to be 1 bigger than 23,578,463, because 27 is 1 bigger than 26. Mira announced that she does that part in her head. Pointing to the equation, she said, "I just look and think that this number [pointing to the 27] is 1 bigger, and so this one [pointing to the *m*] has to be 1 bigger, too."

Number line distance is often used in algebra. For one example, using the Pythagorean equation to compute the distance between two points on the plane first requires finding the lengths of the horizontal and vertical legs of the right triangle, exactly the computation that is being taught on the number line; in Chapter 1 that step was taken further to find the equation of a circle. Besides the benefits of looking at a familiar operation in a new way, practicing distance is an important task in itself. Learning to see subtraction as distance hones skills that these students will need in their algebraic studies. We'll see more about the use of number lines in algebra on page 145.

Adding and Subtracting Decimals and Fractions

Little new needs to be learned to be able to add and subtract decimals and fractions if a student already understands the geography of the number line, the locations of the numbers.

Decimals

We can see what 0.6 + 0.6 is by imagining two rods of length 0.6 laid end to end. We compare that logically with 0.5 + 0.5, which we're probably quite sure about, and the fact that 0.6 + 0.6 is 0.2 longer than 1 also makes sense. It's absolutely clear that 0.12 is *not* the right answer!

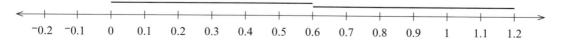

Intermediate "jumps" on the number line can help students navigate the decimal or fractional elements of the problem. Even with integer calculations like 131 − 45, the distance from 45 to 131, picturing subjumps can help: 5 + 50 + 31 (stopping at 50, and then 100 along the way) gives us 86 more easily than crossing out and borrowing in our head. Let's look at some ways students can think about ⁻1.6 − 17.8.

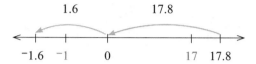

If students treat this subtraction as reporting the *distance* from 17.8 to ⁻1.6, they see that they must add the two legs of the trip. To support that addition, they might (physically or mentally) sketch in two convenient rest stops and reinterpret that total distance as 18 (the distance between rest stops 17 and ⁻1) + 0.8 + 0.6 (the walks between rest stops and endpoints), for a total trip of 19.4. The computation ⁻1.6 − 17.8 is subtracting large from small, so the sign of the distance is negative: ⁻1.6 − 17.8 = ⁻19.4.

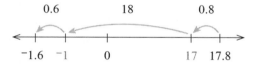

Or they might think of ⁻1.6 − 17.8 as ⁻1.6 + ⁻17.8, starting at ⁻1.6 and moving 17.8 in the negative direction.

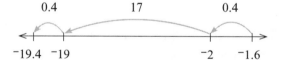

In any case, choosing convenient stopping places can help students think through the calculation. Over time, and with experience, many can learn to make those smaller stops in their head, while retaining the sense making supported by the number line.

Adding and Subtracting Fractions

Treating fractions as "parts of things" builds a mental model that doesn't quite know what to do with $\frac{6}{3}$. If, instead, we think of fractions on the number line, naming their distance from 0 as all other numbers do, then the logic of addition and subtraction remains the same.

For addition: locate the first number; then move in the direction indicated by the *sign* of the second number a distance given by its *magnitude*. For subtraction, find the distance and sign.

Subtraction as distance: $5\frac{3}{8} - 2\frac{7}{8}$.

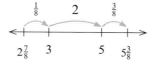

How far from $2\frac{7}{8}$ to $5\frac{3}{8}$?

The travel distance is $2\frac{4}{8}$, which we can reduce to $2\frac{1}{2}$ if we like.

As with the previous example with decimals, choosing convenient stopping places on the number line can help students think through the calculation.

Algebra on the Number Line

Using the number line can also help students think about and understand expressions such as $-4m$ and $\frac{n}{3}$, and solutions for inequalities such as, $2n + 6 > 0$.

We've emphasized that in drawing number line models, we don't have to be precise about length. That imprecision serves in our work with algebra, because an imprecise model is the only one we can use for most work in algebra. In fact, in algebra we generally *can't* be precise about lengths because we don't know them.

Adding and Subtracting

How might $n + 5$ and $n - 5$ look in a number line diagram? Because we know nothing about the value of n—not even whether it is positive or negative—the best we can do is this. It's somewhere!

To plot $n + 5$, we choose a spot to the right of n, being arbitrary about the scale—the placement could be as close or far as we like—but not the order: $n + 5$ *must* go to the right of n. And when we sketch $n - 5$, we must place it to the left of n, and if we're being careful about lengths, symmetrically to the left of n. Both expressions are the same distance (5) from n.

![number line with n − 5, n, n + 5 marked]

The value of n can be positive or negative and the relationship still holds, so there is no need to show 0.

> *If we marked 0 between n and*
> *n + 5 on this number line, what*
> *would we now know about the*
> *value of n? What algebraic notation*
> *encodes the same information as*
> *marking 0 between n and n + 5?*

Precision is important for students learning to understand the relationships among n, $n + 5$, $n - 5$, $n + {}^-5$, and $n - {}^-5$. In our experience, students come to understand this in four steps: First they learn to place n, $n + 5$, and $n - 5$. Then they work through understanding that $n + {}^-5$ is going to be smaller than n, and that $n - {}^-5$ will be larger. It is quite common for students to then label the number line this way:

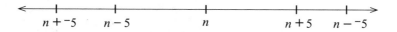

This reflects their hard-won understanding of the placement of $n + {}^-5$ to the left of (smaller than) n and $n - {}^-5$ to the right of (larger than) n. In a final step, usually with a question from the teacher, like "How do you know which is bigger, $n + 5$ or $n - {}^-5$?" they come to think about the relationship between those two values.

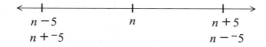

Multiplication and Division

Students generally have an image of multiplication—not correct, but very strong—that can cause trouble: multiplication makes things bigger. They see two counterexamples quite early, but those feel like ignorable exceptions: multiplication by 1 leaves numbers unchanged, and multiplication by 0 always results in 0. The next counterexample to the idea that multiplication enlarges is multiplication by any number between 0 and 1, with multiplication by $\frac{1}{2}$ generally being the first case. Even so, the multiplication-makes-larger image nearly always sticks. Students who really do understand that $^-12 < {}^-6$ can find it unsettling that doubling $^-6$ results in a smaller number!

In one sixth-grade class, a lively debate broke out over whether doubling $^-6$ should result in $^-3$ or $^-12$. The students all knew what the rule said, but some students raised objections that multiplication should make things "bigger" and $^-12$ was smaller than $^-6$. When students sketched the image on the number line, they could see two possible meanings for "bigger"— farther to the right and farther from 0—and were convinced that the more sensible definition for this purpose was the greater distance from 0: doubling $^-6$, to make a sensible, consistent arithmetic, *should* give $^-12$.

What if we are doubling n? If n is positive, $2n$ is twice as far from 0 and to the right of n. And if n is negative, $2n$ is again twice as far from 0, but it is now to the *left* of n. Already, we need to show 0 in order to locate $2n$. So, if we sketch the effect of multiplying or dividing n by a positive number, we do need to show 0. The same is true if we multiply or divide by a negative number. If we pay attention to scale, ^-2n is located twice as far from 0 as n, and on the opposite side of 0 from n; and $\frac{n}{3}$ is located on the same side of 0 as n but at one third of the distance from 0. We can't *draw* these images until we decide whether n is positive or negative. Here are the two possibilities.

That second drawing often looks confounding to students. The minus sign appears on the right! It is worth the extra thought to understand that the number represented by ^-n could be positive, negative, or 0, depending on the value of n. We have found that practicing this idea on the number line really helps students move beyond a surface understanding of both variables and the minus sign. They learn early that the value of n can be positive or negative, but when they are asked to work with a number line where they see $-n$ to the right of 0, it is quite common for them to point out "the mistake" to their teacher. This is an excellent opportunity to help students deepen their understanding of the words that they themselves know how to say. They work through the notion of the possible values of n and the meaning of the minus sign as taking the opposite of whatever number you have. It is often helpful to have them place a few numbers on both sides of 0 on the number line, to imagine numbers on either side being values of p or n or q and so on, and then to place those same numbers prefixed by "$-$" on the other side of 0 at an equal distance.

AREA AS A MODEL FOR MULTIPLICATION, DIVISION, AND FACTORING

We've all seen errors like these.

$(a + b)^2 = \underline{a^2 + b^2}$ (explained "you square each part")

$2(x + 5) = \underline{2x + 5}$ (no explanation given)

$(2a + 5b)(a - 3b + 6) = \underline{2a^2 + 12a + 5ab + 30b}$
(explained "I used FOIL")

Some of the common errors students make are results of treating multiplication like addition. For example, the not-uncommon error $(x + 4)(x + 5) = x^2 + 20$ could well be overgeneralization of ideas about *addition* rather than multiplication—a misapplication of "add like with like" for combining terms.

When the goal is to understand multiplication, division, and factoring algebraic expressions well enough to perform those operations correctly—and, for that matter, when the goal is to understand multiplication and division of numbers including fractions and mixed numbers—area is a more useful mental model builder than distance. Thinking of how one computes the area of a rectangle can help students perform computations in expressions like $4\frac{1}{3} \times 6\frac{1}{2}$, $(3x^2 + 7x - 2)(y + 4)$, and $\frac{3x^2 + 9x + 6}{x + 1}$ and can give the distributive property a strong intuitive grounding.

Although it may be enticing to skip over numerical examples in favor of spending more time on the newer goal of multiplying algebraic expressions, taking the time to rebuild (or, in some cases, build) understanding of multiplication can repay the small amount of time it costs.

Basic Ideas About Area

We start with some features of area that we—and our students—take pretty much for granted. We show how these features explain a few standard facts about area, and then extend those ideas to algebra. For students, the foundations may seem *so* obvious that they are just assumed without real understanding. To apply them to algebra, we have to get them right.

Rearranging Does Not Change Area

Although we might have a hard time saying precisely what we mean by *area*—informally, maybe something like the "inside space" of a two-dimensional figure—we can still use it. It has properties that we take for granted. For one thing, if we cut a two-dimensional figure and rearrange its parts, the shape might change, but what we mean by "its area" does not. For example, we can be sure that figures A and B below have the same area even though, without measuring, we don't know what that area is. Why? Because they are composed of exactly matching parts, just arranged differently, as the middle two pictures show.

Whatever methods or formulas we might cook up for measuring the areas of figures A and B, they had better produce the *same* numbers! Moreover, we take for granted that if we measure the areas of figures C and D separately and then add those smaller measurements, we will get the same result as if we measured the area of figure A or B.

Combining Areas

That last idea—that if we measure the areas of separate parts and then add the areas, we must get the same result as if we combine the parts first and then measure the combined area—tells us one more important thing. If we measure the areas of these 5 × 4 and 5 × 3 rectangles and then add, we *want* the sum to be the same as the area 5 × 7—the two rectangles combined into one. So if the arithmetic expression 5 × 4 + 5 × 3 describes computing and adding the areas of the two smaller rectangles, and if 5 × 7 represents the computation of the area of the larger one, then we *want* those two computations to be equal: 5 × 4 + 5 × 3 = 5(4 + 3) = 5 × 7. We *expect* multiplication to behave in the way we formally call "distributive over addition."

The equivalence of small models like 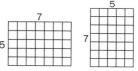 can be verified just by counting. In grade 2, experiences with recognizing and combining small arrays like these can be an excellent foundation for small multiplication facts and for properties of multiplication. In middle and high school, discussion helps students see that they'd expect the same additive principle—which we formalize as the distributive property—to apply to any rectangle regardless of how it is partitioned, regardless of its size, and regardless of whether or not we even knew that size.

Rotation Does Not Change Area

We also expect that the way we hold a figure can't change the area, so 5 × 7 and 7 × 5 must have the same area. For multiplication to help us count the number of tiles in these rectangles, it had better be defined in a way that gives the same answer no matter which way that rectangle is held. If we choose to write the dimensions of each rectangle in the order *base × height*, then we really need 5 × 7 to equal 7 × 5, because that's what we see in the rectangles.

Calculating Area

By middle school, many students take the *base × height* computation for granted, but it is worth taking a moment to make explicit why it works so that students can use area to organize algebraic computations or to think about the distributive property in general. Images like

make it sensible that if we regard □ as 1 unit of area, then ⊞⊞⊞⊞⊞ is 7 units of area, and the large rectangle above is 5

We *define* addition and multiplication to make them behave consistently and suit our purposes, so they make sense in the situation in which we are using them. Multiplication and addition of numbers are defined to make sense of things we can count. When we want to add things like $-7 + 3$ or $\frac{3}{4} + \frac{3}{4}$ or $\sqrt{7} + \sqrt{7}$, or to multiply $4\frac{2}{3} \times 6\frac{1}{2}$, we try to extend our definitions in ways that don't ruin what already worked.

rows of 7 units, or 5 × 7 units. Its area, therefore, is the length of the row times the number of rows. Beginning algebra students presumably know how to calculate the area of a rectangle, but may not have thought through the logic behind the formula. The understanding makes formulas like $A = l \times w$ or $A = bh$ a way of recording what one knows and understands, rather than an incantation to memorize. Understanding in this way can be established solidly early in elementary school, as soon as students begin learning their multiplication facts in grade 2, making it possible to extend later in elementary school to support multidigit multiplication and division.

As obvious as these small integer examples may feel, a brief review is valuable even for high school students because it lets them see under the hood—counting if they like—to build or rebuild the logical foundation before using the model to move on to multiplying larger numbers like 26 × 48, and fractions, and polynomial expressions like $(a + b)(a + b)$, in which the "lengths" are numbers that we do not know. Briefly revisiting the logic of the simple model helps keep the new use we are making of this model—in an algebraic setting—grounded in logic. To be respectful of students' intelligence and sensibilities, we often start this revisiting of multiplication by saying to students that we realize that for a few minutes it's going to feel like they're back in second grade, but we promise they won't be there for long. When using a model in a new way, especially when you make such heavy use of it, it's good to ease the cognitive load by reviewing it first, although the review can be brief.

Connecting Area Models to Multiplication Algorithms

In Chapter 1, we started with a concrete, full-detail array that illustrated 26 × 48 and then we moved to increasingly abstract versions of it. Let's take another look at it.

We already know how to multiply 26 × 48—but now we are trying to understand how that arithmetic algorithm works so that we can apply the relevant parts to algebra. So, instead of just *using* the method, we'll sketch the problem we're trying to solve so that we can study the method. Here's a complete to-scale picture, way more detailed and precise than we'll ever want or need to draw again.

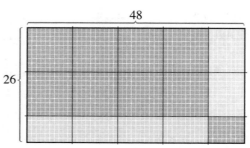

We need to figure out the number of tiles in each shaded region. In the left-hand figure below, we show the multiplications needed for each region. The right-hand figure shows the results of those multiplications, the number of tiles in each region.

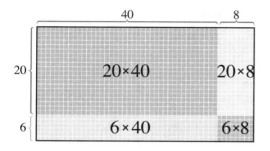

We won't ever count all the small tiles so there's no need to draw them again. We can make the more abstract sketch below (left): it has the (40 + 8) shown as the length of the rectangle and the (20 + 6) shown as the height, but we are not even trying to be approximate about scale. We can figure out the products mentally, using a small set of facts we have memorized and an understanding of the effect of place value (multiplications by 10). The total number of tiles can be found by using a computation like the one below on the right.

	40	8
20	800	160
6	240	48

```
        26
      ×48
       800
       240
       160
        48
      1248
```

We often see students write down calculations like 20 × 4 and 20 × 8. Mental mathematics exercises in which students double numbers like 10, 30, 40, 20, 60, 80, 800, 300 set them up to do these mentally. Then tripling 2, 20, 200, 2000, and then tripling 4, 40, 400, 4000... With experience, the pattern begins to be clear enough to use.

It is worth some time to teach students this notation for multiplication, even if they are capable in multidigit multiplication with "carrying" (and especially if they are not). The benefit to their algebraic understanding of multiplying polynomials is likely to be great enough to repay the additional instructional time this will cost.

The method generalizes completely to any multiplication. Students might use the clues from the numbers already filled in on this partially completed multiplication of 378 × 24 to fill in the remaining numbers.

	300	70	8
20	6000		
4	1200	280	

The form of the multiplication algorithm shown in the previous computation is both completely generalizable and clear. In fact, *this* form—and *not* the algorithm with "carrying" that is still probably more common in elementary school—generalizes to algebra.

With numbers like 26 and 48, it's particularly convenient to split them using place value, because then the resulting multiplications are easy variants on facts we have already memorized, but the way we split the rectangle is totally up to us: instead of computing $(20 + 6)(40 + 8)$, we could compute $(13 + 13)(24 + 24)$ if we felt like it. In fact, *any* way we slice up the rectangle, the result should be the same.

To succeed in algebra, students must get comfortable with this level of generality and choice, so it's worth testing concretely with some extreme cases. Any discussion of the area of rectangles tacitly assumes that the lengths of its sides, though possibly unknown, are positive numbers. It's a leap to assume that the area model works for negatives as well, so that's one extreme case to test. A rectangle that is 2 by 20 will have 40 tiles: what if we *write* those dimensions weirdly as $(3 + {}^-1)$ by $(25 + {}^-5)$?

	25	$^-5$
3	75	$^-15$
$^-1$	$^-25$	5

The width is $25 + {}^-5 = 20$ and the height is $3 + {}^-1 = 2$. The area—the sum of the areas of the four regions in this rectangle—is still 40.

Learning to use the area model supports *choices* in mental calculation: we might compute 5×28 as $5(20 + 8)$, as we did earlier, or as $5(30 - 2)$, mentally computing $150 - 10$, which gives a closer estimate in the first step. And algebra soon generalizes this.

Area Models and Algebra: Multiplying Polynomials

A benefit of revisiting the area model with numbers is that it builds a gut sense of the distributive property. Extending students' work with the area model for multiplication of numbers to multiplication of algebraic expressions helps students to use the same structure and reasoning to make sense of polynomial multiplication. It shows the logic of multiplying each term in one polynomial by each term in the other polynomial, and then adding the results.

Geometrically, $(x + 6)$ and $(40 + y)$ could each be seen as a length split in two parts, in which case their product represents the area of a rectangle with those dimensions. Sketch the rectangle, multiply just as with numbers, and add the results to get the area, the product of $(x + 6)(40 + y)$.

	40	y
x	$40x$	xy
6	240	$6y$

$$(x + 6)(40 + y) = 40x + xy + 240 + 6y$$

Provide students with opportunities to use the area model not just for the multiplication of binomials but also with any pair of polynomials. Because we can split a rectangle in any convenient way, this image can organize the multiplication of polynomials of any order.

	$3x^2$	$7x$	$^-2$
y	$3x^2y$	$7xy$	^-2y
4	$12x^2$	$28x$	$^-8$

$$(3x^2 + 7x - 2)(y + 4) = 3x^2y + 7xy - 2y + 12x^2 + 28x - 8$$

Students who automatically think of an area model to multiply binomials like $(x + 6)(40 + y)$ can succeed not only with those but also with more general polynomials. Students who automatically think FOIL may trip on the computation shown above, which requires six products, not four. The area model organizes this computation: the product is the sum of all of the separate partial products.

EWE ("each with each") would be a more honest mnemonic than the more common FOIL ("first, outer, inner, last").

Building experience using the area model to organize polynomial multiplication establishes a strong foundation for understanding; it is not just a "trick" or a mantra like FOIL. The structure makes the logic clear. As we have described, students get a chance to ask (and check out) questions like "Does it work with negative numbers?"

Other ways to build students' understanding of polynomial multiplication and the use of area models is to introduce puzzles in which students translate between the expressions and the area model, or fill in missing information. Such puzzles might well start just with arithmetic, where the logic may feel more familiar at first.

Oops, some numbers got blotted out!

What is the area of this rectangle?

What are its dimensions?

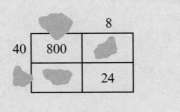

Multiplication distributes over addition and subtraction. Exponentiating—raising to a power or taking roots—does not distribute over addition or subtraction but *does* distribute over multiplication and division!

$$(5ab)^2 = 5^2a^2b^2$$

$$\sqrt{5^2a^2b^2} = \sqrt{5^2} \times \sqrt{a^2} \times \sqrt{b^2}$$

$$\sqrt{\frac{5^2}{a^2b^2}} = \frac{\sqrt{5^2}}{\sqrt{a^2}\sqrt{b^2}}$$

The common error $(a + b)^2 = \underline{a^2 + b^2}$ results from an attempt to "distribute" the exponent into the parentheses the way we'd distribute in the case of $2(a + b)$ to get $2a + 2b$, but the operation of raising to a power does not distribute over addition. The area model gives the distributive property of multiplication (over addition) a clear visual image.

	a	b
a	a^2	ab
b	ab	b^2

	a	b
2	$2a$	$2b$

When students understand what the property really means, they are less likely to overgeneralize.

Area Models and Algebra: Dividing and Factoring Polynomials

Area models with polynomials can also help make sense of division and factoring. With multiplication, we work with the model from the outside in, but students can also consider the meaning of division and factoring by working from the inside out.

Area Model Puzzles

More puzzles! Each of these was once a complete area model, but some of the parts are missing. Which of the four missing parts might you choose to fill in first? How does that help you with others?

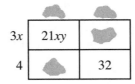

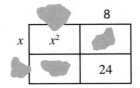

In each puzzle, students rely on their understanding of multiplication and the structure of the model. In the first puzzle, for example, the $3x$ term must have been multiplied by $7y$ to get a product of $21xy$; thus, $7y$ belongs in the blob above the $21xy$. That lets us fill in the blob in the bottom of that column. Area model puzzles such as these require students to factor, multiply, and divide algebraic expressions and to choose among these processes to accord with the placement of the terms and blobs.

Students can also build their own area model puzzles by selecting two polynomial expressions, drawing a model, finding the partial products, and then erasing components until the puzzle becomes interesting to solve.

The puzzles can be tailored to model only one algebraic process. To model only division, we'd start with a product (area) and one factor (dimension) and ask for the other factor.

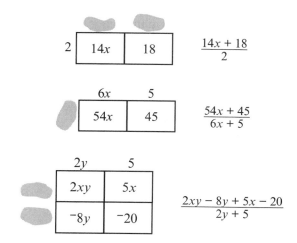

$$\frac{14x + 18}{2}$$

$$\frac{54x + 45}{6x + 5}$$

$$\frac{2xy - 8y + 5x - 20}{2y + 5}$$

To model factoring, only the "area" is given and both factors must be discovered.

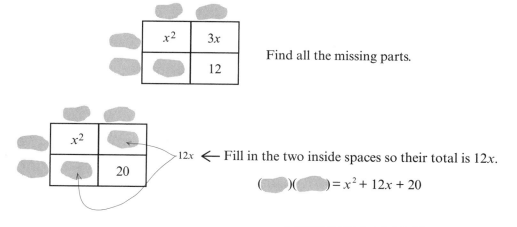

Find all the missing parts.

$12x \leftarrow$ Fill in the two inside spaces so their total is $12x$.

$$(\quad)(\quad) = x^2 + 12x + 20$$

CONCLUSION

We can use what we know about navigating the space around us as a tool to help us navigate the transition from arithmetic to algebra. The geometric notions of distance and area can simplify how we look at the properties of operations and can serve as a strong foundation for the logic of algebra. Those geometric ideas along with a determination to make consistent sense as we extend from whole-number arithmetic through negative- and rational-number arithmetic and then to the greater abstraction of algebra can support logical thinking about addition, subtraction, multiplication, division, and factoring in both arithmetic and algebra.

Thinking Out Loud

> *"The problems we face in science, economics and many other fields are more complex than ever before, and we'll need to stand on one another's shoulders if we can possibly hope to solve them."*
>
> —(Cain, 2012)

In a nuanced article appearing on *The New York Times* opinion pages (January 13, 2012), Susan Cain argues that creativity and productivity depend on effective collaboration, as well as on giving individuals "privacy, personal workspace, and freedom from interruption" (Cain 2012). She argued for both time for individual thought and environments that allow us to share our insights, questions, and problems in a way that feeds others' efforts as well as our own. This is true for students as well as those in the workplace.

Teaching requires maintaining many balances: balance between telling, which is necessary at times because it is efficient, and allowing discovery, which is necessary at times because it is one of the skills we want students to acquire; balance between giving time for students to resolve confusions on their own and formalizing an idea as a class; and balance between individual silent thought and thinking out loud in group discussion.

This chapter focuses on discussion: teaching *how* to discuss; troubleshooting, moderating, and maintaining discussions; and choosing, using, and possibly creating models of mathematical discussions.

BENEFITS OF DISCUSSION IN THE CLASSROOM

Discussions take time, and you almost certainly already have too little of that, so you want discussions to pay off for you and your students. As with investigation, one value of discussion is for students to get the chance to learn how to find their way when approaching a new problem that they have not been taught to solve. Most of life requires us to draw upon what we have learned, but then figure out how to apply it in a novel situation. It is possible, but hard, just from listening to a teacher, to learn to be one's own judge of correctness, to assume "mathematical authority" oneself, rather than believing that correctness can be determined only by consulting an outside authority—the book or the teacher or some website. It is also possible, but hard, to do that alone; one doesn't always catch one's own errors or see alternative routes when one hits a dead end. But discussion helps. When students really discuss, the variety of perspectives makes it possible for students to see how ideas can be generated, validated, and critiqued without appealing only to outside authority.

A good conversation is both a way for students to work out their mathematical ideas and a way for them to develop the mathematical and other academic language for clearly expressing those ideas. A major additional value of student talk is the information that it gives to the teacher about students' mathematical thinking.

Not everything needs to be discussed, of course, but good discussion can be useful in a variety of ways:

- You hear what your students are thinking and gain useful informal data to help you assess your students' understanding and/or guide your teaching.
- Your students hear alternative approaches to problems and learn that alternatives are OK.
- Discussion is likely to clarify a concept or method or give insight into an idea that needs more development.
- Your students have the experience of guiding their own learning.
- The relatively unstructured exchanges of a discussion give your students the opportunity to draw from ideas across mathematical topics, which can strengthen the whole group's understanding of those ideas and validate the usefulness of knowing and summoning material outside of the current class focus.
- Your students learn to express their thinking as a sequence of logically connected statements in a coherent argument; in doing so, they practice academic language they need even outside your classroom.
- Your students are engaged in trying to understand another's argument, and trying to assess it for logical validity and correctness.

These last two bullets are the essence of Standard 3 of the Standards for Mathematical Practice outlined in the Common Core.

TEACHING STUDENTS HOW TO DISCUSS

A teacher guide or professional article or mathematics coach might say something like, "Now have students discuss in small groups or as a whole class." Students, of course, all talk to each other, but focused discussion is different; students in many (most?) classroom cultures have not learned *how* to have a discussion. Having teacher talk dominate can become habit and expectation for both students and teachers. A common scenario is that some question is posed by the teacher, one or two (or no) students respond to the teacher, and none respond to each other. There has been talk, but no discussion.

A lot of effort in early schooling goes into teaching students how to *listen* appropriately to others and *not* just talk. And it is, of course, important for teachers to be able to talk and be heard by everyone, and for students to be able to listen. We may need to give information, explain a particular approach to a problem, or outline important features. When telling suffices, its efficiency in a crowded syllabus is valuable and not to be ignored. But some important mathematical skills and ideas can't be learned this way; for them, other methods must be used. Discussion is one, but students need to *learn* how to hold an academic discussion with each other in an orderly way, remaining good listeners, and providing the structure for the discussion themselves rather than depending on a teacher for direction. Teaching students to talk with each other requires, at least initially, a fair amount of teacher mediation. Yet the goal is to fade that mediation to minimal.

Both of those steps—teaching discussion skills and then getting out of the way—are hard, and take conscious awareness, strategy, and patience. There's no magic bullet, but here are some guidelines we've found helpful for teaching discussion.

Encourage Students to Think First, Then Talk

Discussing and writing our ideas can help us clarify them, but explaining our thinking before we've had a chance to do enough of it—before we've had time to mull over ideas, make some connections on our own, or perhaps even establish and recognize some regularity and structure in those ideas—can actually interfere with thinking. Most of us need a chance to explore a bit, hold at least some internal dialogue, and have ideas of our own before we can participate actively in collaboration or discussion with others. Although it is true that we often get ideas from discussion with others, it's hard to be in the discussion even as a passive listener if we don't bring some initial understanding, however flawed it may be, of what is being discussed. And we can't be contributors without having had the chance to think. We often need at least some (relatively) solitary preparatory time—doing something, noticing something, and thinking *without* the distraction or pressure of doing so in public—to have ideas and to get them into even a rough form that we could then express, even haltingly. For many of us, it is hard to think while others are talking; for some of us, it is hard even to *read* while others are talking. If we must work in small groups before we've had a chance to play with the ideas on our own, we may completely miss the chance to do our own thinking. Premature group work puts some people who could have been genuine collaborators at risk of being mere observers. This, in essence, is a main rationale for the order in the familiar think-pair-share strategy.

Everything in Moderation

Varying the texture of the class adds variety and interest. Time to think and work on one's own is necessary for reasons even beyond those given here, but, of course, collaboration also has huge benefits. Not only do we get mathematical ideas this way, we also see how differently people approach problems and, sometimes, how useful our own ideas can be to others. Thoughtful teaching doesn't treat any classroom structure—for example, small groups, whole-class instruction, or silent work on one's own—as good or bad in itself but recognizes the benefits and limitations of each and chooses strategically. Even the sensible and generally engaging think-pair-share structure can lose its effect if it becomes a mechanical default.

Focus on the Mathematics

Start with visual and experimental situations that use a minimum of text, giving students a chance to explore and acquire mathematical ideas and methods without the added burden of decoding discursive text or complex word problems or creating text to explain one's thinking in writing. We do need, eventually, to be able to decode mathematical text, or text that contains information in it (e.g., a word problem), and to be able to write a piece of mathematical text to explain a process, a concept, or a proof. But decoding and writing text are not themselves the mathematics and can be a barrier, especially for students who are not fluent in English or have other reading, writing, or language issues. And, of course, younger students are less skilled at reading and writing, so the barrier effect is greatest with them.

Teach and Use the Language of Mathematics

Among other things, algebra is a language for communicating mathematical ideas. Statements such as "Given any number, generate a number that is one greater than twice the value of that number" are daunting to express and understand in English text. The algebraic notation, $f(x) = 2x + 1$, once one knows how to read and write it, is much clearer. (There is much more to the discipline we call *algebra* than this notation, but the notation is essential.) The abstraction of this notation is fine for older high school students but is a cognitive stretch for younger students. A concrete version of algebraic notation—like ⧖⧖. as a first way of writing $2x + 1$—retains the clarity of communication, is accessible even to late elementary students, and paves an easy route to standard notation.

Encourage and Model Precision

It's hard to have a productive conversation if it is unclear what is being discussed. For example, when we talk about the sides of a square, we are referring to line segments. When we talk about a cube, the term *sides* becomes ambiguous: presumably we are not referring to the line segments that make up its frame! Do we mean all six faces, or just four sides (as in a room, excluding ceiling and floor), or just *two* sides (as in a classroom, excluding front and back)? To avoid having to explain each time what exactly we mean, we choose a more precise terminology—a language with carefully defined terms. In the case of our cube, we refer to its eight *vertices*, twelve *edges*, and six *faces*.

Learning those precise terms is most easily done the way young children learn any language: from the context in which the words are used. It is important to build in some redundancy, through pictures or examples, so that students have the information to pick up the meaning. Vocabulary learned this way is more fully understood and is remembered better. You are the "native speaker" of mathematics from whom your students will learn. Although you don't want to police their language or make students self-conscious about their communication— that just makes them more hesitant to speak—you do want to model the precision you'd like them to acquire. Of course, be patient with yourself, too: if you become self-conscious about your own language, that will spill onto your students.

Make Sure the Topic Is Discussable

It's easier to discuss a problem when there are multiple ways to approach it or explain one's strategy. Students might then discuss how they figured out where to start, or alternative methods, or simplifications that they found, or related problems that they posed. That doesn't mean that the problem needs to be complex. Even a "naked computation," like $43 + 39 + 7 + 18 + 1$, presented with the question "How might you tackle doing this in your head?" could be discussed because there is some variety of strategies students might use. Richer situations, of course, can offer even more variety.

It also helps spur discussion when a problem is familiar but not "standard" and when the requested answer is not just a number. For example, the answer to "solve $x - 12 = -9$" is just a number, but asking students to explain how to tell whether x is positive or negative *without solving* the equation generates a discussion. Alternately, you could say, "A student said $x = 21$. Explain where she might have gone wrong and how she can get the right answer." This gives students something to explain, which is crucial to good problems of this sort.

Though students can have a discussion about whether an answer is 24 or 40, there's rarely much to say, even if the problem involves a plausible misinterpretation as, for example, $4 + 4 \times 5$ might. The right answer is decided by convention—order of operations—and there's no strategy to discuss or alternative interpretation to consider.

What is discussable depends, in part, on one's knowledge. In the early stages of teaching a class to discuss, you may need to attend both to the topics themselves—choosing ones that seem truly discussable—and also to your students' perception of what is discussable.

Questions that feel too easy don't feel discussable—there seems to be little worth saying, and people don't like to say stuff that feels obvious, that someone else might say "duh!" to. Whether an answer is right or wrong can also feel nondiscussable: nobody wants to be on the wrong side of that fence, so if a confident person who is generally perceived to be correct speaks, the discussion is over. A more effective strategy for starting productive discussion is to ask the students to find what sensible thinking might have led to an answer they agree is wrong.

Avoid Being the One to Respond to Students' Statements

Discussion isn't necessary when the authority is right there to ask! So let any evaluation that happens come from the students, teaching them to analyze each other's thinking and take that critical responding role. Even a "Yes, and what other ideas are there?" can stop discussion by affirming that the current idea is finished and correct, so, by implication, it no longer needs to be discussed.

At first, when you're helping students learn to discuss among themselves, you may need to intervene often, but even then you might try doing it without words, silently gesturing to the others as if you're inviting their comments. Wait time is really critical. Students *expect* you to respond, and so you need to give them time to generate their own thoughts. Counting to 20 in your head while you look as if you're genuinely expecting them to respond is not unreasonable.

Sometimes, of course, that fails, and you need to speak, but remember that your goal is to get students to comment on each other's work, affirming, adding to, asking for clarification, disputing, coming up with alternatives, and so on. One way to help them learn this wide repertoire of responses is to model that variety yourself. Clearly, you can't do this a lot or you wind up taking over the discussion, but you can often get very far with a brief (and genuine) "I'm not sure I understand. Could you say more?" in whatever style suits your personality. That gets a student talking again and frees others to say similar things when they're not sure what has been said. It also expresses interest without evaluation as right or wrong or "Who agrees?" all of which tend to be discussion enders and put you back in the role of moderator and authority. For there to be real conversation among the students, you also want to avoid a "squash court" conversation in which any student's serve bounces off you before another student gets to say anything.

Your interest in what students are saying is a model to them, so allow yourself to show surprise, delight, doubt, interest, confusion, whatever you're comfortable with that shows you are really listening and interested—a participant, and not just running a discussion because that's what you're supposed to do. If you are with twenty-four students, you are one twenty-fifth of that class; you will inevitably participate more than that, but keep your share fair, and certainly not *less* than that. You also have (and, of course, need) a kind of power and control that they don't have, so being fair while maintaining your necessary control is hard.

Sometimes, even comments like "Wait! Is that right?" or "Oh, wow, I hadn't thought about it that way!" can be freeing for a class, suggesting that such statements can be made by others, as well. These can't be frequent, but can be very powerful if they are rare enough. In this same spirit, it's useful—but only if you can do it honestly—to raise doubts about an argument or answer that is actually correct, and then catch yourself, noting the error that you had made. "Oops, you're right. I was adding wrong in my head." That allows others to comment, even knowing they may later discover their comment to be wrong.

Guided by an inspired former teacher of ours, we've found, in our own teaching, that it's easier for us to make honest errors if we are listening closely to what the students are actually saying and not to what we know already to be true about the problem. Students will be just different enough in how they approach things that we can honestly misunderstand or get ourselves honestly confused rather than trying to fake it for effect. In short, it's important to be a complete, honest, fair participant. Not being genuine, in any form, puts a damper on conversation, and not being fair (dominating the conversation) also puts a damper on conversation.

WHEN DISCUSSIONS FALTER

Many factors, including the fact that many adolescents are self-conscious, can lead to truncated or stilted conversations or to students simply saying, "I don't know," and nothing more.

- Students may feel the question, or their observation, is too trivial.
- Students may be afraid to be publicly wrong.
- Students may hold back because they don't feel they can express their thinking well.
- They may feel they can't contribute because they're "not good in math."
- They may not feel that they're allowed to have ideas or that they have mathematical authority.

Again, there is no magic bullet—teaching is more art than science and almost certainly must remain that way as long as students are more human than machine—but here are some ideas.

Feeling That the Topic Is Trivial

Students may (correctly or incorrectly) perceive a problem or question as so trivial that discussing it is embarrassing, an insult to their intelligence. The idea of taking "obvious" or "trivial" observations seriously, using one person's seemingly tiny contribution to lead to a bigger leap, appeared in earlier chapters and is relevant here, too. It is not easy, maybe not possible, to set a classroom tone in which nobody will think "duh" in response to an observation, but you can model it. *Using* students' observations shows their value more than praising the observations. Here's an example.

See Chapter 3 for a description of MysteryGrid puzzles.

Ms. Ames introduced her students to MysteryGrid puzzles and they've already solved one 3 × 3 puzzle as a group. For their second puzzle, Ms. Ames presents a "MysteryGrid 1, 2, 3, 4" puzzle and asks what might be a convenient place to start. This class has already learned to talk some, though they're always a bit slow to start, but this time they're silent. Ms. Ames isn't sure whether the silence is because they're still thinking hard or if they are just reluctant to respond. She waits what seems like a long time—she explained to us how she times herself by briefly looking directly at each student as if she's counting them all, but in some funny random order—but they're still silent, so she adds, "We don't have to be sure we've picked the *most* convenient place to start. Just something that we can do."

Angela tentatively points to the "2,–" cage and says that the numbers in that cage could be 1 and 3. Several classmates nod in agreement. Having had experience with these puzzles, Ms. Ames already realizes that this cage has too many possibilities to be a truly "convenient" place to start: 1 and 3 will work in that cage, as Angela said, but so will 2 and 4, and each of these could be written in either order. But Angela's statement is completely correct—the cells *could* be 1 and 3—and so Ms. Ames writes it in, making no comment. Dean says, "Well, couldn't it also be 2 and 4?" Ms. Ames doesn't speak, but does gesture to the class as if to say, "Well, *could* it?"

After a couple of nods from the class, Ms. Ames nods agreement and moves as if to write that in, too, but then stops and asks, "Well, wait! Before I write more, is there any way we can decide which of these is more likely to work? Or should we just write both for now?" Now the ice is broken. CK takes the easy route: "Just write them both." Josh says, "I agree. We can't decide until we do more." Janette says, "Well, if you use 2 and 4 there, we'll have to put 1 and 3 in the other two spaces," and she actually comes to the front of the room to point at the spaces. Damian says, "And see those two on the bottom? The one that says 'three, plus'? 1 and 2 have to go in there." Janette is still thinking about what she'd just said and now fairly shouts out, "You *hafta* put 2 and 4 there because . . . because see that end space?" and she moves quickly to the board to point at the "3,×" cage. "The 2 and 4 can't go *there*, so they *hafta . . .* !" Angela interrupts, "So I was wrong?" While correcting the cage entries to 2 and 4 instead of the original 1 and 3, Ms. Ames says, "Yup. But only about the final result. You were the one who got us started. You picked that cage and said that 1,3 *could* go in a "2,–" cage. We all agreed that they *could*. Now we know more. In *this* puzzle, they don't."

Fear of Being Wrong

Nobody is comfortable being publicly wrong! Some of us develop thick skin, but nobody likes it. A history of heavy focus on the *answer* instead of the *process*, kids' worries about their image in your eyes, their worries about their grades, all sorts of purely social pressures, and, of course, testing cause students to be naturally uneasy about admitting they do not understand or that they have come to the wrong answer.

It is often possible to reduce this uneasiness, but it takes time, and success doesn't always come. Mostly, and this is surely not news to you, it requires setting up the class so that students know that they are safe—they need not worry about their grade, your opinion of them, or their treatment by others—even when they show that they are uncertain or don't know things, and when they say things that are incorrect. What *may* be a surprise is that this generally means *not* pretending that wrong answers are almost right or that students are "getting warmer," because these ways of softening the truth are often heard by students as if being right is still the *real* goal. If a student, responding to a problem being discussed, computes 6 × 8 as 49, it can work against your interests to say, "Close"; that is just a soft cover for saying "Wrong," a kind of consolation prize that ends the discussion just as completely as saying "Wrong" does. Neither *close* nor *wrong* gives any corrective information to use in reply. Worse, it implies that being wrong is bad enough to *need* a consolation prize—that we need to be comforted when we are told we are wrong.

By contrast, saying, "Oh, but 6 × 8 has to be even" or "Were you thinking of 7 × 7?" says that 49 is wrong, doesn't apologize for saying so or console one for the supposed insult, and, most importantly, provides (or reminds the student of) a piece of information that invites the student to reenter the conversation.

The response "Almost right" to a student's explanation of some method or process has the same risk as "Close" does for a computation. It seems to focus on the endpoint—it's summative, the answer is wrong—even though you probably mean that there's a flaw in some step(s) in an otherwise salvageable argument.

Also, "Almost right" makes you, not the student or class, the judge, and because it also provides no information, it can encourage guessing rather than analysis in the search for the flaw. Of course, you don't want to give so much information about where the flaw is that there's nothing for the student or class to figure out. But in most cases, you do want to indicate that the argument needs to be fixed, not trashed and replaced. "I followed most of those steps, but got lost at some point" doesn't steal the opportunity for students to analyze, but does point specifically to *steps* and affirms that at least some of them could be followed; it encourages a search for a single misstep. The student doesn't need to be consoled for being wrong, because this process of salvaging the argument is affirmation (without calling attention to it) that most of it is *right*. In general, recognizing correct elements of incorrect work seems to make it easier for students to be comfortable, even publicly, with the wrong parts. Also, not being afraid to say that there *are* wrong parts makes them less unspeakably bad. Ms. Ames didn't flinch from saying to Angela that her answer was wrong.

Difficulty Expressing Knowledge They Have

While you are still learning mathematics, talking about it can feel like speaking a different language with its own specialized vocabulary and style. For students who are not yet fully fluent in English, explaining mathematical ideas is even more daunting because they are so well aware that their thinking is deeper than what they are able to communicate! So even when learners have a good understanding of the idea they want to convey, they may not yet be able to translate that into something that they are sure others will understand.

And, frankly, it can be hard, even for articulate adults, to convey ideas coherently. Here is an example from the communication of a ninth grader, fluent in English, average in mathematical achievement, while working with a partner. Trying somewhat excitedly to get the partner to do the next calculation, he said, "You just double it! You have to double!" The partner couldn't see why multiplying by 2 would make sense, but was uncertain, and said only that he didn't understand. Eventually, exasperated, the first student wrote what he meant, and the second said, "Oh! You meant *square* it, not double it!" Both took this just as a slip in communication. The teacher listening in also felt pretty confident that this was neither a conceptual error nor even a lack of the proper vocabulary—just a slip. But the communication didn't work smoothly at first. Situations that don't work out quite as well as this one did—or in which the miscommunication is perceived more negatively—can discourage a student from speaking out in a larger group.

This miscommunication was easy to address—in fact, the students sorted it out themselves—but some miscommunications require new learning. That may mean specialized mathematical vocabulary; it may also require more general academic or logical language (e.g., "if . . . then . . . ," "at most . . . ," "only when . . . but not . . . ," "in every case we tried . . . ," and so on). And, of course, for some, an even more general language issue—lack of complete ease in communication in English—raises the level of effort they must put out to communicate their mathematical thoughts. Mathematical language, like any language, grows with use, not just lessons: the way to learn to communicate is through communicating, however clumsily. Classroom discussions provide opportunities for that practice.

Not Feeling Smart

Even by upper elementary school, some students have begun to think they are just not capable of thinking mathematically. They feel branded: *not smart enough for mathematics.* Carol Dweck (2000) speaks of the fixed mindset, the belief that one's intelligence is a fixed quantity one is endowed with and cannot be changed, and the growth mindset, a belief (backed up by science, though the believer need not know that!) that one's intelligence can grow and that one has control over that growth. People with fixed mindsets tend to want to show their prowess and, as a seemingly paradoxical consequence, avoid problems that they perceive might be too hard for them (and therefore expose a weakness). Those with growth mindsets tend to choose challenges that get them to grow. Interestingly, teachers' actions can have an effect on students' mindsets. When students succeed at a task and are praised for being smart, they tend to be more risk-averse in choosing next problems and to have a more fixed mindset in their approach. Some, instead, rush to the hardest problem to prove how smart they are, and then goof off to cover their inability to solve the problem. By contrast, when students succeed and are praised for the effort and thought they must have put in, they tend to choose greater challenges, to demonstrate all that effort and stamina again. Chess players will tell you that the way to become a better chess player is to play a lot of chess, but especially with players who are better than you. You'll lose most of the time, of course, but you'll gain, too!

Expectations and Success

Teachers, too, feel cornered by labels placed on students. If a class is defined precisely because of its history of difficulty with mathematics, it would be frankly unreasonable for the teacher to expect that those difficulties will just go away and that the students will begin performing on par. It is especially tempting to fall into this kind of thinking when the students are disruptive or disrespectful, but of course, students who feel stuck with something they themselves believe they can't do are especially likely to protest in an age-appropriate (not classroom-appropriate) way. On the other hand, having low expectations—the fixed view of the class—is a trap. One can't achieve what one does not actively try to achieve.

The challenge for you is not to limit your mathematical goals for students in advance. Keeping in mind that the students, especially in a "weak" class, may think they are fixed in that category, part of your job is to *prove* to the students that they can do things they would never have guessed they could do. Pep talks and praise are not enough and may even be counterproductive; no doubt they've all heard "You can do it" or "You just need to work harder" or "You're all smart" or "I believe in you" before. It may well all be true— you do believe in them, and if they work they *can* do it—but if the students don't believe it themselves, they can hear this as empty cheerleading and insincere. They need success, and success at something *they* deem hard enough to be worthy of pride. That is one reason why this book has talked so much about puzzles: for many students who don't see themselves as good at mathematics or school-smart, puzzles present real yet conquerable challenge and can become good routes to getting students to feel smart again. The next challenge, of course, is to get them to believe they can grow. That takes proof, too, and not just telling them, and that is a big part of the utility of well-crafted mental mathematics (see Chapter 2). It's not just that students learn to compute better, though that's valuable, but that they *notice* that they can fairly quickly learn to do something they thought was too hard or impossible, not only for themselves but for most people.

Good Questions

Students for whom the mathematics always feels hard can be important contributors in mathematical discussions because, if they're comfortable enough, they raise questions others might simply have taken for granted. For example, in one of our class observations, a teacher was explaining addition and subtraction with negative numbers. Some students seemed quick to understand intuitively that subtracting negative numbers was like adding positive numbers. But others couldn't reconcile what they heard. "So, wait," one said cautiously, "that makes no sense. If you take away what's already less than 0, how's it like adding?" Two students answered with versions of, "Two negatives make a positive." They had obviously been taught a procedure for dealing with negative-number subtraction. The questioner's eyebrows remained furrowed. "How can you take away something less than 0? And then, like, it's the same as adding?"

The teacher, who had been paying close attention to the exchange, offered a metaphor using hot air (positive numbers) and cool air (negative numbers). What happens when hot air is added to a room? (It gets hotter, or more positive.) When hot air is removed? (It gets colder, or more negative.) What happens when cool air is added to the room? (It gets colder.) And finally, what happens when cool air is *removed*?

The physics and engineering in this example are suspect, but the metaphor was perfect for these students. The room filled with "Oh!"s of understanding, and not just from the students who had not yet grasped the procedure. The students who thought they already understood gained a more robust understanding. The interaction was positive for all involved.

What It Means to Be Smart

Students often think that fast computation or just "knowing" the answer is what distinguishes students who are smart or good at mathematics from those who are not smart or not good at mathematics. Even for a teacher who herself recognizes that being mathematical means being willing to experiment, to puzzle things out, and to approach problems logically—and is not about the speed or background knowledge you have—it takes time and hard work to switch students' beliefs, partly because they get the opposite message outside of school as well as inside: you should know it already, you shouldn't have to think! And a tiny part of that message is sensible: while knowledge and fluency are not synonymous with *being* good at mathematics, they can be ingredients in *becoming* good at mathematics. The basic ingredient, though, is the clear, logical, structured, focused thinking that one learns over time. One way to hone one's thinking is by sharing it with others who are wrestling with the same topics, discussing in an environment that finds sensible elements in nearly every question and idea.

Over time, this will become the culture of the group discussion. In the beginning, modeling and fostering mathematical discussion takes focus and determination on the teacher's part, using even basic questions and ideas as a springboard for starting the discussion. For students, knowing that the teacher and class take their questions and ideas seriously, and seeing how their questions help others' thinking, encourages more effortful participation not only in discussion but potentially in all their work.

Feeling a Lack of Mathematical Authority

Having mathematical authority means recognizing that we can establish the truth or falsity of mathematical ideas through our own logic, without appealing to outside authorities like the teacher or the text. For very many students—and not just those who find mathematics difficult—the idea that *they* are allowed, and able, to establish truth is a total surprise. Often, even when they believe that their answer is correct, they will respond in a questioning tone as if appealing to your authority to evaluate the correctness of their answer. If you respond, "Well, *is* that right?" some will restate their answer with more assurance—the questioning tone is really habit, but they did believe this answer to be correct—but many will assume that your question signifies an error. When students look at you instead of at some diagram on the page to see if their answer is right, they're doing the same thing: it is your assessment of their answer, not their own logic, that they take as authoritative.

As teachers, we may unintentionally and unconsciously propagate this kind of thinking by our own feeling that we need to have the answers (rather than thinking them out), or by answering questions students could solve on their own (confirming our authority), or by feeling undermined when students challenge our reasoning (worrying about losing our authority).

Building Students' Mathematical Authority

There are ways of handing mathematical authority back to the students. Allow students to discuss and ruminate without your input, even if they ask for it. Allow *them* to tell *you* how to approach a problem. Make a point of not always knowing the answer, or telling students how you came to understand a topic. "Actually, I've forgotten. Let's see if we can figure this out without looking it up." And when looking up information seems the best choice, look it up in front of students, or better, have students look it up. Or try, in a serious and non-staged way, to say, "Well, how can we see if that's correct?" or "Two answers have been offered. Are they both correct? What can we do to decide?" or even "How might we attack this problem if we were the very first ones to solve it, and so we did not already have someone else's technique to use?"

Providing closure in each lesson clearly has many advantages, but also some disadvantages. Don't be reluctant, after a good but incomplete discussion, to let students go home with ideas that are not yet entirely correct. Most students, given the time and experience, begin to recognize that in mathematics, as in life, not all discussions wrap up all the loose ends neatly, and they manage the small amount of tension in not having "settled" things by continuing to think long after the discussion is over. In the beginning of setting up this culture, it is not uncommon for students to be surprised, and perhaps upset, that an idea that the group worked out was not entirely correct, or at least not corrected by the teacher. For a few students, the lack of resolution creates more tension than they can get used to, and you need to notice and adjust accordingly, but most, over time, begin even to enjoy the idea of occasional cliff-hangers. And when they come back with new thoughts, acknowledge how glad you are that they continued thinking about the issue and give the class time to continue the discussion now that a student has brought in a new idea. This models how mathematics is done by real mathematicians and makes it clear that students have a genuine role in the thinking about and doing of mathematics in the classroom.

In showing that we are all incomplete mathematical beings, you show students that although they may not be as far in their mathematical development as you are, they can get there if they give themselves the time to talk and try things.

MODELS OF MATHEMATICAL DISCUSSIONS

When we want students to *think differently* about a problem—to see a habit of mind in action and to apply it and make it their own—discovery/discussion among themselves gives no guarantees. And direct instruction on a method isn't quite to the point because what we want to model is not the results of the thinking but the thinking itself.

In principle, we can model the thinking ourselves, working our way through a problem as if it is the very first time we saw it, hitting various dead ends, rethinking, and so on, illustrating the particular habit of mind that pulls us through. Sometimes, that's possible, but it's often hard to do in a realistic and spontaneous and *honest* way; we are almost always too familiar with the problems we are teaching to feel the puzzlement of working them out from scratch. (But recall that focusing on what students know and say rather than on what *you* know can sometimes bring that confusion honestly back to you!) But even when we ourselves can model that habit of mind, we also want students to learn how to arrive at solutions *collaboratively*, through discussion, with *them* applying the mental tools. It's hard to hold an entire discussion all by oneself!

One way to model collaborative use of a mathematical habit of mind, not discussed earlier, is through a scripted dialogue. Many curricula contain brief snippets of imaginable student dialogues, but often only to illustrate two ways of thinking and then ask the student to say which makes more sense and why. Only in three curricula that we know of are the dialogues written with the explicit intent to illustrate mathematical habits of mind or mathematical discussion.

The three curricula are *Math Workshop* (Wirtz et al. 1964), *CME Project* (EDC 2013), and *Transition to Algebra* (Mark et al. 2014).

That is also the explicit purpose of dialogues illustrated in one resource crafted around the Standards for Mathematical Practice—http://mathpractices.edc.org/. Even though that website is designed specifically to support professional development for teachers, the dialogues are crafted to be usable with students as well, to *show* language and approaches that help students explore and better understand important mathematical ideas. These dialogues illustrate principles useful in developing good models of classroom discussion. One advantage of scripted dialogues, by the way, is that by taking on a role in the script, students have the fun of participating in the modeling themselves. In some classrooms in which we've used scripted dialogues as a regular feature of the teaching, students have gotten so "into" them that they've made videos of themselves acting them out.

It would be wonderful to have a public resource of brief videos that model particular aspects of discussion during problem posing and solving, but they're hard to make and share. Spontaneous dialogue is hard to capture, requiring that we know in advance when the camera should be on (or to record a lot and then edit), they require excellent audio, and it's not always possible to get permissions for widespread distribution of videos of children. Although there are a lot of how-to videos, there are very few that show the serious doing of mathematics.

A Sample Dialogue[1]

1	**Anita**	Hey, Dana! Hey, Sam! Remember I told you I found a brand-new way to figure out how to add fractions with unlike denominators? C'mon, lemme show you.
2	**Sam**	It's lunch time. I'm hungry! Oh, whatever. Sure, show us. You've really wanted to for a while.
3	**Anita**	OK. So let's take $\frac{1}{4} + \frac{1}{6}$. The way we were taught to do it was to look for a common denominator and . . .
4	Dana	Yes, we know. Equivalent fractions, all that stuff.
5	**Anita**	But what if we were the very first people to need to figure out how to add $\frac{1}{4} + \frac{1}{6}$?
6	**Sam**	But we're *not*! We *know* how to do it. The common denominator is 12, so we get $\frac{3}{12} + \frac{2}{12} = \frac{5}{12}$. Done! Now let's get lunch.
7	**Anita**	No, wait! Yes, *we* can do it that way, but *someone* was the first to add fractions and she *didn't* already know how.
8	**Sam**	Or *he* didn't.
9	**Anita**	Whatever. How could someone *figure out* what to do if they hadn't already been given a rule?
10	Dana	Here goes another Anita adventure! OK, go on.
11	**Anita**	Here's what I was thinking. I imagined walking $\frac{1}{4}$ mile and then another $\frac{1}{6}$ mile and . . .
12	**Sam**	Ah, and then you would lay out a ruler and measure how far you walked in fractions of a mile?
13	**Anita**	Well, of course, the problem isn't about miles or inches—that's just what I made up to think about it—but yes, actually, I did imagine a ruler, at first, and I didn't even care that this imaginary ruler would have to be a mile long.
14	**Sam**	So, it's solved?
15	**Anita**	But then something occurred to me. For this super-fancy ruler to work, somebody would already have had to figure out how to label it.
16	**Sam**	In twelfths, of course.

---

[1] This dialogue is adapted from http://mathpractices.edc.org/content/anita%E2%80%99s-way-add-fractions-unlike-denominators, which illustrates, among other things, students taking mathematical authority. The topic, addition of fractions with unlike denominators, is late elementary school, but the thinking style is suitable for middle school and even high school. For a similar style, with content suited specifically to high school, see http://mathpractices.edc.org/content/extending-patterns-exponents.

17	**Anita**	Well, *our* problem needs only twelfths of a mile, just like you said, Sam, but if we wanted a general method, that ruler would have to work for other problems, too. It would need sevenths and tenths and thirty-seconds and thirteenths . . . and every fraction.
18	Dana	[intrigued] OK, right, and that's not just *hard*; it's *impossible*! So what *did* you think up? Did you think of breaking each distance, the $\frac{1}{4}$ mile and the $\frac{1}{6}$ mile, into smaller parts that would nicely measure them both?
19	**Anita**	You mean like finding twelfths or twenty-fourths or some other fraction that both the $\frac{1}{4}$ and the $\frac{1}{6}$ can be converted to? That's the equivalent fraction method that we learned. It's fine, but I didn't do it because I couldn't imagine having *thought* of it on my own.
20	Dana	Oh, Anita, you think of *everything* on your own!
21	**Anita**	[sighs] Instead, I pictured the distance, like this. [She draws ▭▭.] The red one is $\frac{1}{6}$ and the blue one is $\frac{1}{4}$. Never mind my terrible drawing. My sixth is *way* too small compared with the quarter, but it really doesn't matter. Ignore the sizes and just use the colors. The problem is to figure out how long that *would* be if I drew it right.
22	Sam	We know the *problem.* What's the *solution*?
23	**Anita**	Then I said, "I don't know how long that is, but if I repeated it six times, like this [draws ▭▭▭▭▭▭], then I would know the length!
24	Dana	That helps?! Now you've just got *six times* who knows what.
25	Sam	Actually, that's quite clever! The six reds are a mile long, because each red is $\frac{1}{6}$ of a mile. And the 6 blues are . . . 6 quarter-miles, um, is a mile and a half. So the total length of this is $2\frac{1}{2}$ miles!
26	**Anita**	Yup. And I could have stopped there, but that still felt too hard to work with, so I made the whole thing twice as long, an even 5 miles.
27	Sam	Five is *odd.*
28	Dana	[groans at Sam] Ha . . . ha . . . ha . . . [then, to Anita] And you now have 12 copies of your original drawing.
29	**Anita**	Right! And if *twelve* copies of my distance makes 5 miles, then my distance is . . .
30	Sam	Oh my gosh, Anita. That really *is* cool! I really *like* that! But now we do need to hurry to lunch.
31	Dana	Oh! And I see how Anita's idea can work with *any* pair of fractions! But you're right, Sam, we'll have to talk about that later. Lunch is almost over.

Key Elements of Successful Dialogues: Choosing, Using, and Creating Them

Some key features of a successful dialogue include acknowledging that they are fiction; giving the characters personality, and in particular, "mathematical personalities"; making mathematical practice visible; using and supporting key habits of mind; and giving students a chance to pause and think about what's happening in the dialogue. In the curricula that use this device to illustrate habits of mind, two or three characters persist throughout the book, and the reader gets to know their habits and personalities. In *Math Workshop*, the characters change by grade but persist through each grade; in *CME* we meet Sasha, Tony, and Derman; in *Transition to Algebra*, we see Michael, Lena, and Jay. In all of these, and in the example you just read, all of the characters are modeling aspects of the thinking and discussion that we want all of our students to acquire.

Writing dialogues that are readable and useful is not easy—it would have been much easier if we were all accomplished Broadway playwrights—but it is possible, and we learned some lessons you might apply yourself. And, by the way, if you do choose to write dialogues, please share them. They can be useful to other teachers. This section describes some features that we have found helpful in selecting and designing good dialogues.

Limited-Realism Fiction

The previous dialogue does not sound like a faithful recording of student talk. It is openly fiction; it does not sound like your class. But like lots of fiction, it contains truth, too.

Though the language is informal, not all in full sentences, it contains no *ums* and *likes* and *you knows* that are easily ignored in speech but make text unreadable. The characters have no trouble figuring out what they're trying to say. Despite playful comments, they stay on-task.

We considered what role a teacher might have in dialogues of this kind but eventually chose not to put in a teacher voice at all. Every attempt to do that sounded corny, as if it were an attempt to say what teachers should do, or what they do sound like. Eventually, we decided to leave the student characters on their own.

That had a benefit: the student reading it can imagine—even knowing that this is fiction—*how* characters who are never told what to do or how to do it can believe and demonstrate that they can figure out mathematical ideas for themselves, using what they already know. This invests mathematical authority in those characters, repeatedly giving the message that mathematical knowledge can be built logically rather than from some external source.

What realities are worth putting into the fiction?

- The characters say what they think, even when confused or outright incorrect.
- The characters may disagree with each others' ideas, posing questions or raising logical objections, but they don't judge. Ideas are logical or not, they can be a surprise or familiar, but they are neither good nor bad.
- The characters process ideas by agreeing, disagreeing, or asking for clarification.
- The characters use their prior knowledge. They do not shy away from traditional algorithms and accepted ways of doing things. They also do not shy away from new ideas.
- The characters use logic to build understanding. They say things like, "We know this is true, so we can also say. . . ."
- The characters draw from each other, not only from outside sources.

Personality

The characters have personality—they are not just an excuse for explaining a method. They interrupt each other, and their interaction is lively. Students acting out these roles in class may get into the personalities even before they get into the ideas these characters bring.

The characters also have distinctive "mathematical personalities" representing different approaches to problems. Anita runs a mile a minute with new and unconventional ideas, and persistence bordering on obsession. Dana knows a lot but takes a more conventional approach. Sam was created with the role of questioner, though in this dialogue he plays that role only a bit. Sam tends to have more questions, and the other two tend to have more answers.

At first, some students see Sam as the "weak" student because of all those questions, but this is part of the reason to craft him this way. His questions often get the conversation going; he is the one most often to wonder *why* a process works; the questions are *smart*. Dana tends to remember and apply perfectly what she learned in school, but is also able to reconsider it, given Sam's questions, and explore the thinking behind her methods. Anita is an outside-the-box thinker who asks off-the-wall questions ("But what if we were the very first people to need to figure out . . .") and brings alternative solution strategies.

Each personality is chosen for a purpose. The questioner role allows the dialogue to illustrate to readers that asking a question—*any* relevant question, even a simple one—can help move a discussion along. The conventional thinker and the out-of-the-box thinker are equally weighted. Dana, though not really catching on to the significance of Anita's approach until the end, is the one who sees how this idea can be generalized.

Making the three personalities different also helped us craft the dialogues: there is always something to talk about, understand better, or disagree on. If, for example, you wish your students understood *why* cross-multiplication works, rather than simply that it does work, send Sam to the rescue! He will ask why, and he will not let up until his question is satisfactorily answered. Your students might never have thought to ask, but Sam asks, and so students reading his lines see how a question they never had elucidates mathematics they thought they understood.

If you'd like your students to think differently about mathematics they've encountered, Anita's unconventional approach pairs well with Dana's book smarts and helps give both styles a contrast. Anita wonders: Why can't we do it another way?

Note that we've focused on these characters' *mathematical* personalities, not other personality traits. One reason was to limit the text. Extraneous text is a burden to all students, and especially those with reading difficulties or nonnative English speakers. Moreover, this is for a mathematics class, not a literature class, so we chose mostly to include only mathematically relevant talk. Students could also be put off by personality traits that seem a little too close to familiar peers, and for that reason instinctively dislike a character and discount his or her mathematical contributions.

Even so, some extraneous talk—talk about lunch or a brief quip—helps to pace the onslaught of mathematical reasoning. Pared only to the mathematical details, the dialogue could feel both lifeless and breathlessly fast.

If you choose to write dialogues of your own—a task for the intrepid—the names can represent your community but probably should not represent particular people or distinguish ethnic groups, precisely because the characters persist and have personalities, and we don't want their (fictional!) characteristics dumped onto real students in class. Leaving the characters' personal traits fairly open and deliberately not "us" leaves room for students to put their own personal traits onto the characters. As students act out these characters in class, they will sometimes add their own slang to personalize the characters. It's as entertaining as it is productive. By projecting bits of their own personality onto the characters, the students more completely assume the roles of the characters, learning their language, borrowing some of their strengths, and, hopefully, developing their thinking habits at the same time. In one classroom, a student paused after she had read aloud some of the questioner's lines and said, "I sound so smart." In "trying on" that character's articulate mathematical talk, she felt what it was like to express herself in this way, and she impressed herself!

Making Mathematical Practice Visible

In leaving out the characters' nonmathematical personalities, we also leave behind any shyness or insecurity they might feel about their mathematical ability. The characters have no qualms expressing confusion, misunderstanding, or even frustration as they work through the mathematics, because they believe—or rather, their authors believe—that there is no such thing as "native" good or bad at mathematics: wherever we find ourselves at the moment, we can deepen, enrich, and extend our understanding through our own work and through interaction with others at any other level of understanding. In expressing all of their thoughts, the dialogue characters are showing mathematics in practice, showing how mathematical knowledge develops.

The formula for the dialogues is fairly simple. Dialogues begin with some piece of content—often an area known to present difficulty for students. Then the characters ask questions, play off each others' responses, and ask more questions as needed, using appropriate tools and resources (e.g., diagrams and other characters' strengths), occasionally pausing to think and reflect before coming to some new understanding. The result presents a new way of thinking about the chosen topic and models mathematical discussion. Sometimes, understanding the ideas offered by the fictional characters who are still in the process of working out the ideas is easier than understanding those same ideas when they are presented in a perfect package from a teacher or another student. And as students read many such dialogues, they come to pick up a coherent picture of solving problems by thinking through them with peers who have different approaches and skills, who don't understand everything right away, who depend on their own logic, and who build on each other's ideas. And they pick up the language, too. With many dialogues, the structure of a coherent discussion recurs until students begin to imitate the characters—often, at first, only to make fun of them, but over time also picking up some of their articulate style.

Pausing to Think

In teaching using a scripted dialogue, we've sometimes found it useful to go through the dialogue more than once. Repetition takes time, and we can't always afford that time, but sometimes it is quite worthwhile. The first time through the dialogue, we read just to get the gist. The next time through, we might pause at certain key places to think through what the character might have meant. The third time through, we really understand the interchange and build fluency with the discourse. We learn to talk like those characters.

What questions might we ask the second time?

In line 16, Sam is right that a ruler measured in twelfths of a mile would work for this problem. But Anita says it will work only for certain problems. What are some other problems it would work for? How well might it work for $\frac{1}{8} + \frac{1}{6}$?

In line 18, Dana says that having a ruler for all cases is "not just *hard*; it's *impossible*." What reason might she give?

Questions that interrupt the dialogue in the most useful ways generally ask how the character knows what he or she knows, what a character means, what a character would say, or how a character will conclude his or her thoughts. As students better understand the characters' process, they begin to understand their own process.

Pausing to think also, perhaps obviously, provides a pause in the action. The dialogues are composed of text rife with mathematical language. Students who have difficulties with reading, comprehension, mathematics, or the dialogue format will need time to integrate and discuss what has happened. You may wish to pause and pose a question any time you feel your students may not understand where a character's thoughts come from, or how a character is conceptualizing the mathematics.

The biggest pause, of course, is the end of the dialogue. The example you read ends without neatly wrapping the discussion up and without revealing Dana's insight in line 31—leaving a cliff-hanger for the real students reading this dialogue. That is an excellent place for students either to continue the discussion themselves, not scripted by the dialogue's authors, or stew over it for a day or two and pick it up later. If you choose to write dialogues for your own use, providing a clear line of reasoning but leaving a step open in the middle for students to fill in or leaving the final step unfinished can provide you a good tool for spurring on student thinking.

Language

If you choose to write a dialogue, pay attention to readability. Casual speech rambles. Sentences start and restart and run on and are incomplete and contain interruptions, but when that's transcribed to text, it's nearly incomprehensible. The opposite is also true: things that are easy to read may sound very unnatural and even hard to understand when spoken. In general, keep sentences short, straightforward, and in active voice. You may be tempted to include "kid-speak" and slang—"like, I'm so 'they won't understand,' but they're, y'know, all 'I'm so smart'"—but this language is way harder to read than one expects it to be, and can really get in the way.

Once you've written a dialogue, read it out loud. If you stumble as you read, change the written text to match what you actually said!

When you do read aloud, even basic sentences can seem awkward or cumbersome, and so it may be tempting to avoid the extra "heaviness" of specialized mathematical vocabulary. Do express things in the clearest possible way—which sometimes is *not* with technical terms. But do not avoid using mathematical language altogether. One of the strengths of the dialogue format is that mathematical language can be modeled naturally, organically, and appropriately in context, sometimes as students rephrase each other's statements (either formal to informal or vice versa).

Avoid having one character give a lengthy explanation while the others listen silently, as this is difficult to read and comprehend. It's also difficult for listeners to comprehend without pauses to process the ideas, and it's not how real discussions happen. We interrupt each other constantly, even if only with a brief "Yup" or "What?" and we complete each others' sentences. This feedback helps moderate a conversation, letting the speaker know whether the listener is understanding or not. We *depend* on these, which you know yourself whenever you're in a conversation—for example, on the phone—and don't get a response for a while. Breaking up long passages with brief interruptions—questions or even the briefest "Got it!" as a way of letting the other characters indicate they're still following—makes the dialogue easier to follow.

Actability is another consideration. Have you written something your students can say and understand? Have you minimized the chance that the wrong combination of students could make the dialogue silly or uncomfortable? It's also nice to have something for the characters to do, like write, draw, or demonstrate, because that's how a *real* mathematical conversation often goes. This gives the actors something to do aside from standing in a line, reading their lines from the script, and it helps both the actors and the audience understand the ideas being discussed in the dialogue.

Performance

Our experience is that students get more out of the dialogues when they read them aloud than when they just read them silently. Too often in silent readings, students skip, skim, or misread the text. Enacting the text, or even just hearing it, makes it more complete and real.

When students are given a bit of time to rehearse, they fare better in front of the class and are more likely to enjoy the experience. One teacher allowed students to practice and rehearse the dialogues in groups of three, and then after a few minutes she asked one of the groups to perform for the class. This way, all students interacted with the dialogue even though only three read to the whole class. Another teacher elected not to have class presenters at all. Instead, the students practiced in small groups and then convened to discuss the dialogue and answer questions. One teacher identified students as they walked into class and asked them to practice a part during that start-of-class time that is often otherwise wasted before the class is fully assembled and ready to begin. These approaches seemed to allow students to engage with the mathematics and have some playful fun taking on the characters. Where dialogues involve writing something, it's also possible to have two students "share" a role, with one speaking and the other doing just the written part.

Pausing and asking questions (as described previously) is a good way to involve the other class members when only three are performing.

CONCLUSION

Discussion isn't just students talking. It takes effort and skill for teachers to nurture those discussions—modeling good collaboration, creating a safe environment for students to take intellectual risks, backing off to give students a chance to take the lead and to take the authority for checking the logic of ideas, helping to restart discussions when they falter, and finding or crafting models of good discussions to help students learn how to have mathematical discussions.

Discussion is certainly not the only way to learn mathematical ideas, but it is one important contributor, and it is well suited to helping students practice effective collaboration. Learning to collaborate is not the job of a mathematics class, but learning to solve problems *is* a part of that job. And as Susan Cain (2012) said in *The New York Times*, the complexity of our modern world demands a level of creativity and productivity that requires, at least in part, for us to collaborate, pooling our skills and energies to find new directions of thought and creative solutions to problems in a rapidly changing living and working environment.

REFERENCES

Atchley, P., and S. Lane. 2014. "Cognition in the Attention Economy." In *The Psychology of Learning and Motivation,* Vol. 61, edited by Brian Ross. Waltham, MA: Academic Press.

Bandura, A. 1997. *Self-Efficacy: The Exercise of Control.* New York: W. H. Freeman and Company.

Benjamin, A. T., and E. J. Brown. 2014. "Challenging Magic Squares for Magicians." *The College Mathematics Journal* 45: 2.

Berlekamp, E., J. H. Conway, and R. K. Guy. 1982. *Winning Ways for Your Mathematical Plays.* New York: Academic Press.

Bierman, K. L., and M. Torres. 2012. "Promoting the Development of Executive Functions Through Early Education and Prevention Programs." In *Executive Function in Preschool Age Children: Integrating Measurement, Neurodevelopment and Translational Research*, edited by J. A. Griffin, L. S. Freund, and P. McCardle. Washington, DC: American Psychological Association.

Blackwell, L., K. Trzesniewski, and C. Dweck. 2007. "Implicit Theories of Intelligence Predict Achievement Across an Adolescent Transition: A Longitudinal Study and an Intervention." *Child Development* 78(1): 246–263.

Bransford, J. D., A. L. Brown, and R. R. Cocking. 2000. *How People Learn: Brain, Mind, Experience, and School.* Washington, DC: National Academy Press.

Brown, R. P., and E. A. Day. 2006. "The Difference Isn't Black and White: Stereotype Threat and the Race Gap on Raven's Advanced Progressive Matrices." *J. Applied Psych.* 91(4): 979–985.

Brown, Stephen I., and Marion Walter. 2005. *The Art of Problem Posing*, 3rd ed. Mahwah, NJ: Lawrence Earlbaum Associates.

Cain, Susan. 2012. "The Rise of the New Groupthink." *New York Times*, January 13.

Center on the Developing Child at Harvard University. 2011. "Building the Brain's 'Air Traffic Control' System: How Early Experiences Shape the Development of Executive Function." Working Paper No. 11. developingchild.harvard.edu/resources/reports_and_working_papers/working_papers/wp11/. Accessed 16 Dec 2014.

Cuoco, A., P. Goldenberg, and J. Mark. 1996. "Habits of Mind: An Organizing Principle for Mathematics Curriculum." *The Journal of Mathematical Behavior* 15(4): 375–402.

———. 2012. "Organizing a Curriculum Around Mathematical Habits of Mind." In *Curriculum Issues in an Era of Common Core State Standards for Mathematics*, edited by C. Hirsch, B. Reys, and G. Lappan. Reston, VA: NCTM. (First appeared in *Mathematics Teacher* 103(9): 682–88, May 2010.)

Dweck, Carol. 2000. *Self-Theories: Their Role in Motivation, Personality, and Development.* New York: Taylor and Francis.

———. 2006. *Mindset: The New Psychology of Success.* New York: Random House.

EDC. 2008. *Think Math!* Nashua, NH: School Specialty.

———. 2013. *CME Project.* Boston: Pearson Education.

Ferland, K. P. 2014. "Record Crossword Puzzles." *The American Mathematical Monthly* 121(6): 534–536. Accessed 16 December 2014 electronically: dx.doi.org/10.4169/amer.math.monthly.121.06.534.

Gardiner, A. 2007. *Discovering Mathematics: The Art of Investigation.* Mineola, NY: Dover. First published 1987 by Oxford University Press.

Gillan, S. Y. 1909. *Problems Without Figures.* Milwaukee, WI: Gillan and Co. www.schoolinfosystem.org/pdf/2008/10/problemswithoutfigures.pdf. Accessed 16 Dec 2014.

Goldenberg, E. P., and N. Shteingold. 2003. "Mathematical Habits of Mind." In *Teaching Mathematics Through Problem Solving: PreKindergarten–Grade 6*, edited by F. Lester et al. Reston, VA: NCTM.

Goldenberg, E. P., J. Mark, and A. Cuoco. 2012. "An Algebraic-Habits-of-Mind Perspective on Elementary School." In *Curriculum Issues in an Era of Common Core State Standards for Mathematics*, edited by C. Hirsch, B. Reys, and G. Lappan. Reston, VA: NCTM. (First appeared in *Teaching Children Mathematics* 16(9): 548–56, May 2010.)

Goldenberg, E. P., and Marion Walter. 2003. "Problem Posing as a Tool for Teaching Mathematics." In *Teaching Mathematics Through Problem Solving: Grades 6–12*, edited by H. L. Schoen and R. I. Charles. Reston, VA: National Council of Teachers of Mathematics.

Goldenberg, E. P. 1996. "'Habits of Mind' as an Organizer for the Curriculum." *J. of Education* 178(1): 13–34.

Kahnemann, Daniel. 2011. *Thinking, Fast and Slow.* New York: Farrar, Straus, and Giroux.

Mark, J., E. P. Goldenberg, M. Fries, J. Kang, and T. Cordner. 2014. *Transition to Algebra: A Habits of Mind Approach.* Portsmouth, NH: Heinemann.

Mark, J., A. Cuoco, E. P. Goldenberg, and S. Sword. 2012. "Developing Mathematical Habits of Mind." In *Curriculum Issues in an Era of Common Core State Standards for Mathematics*, edited by C. Hirsch, B. Reys, and G. Lappan. Reston, VA: NCTM. (First appeared in *Mathematics Teaching in the Middle School* 15(9): 505–509, May 2010.)

Moses, B., E. Bjork, and E. Paul Goldenberg. 1990. "Beyond Problem Solving: Problem Posing." In *Teaching & Learning Mathematics in the 1990s: 1990 Yearbook*, ed. T. Cooney and C. Hirsch, 82–91. Reston, VA: National Council of Teachers of Mathematics. Also reprinted 1993 in Stephen I. Brown and Marion I. Walter, *Problem Posing: Reflections and Applications.* Mahwah, NJ: Lawrence Erlbaum Associates.

Papadopoulos, Ioannis. 2013. "How Archimedes Helped Students to Unravel the Mystery of the Magical Number Pi." *Science and Education.* Published online: August 11, 2013. http://link.springer.com/article/10.1007%2Fs11191-013-9643-0. Accessed 16 Dec 2014.

Pólya, George. 1957. *How to Solve It*, 2nd ed. Princeton, NJ: Princeton University Press.

———. 1981. *Mathematical Discovery: On Understanding, Learning, and Teaching Problem Solving*, combined edition. Hoboken, NJ: John Wiley and Sons.

Pretzlik, U., J. Olsson, M. Nabuco, and I. Cruz. 2003. "Teachers' Implicit View of Intelligence Predict Pupils' Self-Perception as Learners." *Cognitive Development* 18(4): 579-599.

Wirtz, R., M. Botel, M. Beberman, and W. W. Sawyer. 1964. *Math Workshop.* Chicago: Encyclopedia Britannica Press.

Wydick, Richard C. 2005. *Plain English for Lawyers.* Durham, NC: Carolina Academic Press.

Bring COHERENCE and MEANING to algebra

Transition to Algebra is a classroom resource that approaches algebra instruction differently. Instead of reteaching the same algebra curriculum in the same way to struggling students, *Transition to Algebra*'s twelve units use logic puzzles, problems, and explorations to uniquely build essential algebraic understanding. Students are invited to experience the clarity and meaning of mathematics—perhaps for the first time.

Students are encouraged to reason logically and develop confidence in their own mathematical thinking

Puzzles offer a range of entry points and accommodate a range of prerequisite knowledge

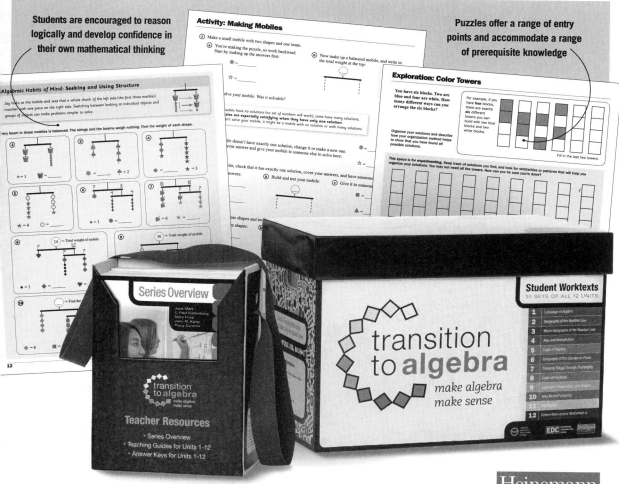

TransitiontoAlgebra.com for samples, resources, and video clips